THE
HINDU
TRADITION

THE
HINDU
TRADITION

EDITED BY

AINSLIE T. EMBREE

Readings in Oriental Thought
General Editor: WILLIAM THEODORE DE BARY

VINTAGE BOOKS
A DIVISION OF RANDOM HOUSE
NEW YORK

VINTAGE BOOKS EDITION, FEBRUARY 1972

Copyright © 1966 by Random House, Inc.

All rights reserved under International and Pan-American
Copyright Conventions. Published in the United States by
Random House, Inc., New York, and simultaneously in
Canada by Random House of Canada Limited, Toronto.
Originally published by The Modern Library in 1966.

ISBN: 0-394-71702-3

Library of Congress Catalog Card Number: 66-13011

Acknowledgments for material used in this volume
appear on the following page.

MANUFACTURED IN THE UNITED STATES OF AMERICA

79C86

ACKNOWLEDGMENTS

The editor wishes to thank the following for permission to reprint material included in this volume:

George Allen & Unwin Ltd and The Macmillan Company—*The Hindu View of Life* by S. Radhakrishnan.

Sri Aurobindo Ashram—*The Life Divine* by Aurobindo Ghose.

Bharatiya Vidya Bhavan—*History and Culture of the Indian People*, Vol. III (*The Classical Age*), ed. by R. C. Majumdar.

The Bodley Head Ltd and T. Werner Laurie—*The Satakas or Wise Sayings* by Bhartrihari, trans. by J. M. Kennedy.

The Christian Literature Society—*The Poems of Tukārām*, trans. by J. N. Fraser and K. B. Marathe.

The Clarendon Press, Oxford—*The Sikh Religion*, Vol. I, by M. A. MacAuliffe, *Tiruvācagam* by Manikkavāchakar, trans. by G. U. Pope, *Bhagavad Gītā*, trans. by K. T. Telang in *Sacred Books of the East*, Vol. VIII, *The Vedānta Sūtra* with commentary of Rāmānuja, trans. by George Thibaut, in *Sacred Books of the East*, Vol. XLVIII.

Columbia University Press—*Introduction to Oriental Civilizations: Sources of the Indian Tradition*, ed. by W. T. de Bary, Stephen Hay, Royal Weiler, and Andrew Yarrow (1958).

Narayan Desai—*The Gita According to Gandhi* by M. K. Desai.

Ganesan & Co. (Madras) Private Ltd.—*Writings and Speeches of Bal Gangadhar Tilak.*

Kutub Popular Private Limited—*Gītā Govinda* by Jayadeva, trans. by George Keyt.

Macmillan & Co. Ltd.—*Nationalism* by Rabīndranāth Tagore, *The Autobiography of Maharishi Devendranath Tagore*, trans. by Satyendranāth Tagore and Indira Devi.

(vi) *Acknowledgments*

The Macmillan Company—*Songs of Kabīr* by Rabīndranāth Tagore. Copyright 1915 by The Macmillan Company, Renewed 1942 by Rathindrinath Tagore.

Lutterworth Press—*A Sixteenth Century Indian Mystic* by W. G. Orr.

Oxford University Press—*The Thirteen Principal Upanishads* by R. E. Hume.

Philosophical Library—*The Mahābhārata*, trans. by P. C. Roy, ed. by S. C. Nott.

Royal Asiatic Society—*Harsacarita* by Bāna, trans. by E. B. Cowell & F. W. Thomas.

Shanti Sadan—*Rāmāyana* by Valmiki, trans. by Hari Prasad Shastri, Vol. I.

M. S. Srinivas—*Artha Śāstra* by Kautilya, trans. by R. Shamasastry.

The Theosophical Publishing House—*Avatāras* by Annie Besant.

Vedanta Society—*The Gospel of Rāmakrishna*, trans. by "M."

YMCA Publishing House—*Hymns from the Rigveda* by A. A. Macdonnell, and *Hymns of the Tamil Śaivite Saints* by F. Kingsbury and G. E. Phillips.

PREFACE

This book is an exploration of the meaning of the Hindu tradition, one of the greatest and most enduring of mankind's many attempts to create an order of existence that would make life both tolerable and meaningful. The physical setting is the land known to the western world since ancient times as India, a word borrowed by the Greeks from the Persians who, because of the difficulty they had with the initial *s*, called the great Sindhu River (the modern Indus) the "Hindu." It was this word that came to be applied by foreigners to the religion and culture of the people who lived in the land watered by the two rivers, the Indus and the Ganges, although the people themselves did not use the term. They had, in fact, no words to describe their religion as distinct from that of others, except those that implied that the way of life known to them and to their fathers was the way of truth. They had, however, a variety of names for their homeland: one, Jambudvīpa, indicated it was the land of the rose-apple tree; another, Bhāratavarsha, indicated it was the land of the sons of a mighty king. But by whatever name they called it, they regarded their land, as one of the scriptures put it, as "the best of the divisions of the world," where gods were glad to be born as mortals, for nowhere else were men so certain of finding "the way to the pleasures of Paradise, or the greater blessings of final liberation" (see page 216).

The method adopted here for the exploration of the Hindu tradition is to give selections from religious, literary, and philosophic works that express the ideas and values, the unquestioned assumptions and the persistent doubts, that have characterized Indian life for the past three thousand years. This method means that certain important aspects of culture have been excluded—any consideration of art and architecture, for example, or any sustained examination of the non-Hindu religions of India—but it also means that much has been included. A fundamental feature of the Hindu tradition is that there is no dividing line between sacred and secular, no area of belief or custom that is alien to religious influence. For this reason there are many selections dealing with the ordering of social life and the management of political relationships, as well as a few that express the Hindu attitude to human love and passion. There are, regrettably, few that touch upon the Hindu scientific contribution. The reason is simply that the texts are too technical or too obscure to yield a meaning comprehensible in ordinary literary terms. It is also true that most of the selections come from what is often referred to as "the high tradition," the literary and learned stratum of society, as distinct from the Hinduism of the common man, who may know nothing of the great works of classical antiquity. But there are numerous examples of the hymns and devotional songs that provide religious sustenance to all classes, and, furthermore, while the Indian villager may not be familiar with the actual Sanskrit texts, their values permeate his thinking and their stories are part of his everyday life.

The arrangement of the material is chronological, not topical. This arises from the conviction that the richness and complexity of the Hindu tradition can be seen only as an attempt is made to suggest its growth and its development over the centuries. Because of the lack of a clear historical framework, this cannot be done with any assurance of success, but at least it is possible to gain some sense of the vitality of a tradition that has frequently, and erroneously, been described as static.

No claim is made that this book represents "what Hindus believe today." Since one purpose is to make clear the extraordinary diversity of Hindu belief, such a claim would be useless. Yet though the emphasis is on the past, the Hindu tradition is today living and vibrant—more so, perhaps, than it has been for two hundred years—and its roots are assuredly in the values and ideals of the great religious and literary works.

In editing a book of this kind, one's debts are so many and so obvious as scarcely to need acknowledgment. The greatest debt, however, is to William Theodore de Bary and his co-workers, particularly Royal Weiler and Stephen Hay, who produced *Sources of Indian Tradition* (Columbia University Press). Not only have many translations been taken from that work, but it has been used as a guide for both fact and interpretation. I am responsible, however, for all the statements made in the introductions and headings to the selections.

AINSLIE T. EMBREE

Columbia University

EXPLANATORY NOTE

With each selection will be found the name of the work from which it is taken, and also the source of the translation. This is expressed as briefly as possible, but the full data can be found by consulting the list of sources at the end of the book.

The transliteration of Indian words follows, in general, that adopted in *Sources of Indian Tradition*, but since the translations are the work of many scholars, there is almost inevitably some variation. Long vowels have been indicated by a macron (ā, ī, ū). The long *ā* is pronounced as *a* in *father*, while the short *a* is pronounced as the *u* in *but*. In some of the selections the long vowels are marked with a slightly different symbol (à). The *sh* sound is, in a few places, indicated with *ś*.

CONTENTS

Part One

THE ROOTS OF THE TRADITION

*(The Age of the Vedas and the
Upanishads, c. 1500-550 B.C.)*

INTRODUCTION

The Ancient Gods—*Varuna*—*Usha, the Dawn*—
Indra—*Agni*—*Soma*. The Origin of the Universe—
Time as Creator—*Sacrifice as Creator*—*The One as
Creator*. The Meaning of Sacrifice. Death.

The Duty of Charity. War. Charms and Spells for a
Good Life—*Against Jaundice*—*Against Serpents*—
To Compel a Woman's Love—*For Success in Trading*. In Praise of the Cow. The Place of the Brāhman. The Crowning of a King—*King of Kings*—*The*

Part Three

THE FLOWERING OF THE TRADITION

(300-1200 A.D.)

Part Four

THE TRADITION AND
THE PEOPLE'S FAITH

INTRODUCTION

Part Five

THE TRADITION AND
THE MODERN WORLD

INTRODUCTION

PART ONE

THE ROOTS OF
THE TRADITION

∽∽∽∽∽∽

(THE AGE OF THE VEDAS AND THE
UPANISHADS, C. 1500-550 B.C.)

INTRODUCTION

The Hindu tradition is rooted in the Vedic Age, the period of Indian history that extends from about 1500 B.C. to 600 B.C. Although this long expanse of time was marked by great religious and social changes, and conditions differed widely throughout the subcontinent, the Age had a unity and style that sets it apart. Chronologically, it was defined on the one side by the disappearance of the ancient Harappa culture and the coming of the Aryan peoples; on the other, by the establishment in the sixth century of important kingdoms in North India. From that time to the present, organized political life has existed in the area. Culturally, the designation "Vedic" indicates the dominant cultural and religious influence of India—the creation of a body of literature, the *Vedas*, which has served to undergird every aspect of the civilization.

The Vedic Age was a time of fusion of different cultures and traditions, concerning the exact origins of which we know little, but whose existence is apparent in the richness and complexities—as well as the contradictions—of the Hindu way of life. One source that almost certainly contributed to this cultural amalgam was the great civilization that centered on the Indus Valley cities of Harappa and Mohenjodaro. The physical remains of this extraordinary culture were only discovered in this century; its existence till then had not even been guessed at. It endured for nearly a thousand years, covering much of northwest India with an elaborately organized commercial and administrative system. Many aspects of later Hinduism—the god Shiva, for example—appear to have had prototypes in the Indus Valley civilization. Another source of the cultural heritage was the widely scattered peoples who spoke Dravidian languages, the modern representatives of which are Tamil and Telugu. It is possible that these peoples were closely related, either ethnically or in terms of cultural influence, with the Indus Valley civilization. Probably such features of popular Hinduism as zoomorphic deities, the use of animals to symbolize the supernatural, were Dravidian in origin, as may have been such important concepts of Indian thought as the belief in transmigration. The third great source of cultural ideas and practices was the peoples who migrated into northwest India in the first half of the second millennium B.C. These were the people known as Aryans, although the word indicates linguistic affinities, rather than a race. Their religious and social concepts, as well as their language, were similar to those of the peoples who migrated westward to Europe.

While not all the chief features of the Hindu tradition can be traced to the Aryans, nevertheless it was they who imposed a distinctive order and character upon the Vedic Age. The evidence of this influence—and the great unifying feature of the period—is a vast body of literature, one of the most magnificent achievements of the human spirit in any place or time. Collectively referred to as the *Veda* it is these writings that provided the roots for the later growth of the Hindu tradition.

The *Veda* is not a book in the ordinary sense, nor even a collection of books, like the Bible. It is, rather, the name given to the extremely diverse materials composed over a period of a thousand years by a priestly class. As such, it exhibits changes and developments within the general structure of the society but it has a unity imposed by a common and continuing concern with the religious ritual.

This vast corpus of scripture can be classified under four headings that indicate both content, and, very roughly, the chronological development of the materials. First of all are the *Samhitās*, collections of hymns used in the ritual. There are four of these collections, the *Rig Veda*, *Yajur Veda*, *Sāma Veda*, and *Atharva Veda*. The *Rig Veda*, the oldest and the most important of these, consists of about one thousand hymns of varying length, some of which may have been written before the Aryans had entered India, while others were written hundreds of years afterwards. Many of the hymns were created by the priests for specific needs of the ritual services that were the heart of Vedic religion, but even those that are from the most ancient strata of the tradition are products of careful literary craftsmanship. They are not, then, the spiritual outpourings of the heart of primitive man at the dawn of history, as has sometimes been suggested; they are the achievement of a highly developed religious system. The *Yajur Veda* and *Sāma Veda* are essentially technical texts and formulae used in the ritual, and are based in large part on the *Rig Veda*. The *Atharva Veda* is different from the other three, consisting largely of spells and incantations. While it is the latest of the *Samhitās* to have received its definitive form, it contains material that is very ancient, and, since it is less concerned with the ritual and more with the problems of ordinary life, provides many insights into the thinking of the people.

The second class of Vedic literature, the *Brāhmanas* are interpretations in prose of the meaning of the ritual acts of the older *Samhitās*. The interpretations frequently take the form of fanciful allegories, with great dependence on supposed etymological derivations of important words, but they provide an indication of the way in which an attempt was made to bring the past into relationship with changing patterns of thought and social life. Within the tradition itself, they fulfilled the valuable function of maintaining the continuity of essential belief and practice, for even though the *Brāhmanas* represented different schools and sects, they all acknowledged the authority of the older texts. A third category of the *Veda*, the *Āranyakas,* or "Forest Books," treated the details of the rituals of the former collections as symbols of hidden truths. The *Upanishads*, the fourth category, are outgrowths of the *Āranyaka* literature, but they display a great freedom of speculation in the discussion of the symbolic meanings of the old ritual. In subsequent Indian thought, the *Upanishads* have a dominant place and quite outshadow the more ancient texts.

This Vedic literature—*Samhitā, Brāhmana, Āranyaka,* and *Upanishad*—was handed down orally, a fact which probably explains such characteristic features as repetition and the use of set modes of expression. Even after the invention of writing the *Veda* was transmitted orally, probably reflecting the enormous emphasis in the tradition on the sanctity of the spoken word. This emphasis meant that great care was taken to see that the text was correctly memorized, and for this reason there is great uniformity in the texts throughout the ages.

Taken together, the four categories of Vedic literature comprise what is accepted by all Hindus as authoritative scripture; indeed, one of the few definitions comprehensive enough to include all Hindus is that they are the people who accept the *Veda* as normative for religious faith and practice. There are, as we shall see, other classes of scripture, but the *Veda* is unique. It is *shruti*, "what is heard," or revealed; another great class of scripture is called *smriti*, "what is remembered," or tradition. For the orthodox, the *Veda* is eternal, and not the product of human minds. Yet it is not like the Bible or the Koran; it is the record of the truth as it was "discovered" by the great rishis, or saints, of ancient time rather than a revelation from God. What is enjoined within the system is not belief in the teachings so much as an attempt to reduplicate the spiritual experiences of these saints; the argument is that they have found truth, and that this can be verified through a repetition of their disciplines. Two important points should be noted. One is that, despite the assertion of the absolute truth of the *Veda*, different interpretations could exist within the framework of orthodoxy because of the variety of ideas within the literature itself. The other is that while the scripture of Hinduism is the *Veda*, the religion of the people of Vedic times was not Hinduism. That is, while Hinduism indubitably has its roots in the Vedic literature, the term "Hinduism" cannot be appropriately applied to the religion of the period. Many scholars prefer the word "Brahmanism" for the ancient religious tradition.

Since few artifacts have survived that can with certainty be identified with the Vedic Age, our knowledge of the social organization and life of the people is based wholly on religious and literary texts, with consequent limitations imposed by their field of concern. They give, nonetheless, a reasonably clear picture of the general outlines of the society. In the earliest period, society is wholly agricultural and pastoral, with an emphasis on stockbreeding. Clans, not kingdoms, were the basic political unit; a tribal chief's main function was to be a leader in time of war. By the end of the Vedic period the Aryans had extended their control from their original homeland in the Panjab to the Gangetic Plain in the region of the modern Benares. The tribal system was replaced by numerous small kingdoms with permanent capitals, and the king became an hereditary ruler through succession from his father, although not necessarily through primogeniture.

The religion of the Vedic people is the subject of an enormous literature; more than almost any other aspect of the life of ancient India, it has attracted great attention since it first became known to the west in the late eighteenth century. This interest was aroused partly by the great antiquity of the surviving religious texts, which gives them a very special place in the history of religion. There are few religious concepts and practices that are not touched upon in some way in the Vedic literature. Beyond this, they are the fundamental sources for the understanding of future developments in both Indian history and religion. As such they have been recognized in modern times as the great glory of the Indian tradition. But above all the records of the Vedic Age are interesting in themselves as expressions of the aspirations and achievements of the human spirit.

CHAPTER I

THE ORDERING OF
THE UNIVERSE

~~~~~~~~~

While it is impossible to reduce the Vedic literature to a
systematic statement, certain general characteristics stand
out. The agricultural life of the people combined with the
special features of the Indian climate—the brilliance of
sunshine, the clarity of atmosphere, the easy beneficence
quickly altering to harsh malevolence—made the people
sensitive to the natural world. Much of the imagery of the
poetry and religion can be understood as the response of
the imagination to a Nature that seemed living and ani-
nate. Related to this response is another characteristic of
the literature of the Vedic Age: the sense of a cosmic
order or law pervading the universe. This cosmic law was
not made by the gods, although they are the guardians of
it. It is reflected not only in the physical regularity of the
night and day and of the seasons but also in the moral order that binds men to each other and to the gods. The
word (rita) used for this cosmic law becomes a synonym
for truth, thus opening up possibilities for the development
of wide-ranging philosophical and theological speculations
as to the nature of the universe.

The concepts of a living nature and a cosmic law find
frequent expression in Vedic mythology. The hymns of
the Rig Veda are addressed to many gods, most of whom

are closely related to the forces of nature, either as contro
ling the natural phenomena or as identified with their e
sential nature. But the gods are not personifications of na
ural forces in the sense that they emerge as clearly define
anthropomorphic beings; with few exceptions, the
characters remain vague and shadowy. The same qualitie
for example, are assigned to different deities, and are give
epithets indicating supremacy. Nor is there any fixed hi
archical structure among the gods, even though some a
regarded as being of greater importance than others. Th
lack of clear distinction between the gods probably mad
possible a belief in multiplicity as representing some mo
fundamental principle of unity.

The Vedic cosmology pictures the universe divided in
three parts—earth, atmosphere and heaven—and this tria
provides an organizing principle for classifying the god
Among those whose functions are related to heaven a
Varuna, one of the greatest of all Vedic deities, Usha, th
goddess of dawn, and Surya, the sun. Indra is the mo
important of all the atmospheric gods, while Soma an
Agni are the chief gods among those classified as having
special relationship to earth. Fuller information on thes
deities is given in the introductory notes to the hymn
There are in addition many divine or semi-divine being
who do not fit into the three-fold classification, such a
family deities, forest spirits, demons, wives of the god
and abstractions derived from human qualities, such a
Faith or Anger.

Questions concerning the creation of the universe an
the origin of gods and men are related to the cosmic law i
a general way, but the Vedic literature presents a numbe
of myths, which are not all consistent with each other, t
explain divine and human existence. Thus at times th
universe is represented as having been created by the god
after the analogy of the work of a carpenter, but at othe
times it is suggested that the whole of creation, includin
the gods, is the product of a process of natural generatio
The gods, quite as much as men, are "this side of crea

ion." *Sometimes the emphasis is on parentage in the human sense; sometimes a complex and subtle reference is made to the evolution of being from non-being. In all these speculations one sees a willingness to move to new positions, even though this means contradicting themes already entrenched within the tradition.*

The concepts and practices of the sacrificial ritual, which was at the heart of Vedic religion, were also linked to the fundamental understanding of the existence of a cosmic law. The central physical feature of the religion was not a temple or an image, but an altar on which the sacred fire was lighted and around which the ritual took place. The sacrifices were mainly things that man himself enjoyed, such as food or the intoxicating soma, a kind of drink whose nature is not now known. These offerings came to be surrounded with rites of extraordinary complexity, the correct performance of which was dependent upon the specialized knowledge of the priests. The belief grew up that the sacrifice was necessary for the maintenance of the cosmic order, and that "without regular sacrifices all cosmic processes would cease, and chaos would come again." [1] From this the conclusion was drawn that what was important was not the gods to whom sacrifice was made, nor the materials of the sacrifice, but the sacrificer, who knew the secret formulae that held the cosmos together. The word that was used for the sacrificer was brāhman, which only by extension of its early meaning came to be used for a whole class of people. Originally brāhman seems to have meant the spoken words of the ritual, but eventually it stood for the power behind the ritual, the principle that lies at the ground of all being, and hence the end of man's spiritual quest.[2]

It might be supposed that the attempt to relate man's

[1] A. L. Basham, *The Wonder That Was India* (New York: Grove Press, 1959), p. 239.
[2] A distinction should be made between *brahman*, the highest principle of the universe; *Brāhman*, a member of the highest social order; and *Brahmā*, one of the great gods.

existence to the cosmic order would have led to considerable interest in the significance of death, but in fact speculation concerning death occupies only a minor place in the
early texts. The ancient Indian peoples desired death for
their enemies and long life on earth for themselves; when
a man died, his soul rose with the smoke of the burning
body to heaven. In the earliest texts there is no certain indication of any belief in transmigration, that most pervasive of later Indian beliefs. Within the Vedic concept,
however, there was possibility for the elaboration of the
belief, particularly in the emphasis on an undeviating cosmic law.

In the following selections, these varied aspects of the
ordering of the universe—the nature of the gods, the creation of the universe, the function of sacrifice, man's fate in
death—are set forth in the words of the saints and seers of
the Vedic Age.

THE ANCIENT GODS

Varuna

Varuna, the greatest of the celestial gods, as the guardian of
the cosmic order (rita), was responsible for the maintenance
of both the physical and moral order. He caused the sun to
rise and set; the stars shone at his command; he bestowed the
rains that gave life to the earth. The moral laws of the universe were no less fixed and immutable than those that governed the natural world, and Varuna administered these with
the same unswerving regularity. For this reason, prayers for
forgiveness for wrongs done to others were addressed to Varuna,
since wrongdoing disturbed the order of the universe. Varuna
eventually faded out of the Indian religious consciousness, but
the emphasis on man's participation in an ordered cosmos became an enduring part of the Hindu tradition. The first two
selections given below are from the Rig Veda, while the third
is from the Atharva Veda, a later compilation of the hymns.

the Vedic people. It is remarkable for the clear assertion of the omnipresence and omniscience of Varuna.

Wise, verily, are creatures through his greatness who stayed
    even spacious heaven and earth asunder;
Who urged the high and mighty sky to motion, the Star
    of old, and spread the earth before him.
With mine own heart I commune on the question how
    Varuna and I may be united
What gift of mine will he accept unangered? When may I
    calmly look and find him gracious?
Fain to know this my sin I question others: I seek the
    wise, O Varuna, and ask them.
This one same answer even the sages gave me, Surely this
    Varuna is angry with thee.
What, Varuna, hath been my chief transgression, that
    thou wouldst slay the friend who sings thy praises?
Tell me, Unconquerable Lord, and quickly sinless will I
    approach thee with mine homage.
Free us from sins committed by our fathers, from those
    wherein we have ourselves offended.
O King, loose, like a thief who feeds the cattle, as from
    the cord a calf, set free Vasishtha.
Not our own will betrayed us, but seduction, thoughtless-
    ness, Varuna! wine, dice, or anger.
The old is near to lead astray the younger: even sleep re-
    moveth not all evil-doing.
Slavelike may I do service to the Bounteous, serve, free
    from sin, the God inclined to anger.
This gentle Lord gives wisdom to the simple: the wiser
    God leads on the wise to riches.
O Lord, O Varuna, may this laudation come close to thee
    and lie within thy spirit.
May it be well with us in rest and labour. Preserve us ever-
    more, ye Gods, with blessings.

(from *Rig Veda*, VII:86, in R. T. H. Griffith, *The Hymns of the Rig Veda*, II, p. 82)

Unto the sovereign lord sing a sublime and solemn prayer (*brahman*), one dear unto glorious Varuna, who has spread out the earth, as the butcher does the hide, by way of a carpet for the sun.

Varuna has extended the air above the trees; he has put strength in horses, milk in cows, will-power in hearts, fire in waters, the sun in the heaven, and soma upon the mountain.

Varuna poured out the leather-bag, opening downward upon the heaven and the earth and the mid-region. Thereby does the lord of the whole creation moisten thoroughly the expanse of earth, as rain does the corn.

He moistens the broad earth and the heaven. When Varuna would have it milked [i.e., would shower rain] then, indeed, do the mountains clothe themselves with clouds and the heroes, showing off their might, loosen those clothes [i.e., disperse the clouds].

This great magic-work (*māyā*) of renowned spiritual Varuna will I proclaim loudly; of Varuna, who, standing in the mid-region, has measured the earth with the sun as with a measuring rod.

No one, indeed, dare impugn this great magic-work of the wisest god, namely, that the many glistening streams, pouring forth, do not fill up one ocean with water.

If we, O Varuna, have offended against a friend, befriended through Aryaman or through Mitra [i.e., gods of hospitality and friendship], or if we have offended against an all-time comrade or a brother or an inmate—whether belonging to us, O Varuna, or a stranger—do you remove that offense from us.

If we have deceived, like gamblers in a game of dice, and whether we really know it or not, all that do you unbind from us, like loosened fetters, O god. Thus may we be dear unto you, O Varuna.

(from *Rig Veda* V:85, in *Sources of Indian Tradition*, pp. 11-12)

As guardian, the Lord of worlds
Sees all things as if near at hand.
In secret what 'tis thought to do
That to the gods is all displayed.

Whoever moves or stands, who glides in secret,
Who seeks a hiding-place, or hastens from it,
What thing two men may plan in secret council,
A third, King Varuna, perceives it also.

And all this earth King Varuna possesses,
His the remotest ends of yon broad heaven;
And both the seas in Varuna lie hidden,
But yet the smallest water-drop contains him.

Although I climbed the furthest heaven, fleeing,
I should not there escape the monarch's power;
From heaven his spies descending hasten hither,
With all their thousand eyes the world surveying.

Whate'er exists between the earth and heaven,
Or both beyond, to Varuna lies open.
The winkings of each mortal eye he numbers,
He wields the universe, as dice a player.

(from *Atharva Veda*, IV:16, in A. Kaegi, *The Rig Veda*, p. 65)

Usha, the Dawn

In the many hymns to the goddess Usha, or Dawn, the descriptions of the beauty of the early morning show the sensitivity of the ancient Indian peoples to the natural world. They are more than nature poems, however, for as elsewhere in the Vedic literature, there is a strong sense of the close relation of the phenomenal world to the deepest concerns of human life. Dawn comes, like a maiden dressed in light, dispelling darkness and driving away evil spirits, making possible a life of ordered regularity. In another poem, the thought that Dawn, the sym-

bol of youthful loveliness, was also ancient, being constantl]
reborn, suggested to a poet the contrast between the "wastin
away of the life of mortals" while the human race itself r
mained (*Rig Veda* I:92). Perhaps at this very early stage ca
be seen the characteristic tendency of Indian literature to se
nature as a frame for human emotions. The natural world
not understood as something apart from man, but as a refle
tion of his moods and passions.

This light has come, of all the lights the fairest:
The brilliant brightness has been born effulgent.
Urged onward for god Savitar's uprising,
Night now has yielded up her place to morning.
Bringing a radiant calf she comes resplendent:
To her the Black One has given up her mansions.
Akin, immortal, following each the other,
Morning and Night fare on, exchanging colours.
The sisters' pathway is the same, unending:
Taught by the gods alternately they tread it.
Fair-shaped, of form diverse, yet single-minded,
Morning and Night clash not, nor do they tarry.
Bright leader of glad sounds she shines effulgent:
Widely she has unclosed for us her portals.
Pervading all the world she shows us riches:
Dawn has awakened every living creature.
Men lying on the ground she wakes to action:
Some rise to seek enjoyment of great riches,
Some, seeing little, to behold the distant:
Dawn has awakened every living creature.
One for dominion, and for fame another;
Another is aroused for winning greatness;
Another seeks the goal of varied nurture:
Dawn has awakened every living creature.
Daughter of Heaven, she has appeared before us,
A maiden shining in resplendent raiment.
Thou sovereign lady of all earthly treasure,
Auspicious Dawn, shine here to-day upon us. . . .
Gone are those mortals who in former ages

Beheld the flushing of the early morning;
We living men now look upon her shining:
Those will be born who shall hereafter see her.
Dispelling foes, observer of world order,
Born in due season, giver of enjoyment,
Wafting oblations, bringing wealth and fortune,
Shine brightly here to-day, O Dawn, upon us. . . .
In the sky's framework she has gleamed with brightness;
The goddess has cast off the robe of darkness.
Rousing the world from sleep, with ruddy horses,
Dawn in her well-yoked chariot is arriving.
She brings upon it many bounteous blessings;
Brightly she shines and spreads her brilliant lustre.
Last of innumerable morns departed,
First of bright morns to come, has Dawn arisen.
Arise! The vital breath again has reached us:
Darkness has gone away and light is coming.
She leaves a pathway for the sun to travel:
We have arrived where men prolong existence.

(from *Rig Veda* I:113, in A. A. Macdonnell, *Hymns from the Rigveda*, p. 38)

Indra

While Varuna was perhaps the most honored of the Vedic deities, it was Indra who was regarded as the particular god of the Aryan peoples. Since his name, unlike that of most of the other gods, does not indicate any connection with a natural phenomenon, it is conceivable that Indra may have been an actual historic figure, a leader of the Aryans who was deified after the defeat of the indigenous people of India by the invaders. In any case, he was clearly the God of Battles, to whom men, "rushing to deadly combat, will cry aloud for protection" (*Rig Veda* IV:24). Indra is also a personification of the thunderstorm, and his weapon is a bolt of lightning. Offerings of the intoxicating *soma* drink are also closely associated with his character, and he is frequently portrayed as a drunken brawler.

A vast number of myths and legends have gathered around

this complex figure. The story of his slaying of the dem
Vritra is the most important of these, for while its meani
for the Vedic peoples is not altogether clear, the many ref
ences to it in the hymns establishes its fundamental charact
Vritra, in the form of a serpent or dragon, has shut up t
waters and the sun, but after a fierce battle Indra slays hi
releasing the life-giving forces. Among the many interpre
tions that have been made of this myth is the suggestion th
it represents the renewal of the year, either through the endi
of the winter or the coming of the monsoons. Another possib
ity is that it represents the actual conflict between the Arya
peoples and those of the Indus Valley civilization. In a wid
sense, Vritra may stand for chaos, upon which Indra impos
form and order.

Indra's heroic deeds, indeed, will I proclaim, the first on
which the wielder of the thunderbolt accomplished. I
killed the dragon, released the waters, and split open tl
sides of the mountains.

He killed the dragon lying spread out on the mountai
for him Tvashtar fashioned the roaring thunderbolt. Lil
bellowing cows, the waters, gliding, have gone dow
straightway to the ocean.

Showing off his virile power he chose soma; from tl
three bowls he drank of the extracted soma. The bount
ous god took up the missile, the vajra; he killed the firs
born among the dragons.

When you, O Indra, killed the first-born among tl
dragons and further overpowered the wily tricks (māyā
of the tricksters, bringing forth, at that very moment, tl
sun, the heaven, and the dawn—since then, indeed, hav
you not come across another enemy.

Indra killed Vritra, the greater enemy, the shoulderle
one, with his mighty and fatal weapon, the thunderbol
Like branches of a tree lopped off with an axe, the drago
lies prostrate upon the earth.

For, like an incapable fighter, in an intoxicated state, h
[Vritra] had challenged the great hero [Indra], th

mighty overwhelmer, the drinker of soma to the dregs. He did not surmount the onslaught of his fatal weapon. Indra's enemy, broken-nosed, was completely crushed.

Footless and handless he gave battle to Indra. He [Indra] struck him with the vajra upon the back. The castrated bull, seeking to become a compeer of the virile bull, Vritra lay shattered in many places.

Over him, who lay in that manner like a shattered bull flowed the waters for the sake of man. At the feet of the very waters, which Vritra had once enclosed with his might, the dragon now lay prostrate.

Vritra's mother had her vital energy ebbing out; Indra had hurled his fatal weapon at her. The mother lay above, the son below; Dānu, his mother lay down like a cow with her calf.

In the midst of the water-streams, which never stood still nor had any resting place, the body lay. The waters flow in all directions over Vritra's secret place; Indra's enemy lay sunk in long darkness.

With the demon as their lord and with the dragon as their warder, the waters remained imprisoned. . . . Having killed Vritra, [Indra] threw open the cleft of waters which had been closed.

You became the hair of a horse's tail, O Indra, when he [Vritra] struck at your sharp-pointed vajra—the one god though you were. You won the cows, O brave one, you won soma; you released the seven rivers, so that they should flow.

Neither did lightning nor thunder, nor mist nor hailstorm, which he [Vritra] had spread out, prove efficacious when Indra and the dragon fought. And the bounteous god remained victorious for all time to come.

Whom did you see, O Indra, as the avenger of the dragon, that fear entered into your heart, after you had killed the dragon, and frightened, you crossed nine and ninety rivers and the aerial regions like the falcon?

Indra, who wields the thunderbolt in his hand, is the lord of what moves and what remains rested, of what is

peaceful and what is horned. He alone rules over the tribe
as their king; he encloses them as does a rim the spokes.

(from *Rig Veda*, I:32, in *Sources of Indian Tradition*, pp. 1
15)

Agni

The god Agni has a special place in the Vedic attempt to cre
ate a model of an ordered cosmos. Although addressed as
person, the description given of him is that of the sacrifici
fire; many-tongued, he is the mouth by which the gods eat th
sacrifices made to them. While in this form he is an earth go
he is also the link with other realms, since he appears in th
atmosphere as lightning and in the heavens as the sun. Th
epithet given to him, "Offspring of the Waters," indicated h
relationship with the primeval waters. On earth, his hidde
home was wood, out of which he could reveal himself as flam
particularly as the flame of the altar. He is both bearer of th
offerings of men to the gods, and the one who brings the go
down to the altar. One may see in these characteristics of Ag
the blurring of distinctions and function, and the attributio
of essentially contradictory qualities, which in later develop
ments was carried to the logical conclusion of denying th
validity of any ultimate differentiation between the gods an
finally, for the quest for a statement of the unity of all bein

I extol Agni, the household priest, the divine minister o
the sacrifice, the chief priest, the bestower of blessings.

May that Agni, who is to be extoled by ancient an
modern seers, conduct the gods here.

Through Agni may one gain day by day wealth and we
fare which is glorious and replete with heroic sons.

O Agni, the sacrifice and ritual which you encompass o
every side, that indeed goes to the gods.

May Agni, the chief priest, who possesses the insight o
a sage, who is truthful, widely renowned, and divine, com
here with the gods.

O Agni, O Messenger, whatever prosperity you bring t

the pious is indeed in accordance with your true function.

O Agni, illuminator of darkness, day by day we approach you with holy thought bringing homage to you,

Presiding at ritual functions, the brightly shining custodian of the cosmic order (rita), thriving in your own realm.

O Agni, be easy of access to us as a father to his son. Join us for our wellbeing.

(from *Rig Veda*, I:1, in *Sources of Indian Tradition*, pp. 9-10)

Soma

Like Agni, Soma has few anthropomorphic characteristics, and is usually described either in terms of the effect the beverage known as *soma* had on those who drank it or of its power over the gods, especially Indra. Just what *soma* was cannot be decided with certainty, but it was apparently a drink made from a plant, and produced hallucinations of the kind made familiar by modern experiments with a variety of drugs and herbs. It was the essential ingredient of the Vedic rituals, and while it was preeminently the offering made to Indra, it was used in the sacrifices made to all the gods. It conferred on men some of the qualities of gods, including immortality. It had, moreover, the power to cause the sun to rise and set, as well as the ability to confer the blessings of riches and long life. One sees here, then, the tendency already noted of assigning the same functions to different gods—in this case, Soma is given powers normally ascribed to Indra and Varuna. The verses that follow here are from a hymn addressed to Soma. They express very vividly the effects *soma* was supposed to have.

We have drunk Soma and become immortal; we have attained the light the Gods discovered.
Now what may foeman's malice do to harm us? What, O Immortal, mortal man's deception?
Absorbed into the heart, be sweet, O Indu, as a kind father to his son, O Soma,

As a wise Friend to friend: do thou, wide ruler, O Soma,
  lengthen out our days for living.
These glorious drops that give me freedom have I drunk.
  Closely they knit my joints as straps secure a car.
Let them protect my foot from slipping on the way: yea,
  let the drops I drink preserve me from disease.
Make me shine bright like fire produced by friction: give
  us a clearer sight and make us better.
For in carouse I think of thee, O Soma: Shall I, as a rich
  man, attain to comfort?
May we enjoy with an enlivened spirit the juice thou givest
  like ancestral riches.
O Soma, King, prolong thou our existence as Surya makes
  the shining days grow longer.
King Soma, favour us and make us prosper: we are thy
  devotees; of this be mindful.
Spirit and power are fresh in us, O Indu: give us not up
  unto our foeman's pleasure.
For thou hast settled in each joint, O Soma, aim of men's
  eyes and guardian of our bodies.
When we offend against thine holy statutes, as a kind
  Friend, God, best of all, be gracious.
May I be with the Friend whose heart is tender, who, Lord
  of Bays! when quaffed will never harm me—
This Soma now deposited within me. For this, I pray for
  longer life to Indra.
Our maladies have lost their strength and vanished: they
  feared, and passed away into the darkness.
Soma hath risen in us, exceeding mighty, and we are come
  where men prolong existence.
Fathers, that Indu which our hearts have drunken, Im
  mortal in himself, hath entered mortals.
So let us serve this Soma with oblation, and rest securely in
  his grace and favour.
Associate with the Fathers thou, O Soma, hast spread thy
  self abroad through earth and heaven.
So with oblation let us serve thee, Indu, and so let us be
  come the lords of riches,

Give us your blessing, O ye Gods, preservers. Never may
  sleep or idle talk control us.
But evermore may we, as friends of Soma, speak to the
  assembly with brave sons around us.
On all sides, Soma, thou art our life-giver: aim of all eyes,
  light-finder, come within us.
Indu, of one accord with thy protections both from behind and from before preserve us.

(from *Rig Veda*, VIII:48, in Griffith, *The Hymns of the Rig
Veda*, II, pp. 198-99)

THE ORIGIN OF THE UNIVERSE

Indra and Varuna are frequently referred to as the creators of
the universe, but from very early times an attempt was made
to go beyond the concept of the world having been created
after the model of a carpenter constructing a building. The
origin of the visible and invisible universe was sought in some
primary principle, rather than in the action of a deity. One of
the most interesting examples of this is seen in the *Atharva
Veda* in a hymn to Kāla, or Time. Kāla is an intellectual abstraction, not a god, and is more correctly thought of as the
source of the universe, rather than as creator. Another abstract
deity, Prajāpati, "Lord of Offspring," seems to be a designation
for the same principle. A hymn to Kāla is given in the first
selection below.
  A very different kind of speculation concerning the origin
of the universe is given in one of the most famous hymns of
the *Rig Veda*, the *Purusha Sukta*, or Hymn of Man. Here the
emphasis is on the creation of animate life and society, rather
than on the physical world. A Primal Man, whose origin is
unexplained in the text, is sacrificed by the gods, and all of
life, including the orders of society, comes into existence. This
concept had an important place in the development of the
sacrificial ritual, for, through analogical reasoning, each ritual
performance was seen as a repetition of the primeval sacrifice.

Each succeeding ritual act was understood to sustain the universe, just as did the first great sacrifice.

Another very fascinating speculation concerning creation is given in the great Creation Hymn of the *Rig Veda*. After a complex statement of the origin of the world, the poet concludes by saying that only the First Principle knows how the earth was created; and then suddenly adds, "or perhaps he knows it not." This phrase is often quoted as evidence of the skeptical mind of the ancient poet, but more probably it indicates the willingness within the Indian tradition to push inquiry to an extreme in the search for some ultimate principle that can be accepted as final and unchanging.

Time as Creator

Time carries [us] forward, a steed, with seven rays, a thousand eyes, undecaying, full of fecundity. On him intelligent sages mount; his wheels are all the worlds. This Time moves on seven wheels; he has seven naves; immortality is his axle. He is at present all these worlds. Time hastens onward, the first god. A full jar is contained in Time. We behold him existing in many forms. He is all these worlds in the future. They call him Time in the highest heaven. It is he who drew forth the worlds, and encompassed them. Being the father, he became their son. There is no other power superior to him. Time generated the sky and these earths. Set in motion by Time, the past and the future subsist. Time created the earth; by Time the sun burns; through Time all beings [exist]; through Time the eye sees. Mind, breath, name, are embraced in Time. All these creatures rejoice when Time arrives. In Time rigorous abstraction, in Time the highest, in Time divine knowledge, is comprehended. Time is lord of all things, he who was the father of Prajāpati. That [universe] has been set in motion by him, produced by him, and is supported on him.

(from *Atharva Veda* XIX:531-38, in Muir, *Original Sanskrit Texts*, V, p. 408)

Sacrifice as Creator

Thousand-headed Purusha, thousand-eyed, thousand-footed—he having pervaded the earth on all sides, still extends ten fingers beyond it.

Purusha alone is all this—whatever has been and whatever is going to be. Further, he is the lord of immortality and also of what grows for food.

Such is his greatness; greater, indeed, than this is Purusha. All creatures constitute but one quarter of him, his three quarters are the immortal in heaven. . . . Being born, he projected himself behind the earth as also before it.

When the gods performed the sacrifice with Purusha as the oblation, then the spring was its clarified butter, the summer the sacrificial fuel, and the autumn the oblation.

The sacrificial victim, namely, Purusha, born at the very beginning, they sprinkled with sacred water upon the sacrificial grass. With him as oblation the gods performed the sacrifice, and also the Sādhyas [a class of semidivine beings] and the rishis [ancient seers].

From that wholly offered sacrificial oblation were born the verses and the sacred chants; from it were born the meters; the sacrificial formula was born from it.

From it horses were born and also those animals who have double rows of teeth; cows were born from it, from it were born goats and sheep.

When they divided Purusha, in how many different portions did they arrange him? What became of his mouth, what of his two arms? What were his two thighs and his two feet called?

His mouth became the brāhman; his two arms were made into the rājanya; his two thighs the vaishyas; from his two feet the shūdra was born.

The moon was born from the mind, from the eye the sun was born; from the mouth Indra and Agni, from the breath the wind was born.

From the navel was the atmosphere created, from the head the heaven issued forth; from the two feet was born the earth and the quarters (the cardinal directions) from the ear. Thus did they fashion the worlds.

Seven were the enclosing sticks in this sacrifice, thrice seven were the fire-sticks made, when the gods, performing the sacrifice, bound down Purusha, the sacrificial victim.

With this sacrificial oblation did the gods offer the sacrifice. These were the first norms (*dharma*) of sacrifice. These greatnesses reached to the sky wherein live the ancient Sādhyas and gods.

(from *Rig Veda* X:90, in *Sources of Indian Tradition*, pp. 16-17)

The One as Creator

Then was not non-existent nor existent: there was no realm of air, no sky beyond it.

What covered in, and where? and what gave shelter? Was water there, unfathomed depth of water?

Death was not then, nor was there aught immortal: no sign was there, the day's and night's divider.

That One Thing, breathless, breathed by its own nature: apart from it was nothing whatsoever.

Darkness there was: at first concealed in darkness this All was undifferentiated chaos.

All that existed then was void and formless: by the great power of Warmth was born that One.

Thereafter rose Desire in the beginning, Desire, the primal seed and germ of Spirit.

Sages who searched with their heart's thought discovered the existent's kinship in the non-existent.

Transversely was their severing line extended: what was above it then, and what below it?

There were begetters, there were mighty forces, free action here and energy up yonder.

Who verily knows and who can here declare it, whence it
     was born and whence comes this creation?
The Gods are later than this world's creation. Who knows
     then whence it first came into being?
He, the first origin of this creation, whether he formed it
     all or did not form it,
Whose eye controls this world in highest heaven, he verily
     knows it, or perhaps he knows not.

(from *Rig Veda* X:129, in Griffith, *The Hymns of the Rig
Veda*, II, pp. 575-76)

THE MEANING OF SACRIFICE

While the centrality of the sacrificial rituals in early Indian
religion is clear, the nature and meaning of the actual performances is often obscure. This is due partly to developments that
took place throughout the centuries in the religious tradition
and partly to the complexity of the concepts involved. In the
earliest period the sacrifice seems to have been performed in
order to win the favor of a god by making a gift for which he
would return riches and a long life. Thus in one hymn offerings
are made to Indra who is told, in a rather peremptory fashion,
to accept them and "then fix thy mind upon bestowing treasure." (*Rig Veda* I:54). Related to this was the thought of
the sacrifice as a thank-offering, a gift made for favors received.
     An important development took place when the conclusion
was reached that if a sacrifice were properly performed the gods
could not withhold the boon requested. In other words, the
sacrifice was understood to be able to provide the results desired, and the will of the gods became almost irrelevant. The
power of sacrifice in bringing about the creation of the world
has already been noted in the Hymn of Man, and the sacrificial
ritual thus assumed enormous importance within the whole
cultural tradition. One result of this belief in the potency of
the ritual was an exaltation of the role of the performer. Since
the ritual was of such great consequence, it had to be correctly

performed; the misuse of a word or phrase might lead to disaster. The sacrificer was thus regarded as controlling a power tha
could bring blessing or destruction. The priest therefore be
came a key figure in the whole drama of the cosmic order. Thi
development undoubtedly explains in part at least the uniqu
function of the Brāhman in Indian culture, for he was a ma
who controlled the secrets of the universe. A further result o
this attitude towards sacrifice and the role of the sacrificer wa
that the gods became less important than the performer an
the ritual act.

The following selections are taken from a *Brāhmana*, on
of a class of Vedic literature that deals, in great detail, witl
the ritual performances. They illustrate the way in which th
significance of the sacrifice was heightened by seeing analogie
and correspondences between the materials of the sacrifice an
other materials. Especial significance was seen in word sim
larities, and the kind of etymological reasoning shown her
occupies an important place in Indian literature. The secon
selection indicates the extent of the claims made by the Brāh
man priests.

After that (the priest) pronounces the offering-prayer t
Tanūnapāt. Tanūnapāt, doubtless, is the summer; for th
summer burns the bodies (tanūn tapati) of these creature
The gods, at that time, appropriated the summer, and de
prived their rivals of the summer; and now this one als
appropriates the summer, and deprives his rivals of th
summer: this is the reason why he pronounces the offering
prayer to Tanūnapāt.

He then pronounces the offering-prayer to the Iḍs. Th
Iḍs (praises), doubtless, are the rains; they are the rains
inasmuch as the vile, crawling (vermin) which shrink du
ing the summer and winter, then (in the rainy season
move about in quest of food, as it were, praising (īḍ) th
rains: therefore the Iḍs are the rains. The gods, at tha
time, appropriated the rains, and deprived their rivals o
the rains; and now this one also appropriates the rains, an
deprives his rivals of the rains: this is the reason why h
pronounces the offering-prayer to the Iḍs.

He then pronounces the offering-prayer to the barhis (covering of sacrificial grass on the altar). The barhis, doubtless, is the autumn; the barhis is the autumn, inasmuch as these plants which shrink during the summer and winter grow by the rains, and in autumn lie spread open after the fashion of barhis: for this reason the barhis is the autumn. The gods, at that time, appropriated the autumn, and deprived their rivals of the autumn; and now this one also appropriates the autumn, and deprives his rivals of the autumn; this is why he pronounces the prayer to the barhis.

(from *Śātapatha Brāhmana*, I:5:3:10-27, in *Sacred Books of the East*, XII, p. 147)

DEATH

When the Vedic people thought of the future life they generally pictured a place where those who had satisfied the gods —both through the performance of sacrifices and the living of a life in accordance with the moral order—enjoyed pleasures which were an extension of those of life on earth, differing in quantity but not in kind. On a more sophisticated level, death was also equated with that state of non-existence (*asat*) of which the hymns speak so frequently. To live, was to be ruled by cosmic law, that ordering of existence that applied to both men and gods; to die, was to pass into the order of non-existence, a realm in some way outside the cosmic law. This sense that death was identified with non-existence is reflected in the reiterated desire to live "a hundred autumns," and, quite probably, in the attempt through ritual and sacrifice to set a limit to Death's claims.

Go hence, O Death, pursue thy special pathway apart from that which Gods are wont to travel.

To thee I say it who hast eyes and hearest: Touch not our
offspring, injure not our heroes.

Divided from the dead are these, the living: now be our
calling on the Gods successful.

We have gone forth for dancing and for laughter, to further times prolonging our existence.

Here I erect this rampart for the living; let none of these,
none other, reach this limit.

May they survive a hundred lengthened autumns, and may
they bury Death beneath this mountain.

As the days follow days in close succession, as with the
seasons duly come the seasons,

As each successor fails not his foregoer, so form the lives of
these, O great Ordainer.

Live your full lives and find old age delightful, all of you
striving one behind the other.

May Tvashtar, maker of fair things, be gracious and
lengthen out the days of your existence.

Let these unwidowed dames with noble husbands adorn
themselves with fragrant balm and unguent.

Decked with fair jewels, tearless, free from sorrow, first let
the dames go up to where he lieth.

Rise, come unto the world of life, O woman: come, he is
lifeless by whose side thou liest.

Wifehood with this thy husband was thy portion, who
took thy hand and wooed thee as a lover.

From his dead hand I take the bow he carried, that it may
be our power and might and glory.

There art thou, there; and here with noble heroes may we
o'ercome all hosts that fight against us.

Betake thee to the lap of Earth the Mother, of Earth far
spreading, very kind and gracious.

Young Dame, wool-soft unto the guerdon-giver, may she
preserve thee from Destruction's bosom.

Heave thyself, Earth, nor press thee downward heavily:
afford him easy access, gently tending him.

Cover him, as a mother wraps her skirt about her child, O
Earth.

Now let the heaving earth be free from motion: yea, let a
thousand clods remain above him.

Be they to him a home distilling fatness, here let them
ever be his place of refuge.

I stay the earth from thee, while over thee I place this
piece of earth. May I be free from injury.

Here let the Fathers keep this pillar firm for thee, and
there let Death make thee an abiding-place.

(from *Rig Veda* X:18, in Griffith, *The Hymns of the Rig
Veda*, II, pp. 406-07)

CHAPTER II

THE SOCIAL ORDER

∞∞∞∞∞∞

For an understanding of the development of the Hindu tradition some knowledge is necessary of the social life of the people in the great creative periods, for very frequently the religious and philosophical ideas appear in a quite new light when they are seen reflected through the patterns of the lives of the people in their ordinary concerns. And while it is probably true that it is difficult to consider religious ideas apart from social structure in any society, in Indian culture it is manifestly impossible. Not only was every stage of life from birth to death marked by formal sacramental acts, but there was scarcely an action or custom, however trivial or commonplace, that did not have a sanction beyond mere utility. This means that while Indian culture is probably more "religious" than almost any other, at the same time religious rites and practices often have a very casual performance, sometimes suggesting to outsiders a lack of genuine piety. The explanation is, of course, a different understanding of the nature of the secular and sacred. It may be noted in passing that the religious consciousness that surrounds commonplace acts is an important element in transmitting the heritage, since the style and tone of the high culture can penetrate in this way to cultural levels that may be quite unfamiliar with the philosophical presuppositions underlying them.

The selections included in this chapter are intended to suggest how some aspects of ancient Indian experience have had a particularly influential role in the growth of the Hindu tradition. Many of the passages are from the Atharva Veda, which is largely a collection of incantations and charms that have an intimate relationship to the everyday lives of the people. A distinction is sometimes made between the levels of religious and cultural experience displayed in the Rig Veda and the Atharva Veda, with the suggestion that the Atharva Veda preserves the record of a more primitive religious understanding, with an emphasis on magic. This distinction probably should not be stressed too much, however, for both in the great sacrificial rituals of the Rig Veda and in the rather crude charms and spells of the Atharva Veda a comparable spirit can be recognized. There is in both an almost unbounded faith in the power of the priestly class to control the processes of life, and, linked to this, a feeling that while the universe may contain many elements hostile to man, nevertheless, means of control are available. This point is worth stressing in connection with the Indian social order, for there seems to be little evidence, at least in the early literature, of any acquiescence on the part of man to natural forces or any sense of fatalism, those two attitudes popularly attributed to Indian society.

THE DUTY OF CHARITY

The stress in the Vedic hymns on the offering of gifts to the gods as an essential feature of religious experience was generalized to include the concept of the duty of liberality to all who were in need. The motivation for charity is not, therefore, an appeal to compassion based on an understanding of human suffering or of common brotherhood, but rather a recognition of the right of the recipient of a gift to share in the good fortune of the donor. The duty of almsgiving, which is a prominent feature of all Indian religions, is clearly foreshadowed in the following hymn from the *Rig Veda*.

The Gods have not ordained hunger to be our death: even to the well-fed man comes death in varied shape.

The riches of the liberal never waste away, while he who will not give finds none to comfort him.

The man with food in store who, when the needy comes in miserable case begging for bread to eat,

Hardens his heart against him—even when of old he did him service—finds not one to comfort him.

Bounteous is he who gives unto the beggar who feebly comes to him in want of food.

Success attends him in the shout of battle. He makes a friend of him in future troubles.

No friend is he who to his friend and comrade, who comes imploring food, will offer nothing.

Let him depart—no home is that to rest in—, and rather seek a stranger to support him.

Let the rich satisfy the poor implorer, and bend his eye upon a longer pathway.

Riches come now to one, now to another, and like the wheels of chariots are ever moving.

(from *Rig Veda*, X:117, in Griffith, *The Hymns of the Rig Veda*, II, p. 561, revised)

WAR

In recent years the place of non-violence in the Indian tradition has received much emphasis, but it is worth remembering that throughout India's history military prowess has been exalted and the waging of war has been regarded as an essential feature of political life. The early Aryans gloried in the ability of their horses and chariots to strike terror into the hearts of their enemies, the people of the land, and their favorite god, Indra, was a great military hero. The selection given here was probably a kind of incantation which, when recited before battle, gave special potency to the weapons of the warriors.

The warrior's look is like a thunderous rain-cloud's, when, armed with mail, he seeks the lap of battle.

Be thou victorious with unwounded body: so let the thickness of thy mail protect thee.

With Bow let us win kine, with Bow the battle, with Bow be victors in our hot encounters.

The Bow brings grief and sorrow to the foeman: armed with the Bow may we subdue all regions.

Close to his ear, as fain to speak, She presses, holding her well-loved Friend in her embraces.

Strained on the Bow, She whispers like a woman—this Bowstring that preserves us in the combat.

These, meeting like a woman and her lover, bear, motherlike their child upon their bosom.

May the two Bow-ends, starting swift asunder, scatter, in unison, the foes who hate us.

With many a son, father of many daughters, He clangs and clashes as he goes to battle.

Slung on the back, pouring his brood, the Quiver vanquishes all opposing bands and armies.

Upstanding in the Car the skilful Charioteer guides his strong Horses on whithersoe'er he will.

See and admire the strength of those controlling Reins which from behind declare the will of him who drives.

Horses whose hoofs rain dust are neighing loudly, yoked to the Chariots, showing forth their vigour.

With their forefeet descending on the foemen, they, never flinching, trample and destroy them. . . .

He lays his blows upon their backs, he deals his blows upon their thighs.

Thou, Whip, who urgest horses, drive sagacious horses in
  the fray.
It compasses the arm with serpent windings, fending away
  the friction of the bowstring:
So may the Brace, well-skilled in all its duties, guard man-
  fully the man from every quarter.
Now to the Shaft with venom smeared, tipped with deer-
  horn, with iron mouth.
Celestial, of the Rain God's seed, be this great adoration
  paid.
Loosed from the Bowstring fly away, thou Arrow, sharpened by our prayer.
Go to the foemen, strike them home, and let not one be
  left alive.

(from *Rig Veda*, VI:75, in Griffith, *The Hymns of the Rig
Veda*, I, pp. 645-47)

CHARMS AND SPELLS
FOR A GOOD LIFE

Valuable sources of information regarding the everyday life of
the ancient Indian peoples are contained in the numerous incantations and spells of the *Atharva Veda*. They feared the
demons and evil spirits who haunted the forests, but, even
more, they feared the sorcerers who had the power to control
the forces of evil. Scarcely differentiated from the malign spiritual forces were the natural sources of death and injury—dis-
eases, wild beasts, serpents. In their world, as in the Psalmist's,
pestilence walked in darkness, and destruction wasted at noon-
day. This did not mean, however, that they felt helpless before
the dark powers; on the contrary, through their armory of spells
and magic formulae they were confident of their ability to
meet and master the external world. And in addition to charms
for protecting life, they had a wide variety of spells to bring

about the birth of sons, to gain success in trading, and to compel the love of men and women.

Examples of these ancient spells are given here. Presumably they were accompanied by symbolic actions which, in consort with the spoken word and the proper materials, brought about the desired ends. This process of "sympathetic magic" is found in many cultures, but it appears to have been elaborated to an unusual degree within the Indian tradition and, through being related to the high religious and philosophical tradition, to have played a unique part in the development of society.

Against Jaundice

Unto the sun let them both go up—your heartburn and your yellowness; with the color of the red bull do we envelop you.

With red colors do we envelop you for the sake of long life; so that this person may be free from harm and may become non-yellow.

Those cows that have Rohinī [the Red One] as presiding divinity, as also cows which are red—their every form and every power—with them do we envelop you.

Into the parrots do we put your yellowness and into the yellow-green birds. Similarly into the turmeric [or yellow wagtail?] do we deposit your yellowness.

(from *Atharva Veda*, I:22, in *Sources of Indian Tradition*, p. 20)

Against Serpents

Let not the serpent, O gods, slay us with our children and with our men. The closed jaw shall not snap open, the open one shall not close. Homage to the divine folk [i.e., the serpents, by way of exorcistic euphemism].

Homage be to the black serpent, homage to the one with stripes across its body, homage to the brown constrictor [?], homage to the divine folk.

I smite your teeth with tooth, I smite your two jaws
with jaw; I smite your tongue with tongue; I smite your
mouth, O Serpent, with mouth.

(from *Atharva Veda*, VI:56, in *Sources of Indian Tradition*,
p. 20)

To Compel a Woman's Love

As the wind shakes this Tuft of Grass hither and thither
on the ground,
So do I stir and shake thy mind, that thou mayst be in love
with me, my darling, never to depart.
Ye, Asvins, lead together, ye unite and bring the loving
pair.
Now have the fortunes of you twain, now have your vows
and spirits met.
When eagles, calling out aloud, are screaming in the joy of
health,
Then to my calling let her come, as to the arrow's neck the
shaft.
Let what is inward turn outside, let what is outward be
within:
Seize and possess, O Plant, the mind of maidens rich in
every charm.
Seeking a husband she hath come! and I came longing for
a wife:
Even as a loudly-neighing steed my fate and fortune have I
met.

(from *Atharva Veda*, II:30, in Griffith, I, pp. 70-71)

For Success in Trading

I stir and animate the merchant Indra: may he approach
and be our guide and leader.

Chasing ill-will, wild beast, and highway robber, may he
    who hath the power give me riches.
The many paths which Gods are wont to travel, the paths
    which go between the earth and heaven,
May they rejoice with me in milk and fatness that I may
    make rich profit by my purchase.
With fuel, Agni! and with butter, longing, mine offering I
    present for strength and conquest;
With prayer, so far as I have strength, adoring—this holy
    hymn to gain a hundred treasures.
Pardon this stubbornness of ours, O Agni, the distant
    pathway which our feet have trodden.
Propitious unto us be sale and barter, may interchange of
    merchandise enrich me.
Accept, ye twain, accordant, this libation! Prosperous be
    our ventures and incomings.
The wealth wherewith I carry on my traffic, seeking, ye
    Gods! wealth with the wealth I offer,
May this grow more for me, not less: O Agni, through
    sacrifice chase those who hinder profit!

(from *Atharva Veda*, III:15, in Griffith, I, pp. 116-17)

IN PRAISE OF THE COW

Although the unique place accorded to the cow is one of the
best-known features of the Hindu tradition, it is difficult to define the nature of the relationship of the cow to the religious
structure. This is probably partly to be explained by the fact
that no very close analogy exists elsewhere, and therefore one
cannot draw upon other cultural examples to illumine the situation, but it is also to be explained in terms of changing
values within the tradition itself. To say that the cow is regarded as sacred is probably correct, but in a tradition notable
for the proliferation of deities and for the willingness of people
to create plastic representations, it is remarkable that there is

no "cow goddess" nor is the cow—as distinct from the bull—found in the form of an idol in temples. Furthermore, the prohibition on cow-killing and the eating of beef, which characterizes Hinduism from the early centuries of the Christian era, was apparently unknown in Vedic times.

From very early times, however, the cow was revered as the possessor of great power. It is frequently suggested this is the natural reaction of an agricultural people to an animal valuable for plowing, transportation, fertilizer, and food, but this naturalistic interpretation would scarcely seem to account for the quite extraordinary sanctity that is associated with the cow. Probably one must look for the explanation in some very primitive acceptance of the cow as a totem, and then, at a later stage, in the tendency for Indian thinkers to see special significance in finding identities between the cosmic order and the familiar objects of the everyday world. The cow and her manifold useful properties provided a peculiarly satisfying object for identification. The following verses in praise of the cow are taken from a long hymn where, through a process of mystical identifications, the cow becomes the whole visible universe.

Worship to thee, springing to life, and worship to thee when born!
Worship, O Cow, to thy tail-hair, and to thy hooves, and to thy form!
Hitherward we invite with prayer the Cow who pours a thousand streams,
By whom the heaven, by whom the earth, by whom these waters are preserved. . . .
Forth from thy mouth the songs came, from thy neck's nape sprang strength, O Cow.
Sacrifice from thy flanks was born, and rays of sunlight from thy teats.
From thy fore-quarters and thy thighs motion was generated, Cow!
Food from thine entrails was produced, and from thy belly came the plants. . . .
They call the Cow immortal life, pay homage to the Cow as Death.

She hath become this universe, Fathers, and Rishis, hath
become the Gods, and men, and Spirits.

The man who hath this knowledge may receive the Cow
with welcoming.

So for the giver willingly doth perfect sacrifice pour
milk. . . .

The Cow is Heaven, the Cow is Earth, the Cow is Vishnu,
Lord of Life.

The heavenly beings have drunk the out-pourings of the
Cow.

When these heavenly beings have drunk the out-pourings
of the Cow,

They in the Bright One's dwelling-place pay adoration to
her milk.

For Soma some have milked her: some worship the fatness
she hath poured.

They who have given a cow to him who hath this knowledge have gone up to the third region of the sky.

He who hath given a Cow unto the Brāhmans winneth all
the worlds.

For Right is firmly set in her, devotion, and religious zeal.

Both Gods and mortal men depend for life and being on
the Cow.

She hath become this universe: all that the Sun surveys is
she.

(from *Atharva Veda* X:10, in Griffith, II, pp. 45-56, revised)

THE PLACE OF THE BRĀHMAN

The nature of the class divisions of Indian society will be noted
in more detail in Chapter IV, but reference must be made here
to the unique role of the Brāhman. While the class structure is
immensely complicated, and varies in character from region to
region, everywhere the highest role is assigned to the priestly

class, the Brāhmans. That the four classes—the priests (*Brāh-man*), warrior (*kshatriya*), peasant (*vaishya*), and serf (*shūdra*) —were regarded as the basic form of the special order is shown in the Hymn of Man in the *Rig Veda*, which is quoted in Chapter I. In social terms, the highest and lowest classes were probably the most important, since the Brāhmans controlled the religious institutions and the shūdras composed the bulk of the composition.

The selection given here indicates the extent of the claims made by the priests, and while the literature from which this type of statement comes was written by Brāhmans who would presumably forward their own class interests, it represents the ideal generally accepted by all classes in the society. Over against the assertion of rights made by the Brāhmans for themselves must be set the role they assigned the shūdras. The general implication is that the lower orders have obligations which can be understood as rights only in a secondary way.

A number of possibilities ought to be kept in mind in reading passages from the ancient texts dealing with class structure. On the one hand, they may be statements of hard social fact, a description of the ways things were, and not the definition of an ideal society. On the other hand, the passages may be examples of rather fanatical pretensions by priests, who while anxious to define the boundaries of the classes, were never actually able to carry out their prescriptions. This would seem, for example, to be the only explanation possible for such statements as "a shūdra is the servant of another, to be slain at will." Such a policy would have led to social anarchy, whereas the emphasis was always on social order.

. . . . Those who spit, or throw filth upon a Brāhman, sit eating hair in the midst of a stream of blood. So long as this Brāhman's cow is cut up and cooked, she destroys the glory of the kingdom; no vigorous hero is born there. It is cruel to slaughter her; her ill-flavoured flesh is thrown away. When her milk is drunk, that is esteemed a sin among the Forefathers. Whenever a king, fancying himself mighty, seeks to devour a Brāhman, that kingdom is broken up, in which a Brāhman is oppressed. Becoming eight-footed, four-eyed, four-eared, four-jawed, two-faced, two-tongued, she (the cow) shatters the kingdom of the oppressor of Brāhmans. (Ruin) overflows that kingdom, as water swamps a leaky boat: calamity smites that country in which a priest is wronged. Even trees, O Nārada, repel, and refuse their shade to, the man who claims a right to the property of a Brāhman. This (property), as king Varuṇa hath said, has been turned into a poison by the gods. No one who has eaten a Brāhman's cow continues to watch (*i.e.* to rule) over a country. . . .

The gods have declared that the cloth wherewith a dead man's feet are bound shall be thy pall, thou oppressor of priests. The tears which flow from a persecuted man as he laments,—such is the portion of water which the gods have assigned to thee, thou oppressor of priests. The gods have allotted to thee that portion of water wherewith men wash the dead, and moisten beards. The rain of Mitra and Varuṇa does not descend on the oppressor of priests. For him the battle has never a successful issue; nor does he bring his friend into subjection.

(from *Atharva Veda*, V:19, in Muir, I, pp. 286-87)

THE CROWNING OF A KING

In the early Indian tradition there is nothing that quite corresponds to western political thinking, but this does not mean that questions concerning the nature of human government were not asked. It only means that different questions were asked, and they were answered in a different way. As will be seen (in Chapter V), statecraft understood as the techniques of political control, became the subject matter of an important branch of literature. In the early period, interest centered on the relation of the king to the ritual practices of the religion and his place in the divine order.

Although there are some passages that suggest the king was elected by the people, normally this could have only meant some measure of control by the tribal or village elders. From quite early times—certainly by 600 B.C.—the king was re garded as surrounded by a special sanctity. Two things prob ably contributed to this. One was the king's participation in the great sacrifices, most notably the horse sacrifice; the othe was his membership in a class that was itself divinely ordained The selections given here, the first of which is taken from description of the coronation rites and the second of whic is from hymns probably sung at the ceremony, emphasize bot the king's power and his duty to rule according to the sacre laws of society.

King of Kings

This is the Lord of Indra, this the Lord of Heaven, th Lord of Earth,
The Lord of all existing things: the one and only Lord b thou.
The Sea is regent of the floods, Agni is ruler of the land,
The Moon is regent of the stars: the one and only Lord b thou.
Thou art the King of Earthly Kings, the crown and sun mit of mankind:
Thou art the partner of the Gods: the one and only Lor be thou.

The Chosen One

Here art thou: I have chosen thee. Stand steadfast an immovable.
Let all the clans desire thee: let not thy kingdom fall awa
Be even here: fall not away: be like a mountain unr moved.
Stand steadfast here like Indra's self, and hold the kingshi in thy grasp.
This man hath Indra stablished, made secure by constan sacrifice.

Soma, and Brahmanaspati here present bless and comfort him!

The Enduring Ruler

Firm is the sky, firm is the earth, and firm is all this living world;

Firm are these mountains on their base, and steadfast is this King of men.

Steadfast may Varuna the King, steadfast the God Brihaspati,

Steadfast may Indra, steadfast, too, may Agni keep thy steadfast reign.

Firm, never to be shaken, crush thy foemen, under thy feet lay those who strive against thee.

One-minded, true to thee be all the regions: faithful to thee, the firm, be this assembly!

(from *Atharva Veda*, VI:86,87,88, in Griffith, I, pp. 292-293, revised)

EARTH AS MOTHERLAND

One of the most enduring and vital features of the Hindu tradition is the concept of the earth as motherland. Hinduism is very firmly rooted in the Indian soil, and, unlike the other great religions, has tended to be confined to the region of its origin. The geography of the great myths and legends is the actual geography of India, and almost every hill and river has some association that is a constant reminder of the great deeds of the gods. The importance of this "sacred geography" in maintaining the tradition, and of continually renewing its meaning to the people, can scarcely be overestimated. The magnificent Hymn to Earth (or *Prithivī*) is one of the clearest expressions of the conviction that the Earth is a fitting symbol for the deepest of religious impulses.

Truth, high and potent Law, the Consecrating Rite, Fervour, Brahma, and Sacrifice uphold the Earth.

May she, the Queen of all that is and is to be, may Earth make ample space and room for us.

Not over-crowded by the crowd of Manu's sons, she who hath many heights and floods and level plains;

She who bears plants endowed with many varied powers, may Earth for us spread wide and favour us.

In whom the sea, and the great river, and the waters, in whom our food and corn-lands had their being,

In whom this all that breathes and moves is active, this Earth assign us foremost rank and station!

She who is Lady of the earth's four regions, in whom our food and corn-lands had their being,

Nurse in each place of breathing, moving creatures, this Earth vouchsafe us kine with milk that fails not!

On whom the men of old before us battled, on whom the Gods attacked the hostile demons,

The varied home of bird, and kine and horses, this Earth vouchsafe us luck and splendour! . . .

O Earth, auspicious be thy woodlands, auspicious be thy hills and snow-clad mountains.

Unslain, unwounded, unsubdued, I have set foot upon the Earth,

On earth, brown, black, ruddy and every-coloured, on the firm earth that Indra guards from danger.

O Earth, thy centre and thy navel, all forces that have issued from thy body—

Set us amid those forces; breathe upon us. I am the son of Earth, Earth is my Mother. The Rain God is my Sire; may he promote me.

Earth on whose surface they enclose the altar, and all performers spin the thread of worship;

In whom the stakes of sacrifice, resplendent, are fixed and raised on high before the oblation, may she, this Earth prospering, make us prosper.

The man who hates us, Earth! who fights against us, who

threatens us with thought or deadly weapon, make him our thrall as thou hast done aforetime.

(from *Atharva Veda*, XII:1, in Griffith, II, pp. 93-101, revised)

CHAPTER III

THE CROWN OF
THE VEDIC AGE:
THE UPANISHADS

∾∾∾∾∾

The designation of the Upanishads as "the end of th
Veda" (Vedānta) indicates both their place in the tem
poral sequence of the Vedic literature and their position
within the canon of Hindu scripture as the summation o
the truth contained in all the previous works. Over a hun
dred works are given the name of "Upanishad" but onl
about thirteen of these can be dated with assurance as be
longing to the Vedic Age. They do not present any con
sistent religious or philosophical system, and even within
single work there may be contradictions; nor do they claim
to present new truths. It is sometimes suggested that th
Upanishads are the product of a religious revolt, a turnin
away from the rigid ritualistic formulations of the past, bu
there actually is little within the works themselves to sug
gest any such origin. There is no attack on the old ways, n
demand for reform; at most, there is an indifference t
some features of the older Vedic sacrificial tradition. I
general, the ideas of the Upanishads can be traced to de
velopments which had already made their appearance i
the older texts.

Yet having emphasized their continuity with the trad
tion, it must be recognized that the spirit and temper o
the Upanishads is remarkably different from that of th

earlier literature. New questions were ___
form determined the answers given to the ___
most notable transformations that took place ___
tion related to the understanding of sacrifice. ___
in ritualistic performance, with fantastic attentio___ details, was replaced by an interest in attaining the same
goals through meditation and concentration, with the
physical materials of the old sacrifices being treated in a
symbolic fashion. Related to this was a turning inward to
examine the nature of reality, rather than studying the
external world. The aim of this examination of the self was
not, however, psychological understanding; it was motivated by the conviction that "underlying the exterior
world of change there is an unchangeable reality which is
identical with that which underlies the essence of man." [1]

The Vedic thinkers had been inclined to identify some
particular phenomenon—wind or water, for example—as a
god, and to see this as the ultimate source of the universe.
In the Upanishads this unifying principle is seen to be not
a deity or any physical property but brahman, that myste-
rious principle that even in early thought is regarded as
forming the substratum of the universe. At the same time,
the basis of human selfhood was understood to be the ātman, the self or soul. One conclusion that the sages of the
Upanishads reached was that these two principles, brahman and ātman, were identical, and that the essence of
being underlying both the self and the external was absolutely undifferentiated. This doctrine is summed up in the
famous formula, tat tvam asi, "that art thou," with "that"
standing for the universal brahman, "thou" for the individual ātman. An exposition of this is given in the selection
below entitled "The Identity of Brahman and Ātman."

Although this assertion of the ultimate identity of brahman and ātman seems to be the dominating theme of the
Upanishads, there are other interpretations of the nature
of the relationship between the two principles. One of the

---

[1] S. N. Dasgupta, A History of Indian Philosophy (Cambridge:
1922), I, p. 42.

panishads, Śvetāśvatara, *speaks of* brahman *as* God, *making a distinction between this and the external world. In addition to this theistic interpretation, there is also a movement towards pantheism, a tendency to think of the natural universe and the individual soul as* God.

These varying interpretations could exist side by side because the sages and teachers were not seeking to formulate a statement of belief but something entirely different, "a radical alteration in the mode of consciousness . . . with a view to gaining intuitive knowledge of reality." [2] They defined this reality in terms of the brahman-ātman equation, but their quest can probably also be understood in western terminology as an attempt to experience a sense of the immortality of the soul, to find a self more permanent than the ego immediately known to consciousness. At this level of the Indian tradition, therefore, the religious concern is not with a relationship between man and God, but with the realization of the nature of the self. This is brought out in the selection, "Ātman: the Real Self."

Underlying much of the speculation of the Upanishads are the two closely related concepts, karma and transmigration. Karma, literally "action," is the belief that every act produces an effect which inevitably finds fruition. One of the great unquestioned assumptions of the Indian tradition, this doctrine may have its roots in the idea of rita, the cosmic principle that the early Vedic peoples saw as ordering the whole universe. The prominence of the idea of sacrifice must also have been a contributing factor in the development of the belief in karma, for sacrifice was the supreme action that men could perform, and the performance of the ritual led inevitably to certain results.

Indissolubly linked with the concept of karma is the other great characteristic feature of Indian thought, the belief in transmigration. The idea that the human soul on death finds lodging in another body is widespread, but by being linked with the doctrine of karma it took on special

[2] R. C. Zaehner, *At Sundry Times* (London: Faber and Faber 1958), p. 37.

significance. Since every act carries with it an inevitable result, the span of one lifetime may not suffice as a field for the working out of all the implications of action. Transmigration makes possible, therefore, a belief in the strict justice of the universe, with each action reaping its due reward of good or evil fruit. Conversely, the two concepts can be used to explain the seeming injustices and inequities of the world.

The concepts of karma and transmigration have had enormous influence on every aspect of the Indian tradition, and were accepted in some form not only by Hinduism but also by Jainism and Buddhism, both of which rejected the Vedic scriptures. Readings to illustrate them have been included in this section because they are accepted without question as part of the structure of the universe.

THE NEW MEANING
OF SACRIFICE

While the Upanishadic thinkers turned to new concepts of religion, they did not abandon the old ritual forms, but transformed what had been actual physical acts into symbolic representations. One of the best examples of this is the elaborate allegorization of the Horse Sacrifice, the greatest of the Vedic rituals. Involving large numbers of priests and great preparations, it exemplified the extreme development of external ritual. Basically, it was the act whereby a king proclaimed his intention to become a "world ruler," or, more prosaically, to extend his territory, and the horse represented such qualities as virility, power, and majesty. To the Upanishadic thinker, the significance of the sacrifice was in the identities he saw between the great sacrificial animal and the cosmos. Through this process of symbolic identification the sage moved towards a statement of the unity of the disparate parts of the universe and also linked his meditations with the sacrificial ritual, whose power and potency had long been accepted as a fundamental feature of existence.

Dawn verily is the head of the sacrificial horse. The sun is his eye; the wind, his breath; the universal sacrificial fire, his open mouth; the year is the body (ātman) of the sacrificial horse. The sky is his back; the atmosphere, his belly; the earth, his underbelly; the directions, his flanks; the intermediate directions, his ribs; the seasons, his limbs; the months and half-months, his joints; days and nights, his feet; the stars, his bones; the clouds, his flesh. Sand is the food in his stomach; rivers, his entrails; mountains, his liver and lungs; plants and trees, his hair; the rising sun, his forepart; the setting sun, his hindpart. When he yawns, then it lightnings; when he shakes himself, then it thunders; when he urinates, then it rains. Speech (vāc) is actually his neighing (vāc).

(from *Brihad Āranyaka*, I:1:1, in *Sources of Indian Tradition* pp. 27-28)

BRAHMAN: THE SEARCH FOR
THE GROUND OF THE UNIVERSE

In their quest for some ultimate ground for the world o natural phenomena, of time and space, and of human exist ence, the Upanishadic sages came to the conception of *brah man*, an undefinable, impersonal, unknowable power. One o the most interesting discussions of this absolute principle i given in the form of a dialogue between Gārgī, a woma philosopher, and Yājnavalkya, a great sage. Although in th preceding dialogues Gārgī had been warned not to ask to many questions, lest her head fall off, she persisted, and wa rewarded with answers to her questions.

Yājñavalkya said: 'Ask, Gārgī.'

She said: 'That, O Yājñavalkya, which is above the sky, that which is beneath the earth, that which is between these two, sky and earth, that which people call the past and the present and the future—across what is that woven, warp and woof?'

He said: 'That, O Gārgī, which is above the sky, that which is beneath the earth, that which is between these two, sky and earth, that which people call the past and the present and the future—across space is that woven, warp and woof.'

She said: 'Adoration to you, Yājñavalkya, in that you have solved this question for me. Prepare yourself for the other.'

'Ask, Gārgī.'

She said: 'That, O Yājñavalkya, which is above the sky, that which is beneath the earth, that which is between these two, sky and earth, that which people call the past and the present and the future—across what is that woven, warp and woof?'

He said: 'That, O Gārgī, which is above the sky, that which is beneath the earth, that which is between these two, sky and earth, that which people call the past and the present and the future—across space alone is that woven, warp and woof.'

'Across what then, pray, is space woven, warp and woof?'

He said: 'That, O Gārgī, Brāhmans call the Imperishable (*akṣara*). It is not coarse, not fine, not short, not long, not glowing [like fire], not adhesive [like water], without shadow and without darkness, without air and without space, without stickiness, (intangible), odorless, tasteless, without eye, without ear, without voice, without wind, without energy, without breath, without mouth, (without personal or family name, unaging, undying, without fear, immortal, stainless, not uncovered, not covered), without measure, without inside and without outside.

> *It consumes nothing soever.*
> *No one soever consumes it.*

Verily, O Gārgī, at the command of that Imperishable
the sun and the moon stand apart. Verily, O Gārgī, at the
command of that Imperishable the earth and the sky stand
apart. Verily, O Gārgī, at the command of that Imperishable the moments, the hours, the days, the nights, the
fortnights, the months, the seasons, and the years stand
apart. Verily, O Gārgī, at the command of that Imperishable some rivers flow from the snowy mountains to the
east, others to the west, in whatever direction each flows.
Verily, O Gārgī, at the command of that Imperishable
men praise those who give, the gods are desirous of a sacrificer, and the fathers [are desirous] of the Manes-sacrifice.

Verily, O Gārgī, if one performs sacrifices and worship
and undergoes austerity in this world for many thousands
of years, but without knowing that Imperishable, limited
indeed is that [work] of his. Verily, O Gārgī, he who departs from this world without knowing that Imperishable
is pitiable. But, O Gārgī, he who departs from this world
knowing that Imperishable is a Brāhman.

Verily, O Gārgī, that Imperishable is the unseen Seer,
the unheard Hearer, the unthought Thinker, the ununder-
stood Understander. Other than It there is naught that
sees. Other than It there is naught that hears. Other than
It there is naught that thinks. Other than It there is
naught that understands. Across this Imperishable, O
Gārgī, is space woven, warp and woof.'

She said: 'Venerable Brāhmans, you may think it a great
thing if you escape from this man with [merely] making a
bow. Not one of you will surpass him in discussions about
Brahman.'

Thereupon [Gārgī] held her peace.

(from *Brihad Āranyaka*, III:8:2-12, in Hume, *The Thirteen
Principal Upanishads*, pp. 118-19)

ĀTMAN: THE REAL SELF

Over against the questions concerning the ground of the external world are to be set those that probe inward, asking what is meant by the concept of the Self. The Self could be identified with the physical body, or "food," as some of the Upanishadic thinkers were inclined to say. But consciousness, breath, will, all had claims to be regarded as the Self, and all were unsatisfactory as final definitions. What was needed was something that could be identified as being beyond change, something that was in fact immortal. This was found in the conception of the *ātman* as given in the following parable. Here the Self is, as another *Upanishad* says, "the shining, immortal Person." The search for this permanent and unchanging reality found expression in the famous prayer, in the *Brihad Aranyaka*:

> From the unreal lead me to the real;
> From darkness lead me to the light;
> From death lead me to deathlessness.

The Self (ātman) who is free from evil, free from old age, free from death, free from grief, free from hunger, free from thirst, whose desire is the Real, whose intention is the Real—he should be sought after, he should be desired to be comprehended. He obtains all worlds and all desires, who, having found out that Self, knows him." Thus, indeed, did the god Prajāpati speak. Verily, the gods and the demons both heard this. They said among themselves: "Aha! Let us seek after that Self—the Self, having sought after whom one obtains all worlds and all desires." Then Indra from among the gods went forth unto Prajāpati, and Virochana from among the demons. Indeed, without communicating with each other, those two came into the presence of Prajāpati with sacrificial fuel in hand [i.e., as students willing to serve their preceptor]. For thirty-two years the two lived under Prajāpati the disci-

plined life of a student of sacred knowledge. Then Praj
pati asked them: "Desiring what have you lived the dis
plined life of a student of sacred knowledge under me
They said: " 'The Self, who is free from evil, free from o
age, free from death, free from grief, free from hunge
free from thirst, whose desire is the Real, whose intentic
is the Real—he should be sought after, he should l
desired to be comprehended. He obtains all worlds and
desires, who, having found out that Self, knows him
These, people declare to be the venerable master's worc
Desiring him [the Self] have we lived the student's life u
der you." Prajāpati said to them: "That Purusha who
seen in the eye—he is the Self (ātman)," said he. "That
the immortal, the fearless; that is Brahman." "But th
one, Sir, who is perceived in water and in a mirror—who
he?" Prajāpati replied: "The same one, indeed, is pe
ceived in all these." "Having looked at yourself in a pan
water, whatever you do not comprehend of the Self, te
that to me," said Prajāpati. They looked at themselves
the pan of water. Prajāpati asked them: "What do ye
see?" They replied: "We see here, Sir, our own selves
entirety, the very reproduction of our forms, as it wer
correct to the hairs and the nails." Then Prajāpati said
them: "Having become well ornamented, well dresse
and refined, look at yourselves in a pan of water." Havi
become well ornamented, well dressed, and refined, th
looked at themselves in a pan of water. Thereupon Pra
pati asked them: "What do you see?" They replied: "Ju
as we ourselves here are, Sir, well ornamented, we
dressed, and refined. . . ." "That is the Self," said l
"That is the immortal, the fearless; that is Brahmar
Then they went away with a tranquil heart. Having look
at them, Prajāpati said to himself: "They are going aw
without having realized, without having found out tl
Self. Whosoever will accept this doctrine as final, be th
gods or demons, they shall perish." Then Virochana, ve
ily, with a tranquil heart, went to the demons and declar
to them that doctrine, namely: One's self [one's bodi

elf] alone is to be made happy here; one's self is to be
erved. Making oneself alone happy here, serving oneself,
oes one obtain both worlds, this world and the yonder.
Therefore, here, even now, they say of one who is not a
iver, who has no faith, who does not offer sacrifices, that
e is, indeed, a demon; for this is the doctrine of the demons. They adorn the body of the deceased with per-
umes, flowers, etc., which they have begged, with dress
nd with ornaments, for they think they will thereby win
he yonder world.

But then Indra, even before reaching the gods, saw this
danger: "Just as, indeed, the bodily self becomes well ornamented when this body is well ornamented, well dressed
when this body is well dressed, and refined when this body
s refined, even so that one becomes blind when this body
s blind, lame when this body is lame, and maimed when
his body is maimed. The bodily Self, verily, perishes immediately after the perishing of this body. I see no good in
his." With sacrificial fuel in hand, he again came back to
Prajāpati. [Indra states his objection to Prajāpati, who admits its truth and asks him to live as a student under him
for another thirty-two years.] Indra lived a student's life
under Prajāpati for another thirty-two years. Then, Prajāpati said to him: "He who moves about happy in a dream
—he is the Self," said he. "That is the immortal, the fear-
ess; that is Brahman." Thereupon, with a tranquil heart,
ndra went away.

But then, even before reaching the gods, he saw this
danger: "Now, even though this body is blind, the Self in
he dream-condition does not become blind; even though
his body is lame, he does not become lame; indeed, he
does not suffer any defect through the defect of this body.
He is not slain with the slaying of this body. He does not
become lame with the lameness of this body. Nevertheless,
hey, as it were, kill him; they, as it were, unclothe him.
He, as it were, becomes the experiencer of what is not
agreeable; he, as it were, even weeps. I see no good in
his." [Again Indra returns to Prajāpati with his objection.

The latter admits its truth but asks Indra to be his studen
for another thirty-two years.] Then Prajāpati said to him
"Now, when one is sound asleep, composed, serene, an
knows no dream—that is the Self," said he. "That is th
immortal, the fearless; that is Brahman." Thereupon, wi
a tranquil heart, Indra went away.

But then, even before reaching the gods, he saw th
danger: "Assuredly, this Self in the deep sleep conditic
does not, indeed, now know himself in the form: 'I a
he'; nor indeed does he know these things here. He, as
were, becomes one who has gone to annihilation. I see
good in this." [Indra once more returns to Prajāpati, wh
promises to tell him the final truth after another five yea
of studentship.] Indra lived a student's life under Praj
pati for another five years. The total number of these yea
thus came to one hundred and one; thus it is that peop
say that, verily, for one hundred and one years Maghava
[Indra, the Rewarder] lived under Prajāpati the dis
plined life of a student of sacred knowledge. Then Praj
pati said to him: "O Maghavan, mortal, indeed, is th
body; it is taken over by death. But it is the basis of th
deathless, bodiless Self. Verily, the Self, when embodie
is taken over by pleasure and pain. Verily, there is no fre
dom from pleasure and pain for one who is associated wi
the body. The wind is bodiless; cloud, lightning, thund
—these are bodiless. Now as these, having risen up fro
yonder space and having reached the highest light, appe
each with its own form, even so this serene Self, havi
risen up from this body and having reached the highe
light, appears with its own form. That Self is the Suprer
Person."

(from *Chāndogya*, VIII:7-12, in *Sources of Indian Traditic*
pp. 30-33).

THE IDENTITY OF BRAHMAN AND ĀTMAN

In the macrocosm of the universe, the sages saw *brahman*; in the microcosm of their own being they saw the *ātman*. The realization that there is no distinction between the two, that the ground of one's own being is identical with the ground of the universe, is the great discovery of the Upanishadic thinkers. "Whoever thus knows, 'I am *brahman*,'" declares the sage, "becomes this all. Even the gods have not the power to prevent him from becoming thus, for he thus becomes the self." The best-known statement of this identity of individual self and universal self is given here. It should be carefully noted that this is not described as merging with the divine or union between God and man or reaching a state of unity. It is rather a recognition that there is no "divine" as distinct from the individual, no being over against the self, no process of becoming what once was not, but only the knowledge of the truth that always existed.

There, verily, was Shvetaketu, the son of Uddālaka Āruni. To him his father said: "O Shvetaketu, live the disciplined life of a student of sacred knowledge (brahmacharya). No one, indeed, my dear, belonging to our family, is unlearned in the Veda and remains a brāhman only by family connections as it were." He, then, having approached a teacher at the age of twelve and having studied all the Vedas, returned at the age of twenty-four, conceited, thinking himself to be learned, stiff. To him his father said: "O Shvetaketu, since, my dear, you are now conceited, think yourself to be learned, and have become stiff, did you also ask for that instruction whereby what has been unheard becomes heard, what has been unthought of becomes thought of, what has been uncomprehended becomes comprehended?" "How, indeed, Sir, is that instruction?" asked Shvetaketu. "Just as, my dear, through the

comprehension of one lump of clay all that is made of cla
would become comprehended—for the modification is o
casioned only on account of a convention of speech, it
only a name; while clay as such alone is the reality. Just a
my dear, through the comprehension of one ingot of irc
all that is made of iron would become comprehended—fe
the modification is occasioned only on account of a con
vention of speech, it is only a name; while iron as suc
alone is the reality. . . . So, my dear, is that instruction
"Now, verily, those venerable teachers did not know thi
for, if they had known it, why would they not have tol
me?" said Shvetaketu. "However, may the venerable s
tell it to me." "So be it, my dear," said he.

"In the beginning, my dear, this world was just bein
one only, without a second. Some people, no doubt, sav
'In the beginning, verily, this world was just nonbeing, or
only, without a second; from that nonbeing, being wa
produced.' But how, indeed, my dear, could it be so?" sai
he. "How could being be produced from nonbeing? O
the contrary, my dear, in the beginning this world was b
ing alone, one only, without a second. Being thought t
itself: 'May I be many; may I procreate.' It produced fir
That fire thought to itself: 'May I be many, may I procr
ate.' It produced water. Therefore, whenever a perso
grieves or perspires, then it is from fire [heat] alone tha
water is produced. That water thought to itself: 'May I b
many; may I procreate.' It produced food. Therefor
whenever it rains, then there is abundant food; it is fro
water alone that food for eating is produced. . . . Tha
divinity (Being) thought to itself: 'Well, having entere
into these three divinities [fire, water, and food] by mear
of this living Self, let me develop names and forms. Let m
make each one of them tripartite.' That divinity, accor
ingly, having entered into those three divinities by mear
of this living Self, developed names and forms. . . .
made each one of them tripartite. . . .

"Bring hither a fig from there." "Here it is, sir." "Brea
it." "It is broken, sir." "What do you see there?" "The

extremely fine seeds, sir." "Of these, please break one." "It is broken, sir." "What do you see there?" "Nothing at all, sir." Then he said to Shvetaketu: "Verily, my dear, that subtle essence which you do not perceive—from that very essence, indeed, my dear, does this great fig tree thus arise. Believe me, my dear, that which is the subtle essence—this whole world has that essence for its Self; that is the Real; that is the Self; that subtle essence art thou, Shvetaketu." "Still further may the venerable sir instruct me." "So be it, my dear," said he.

"Having put this salt in the water, come to me in the morning." He did so. Then the father said to him: "That salt which you put in the water last evening—please bring it hither." Even having looked for it, he did not find it, for it was completely dissolved. "Please take a sip of water from this end," said the father. "How is it?" "Salt." "Take a sip from the middle," said he. "How is it?" "Salt." "Take a sip from that end," said he. "How is it?" "Salt." "Throw it away and come to me." Shvetaketu did so thinking to himself: "That salt, though unperceived, still persists in the water." Then Āruni said to him: "Verily, my dear, you do not perceive Being in this world; but it is, indeed, here only: That which is the subtle essence—this whole world has that essence for its Self. That is the Real. That is the Self. That art thou, Shvetaketu." "Still further may the venerable sir instruct me." "So be it, my dear," said he.

"Just as, my dear, having led away a person from Gandhāra with his eyes bandaged, one might then abandon him in a place where there are no human beings; and as that person would there drift about toward the east or the north or the south: 'I have been led away here with my eyes bandaged, I have been abandoned here with my eyes bandaged'; then as, having released his bandage, one might tell him: 'In that direction lies Gandhāra; go in that direction.' Thereupon he, becoming wise and sensible, would, by asking his way from village to village, certainly reach Gandhāra. Even so does one who has a teacher here know:

'I shall remain here [in this phenomenal world] only a
long as I shall not be released from the bonds of nescience
Then I shall reach my home.' "

(from *Chāndogya*, VI:1-14, *passim*, in *Sources of Indian Tra
dition*, pp. 33-36)

KARMA AND TRANSMIGRATION

The conviction that *karma*, the law of cause and effect, worke
so that every action must have a result, was well-established
when the earliest *Upanishads* were written. The fruits of ac
tion—which included thoughts and desires as well as actua
deeds—are inexorably fulfilled and according to necessity buil
into the structure of the universe. The idea of rebirth of th
soul may well have been an older idea, but in any case th
two concepts fitted together, with actions in one life determin
ing the conditions of future existences, and producing an end
less cycle of rebirths. In this conception there is no though
of punishment and reward given by some deity external t
man; indeed, many schools of thought which explicitly rejec
belief in gods accept the doctrine of *karma*. The system i
one of perfect justice—a man reaps precisely what he sows
Nor is there anything inherently pessimistic about the scheme
since man is master of his fate.

According as one acts, according as one conducts himself,
so does he become. The doer of good becomes good. The
doer of evil becomes evil. One becomes virtuous by virtu
ous action, bad by bad action.

But people say: "A person is made not of acts, but o
desires only." In reply to this I say: As is his desire, such is
his resolve; as is his resolve, such the action he performs;
what action (*karma*) he performs, that he procures fo
himself.

On this point there is this verse:—

Where one's mind is attached—the inner self
Goes thereto with action, being attached to it alone.

> *Obtaining the end of his action,*
> *Whatever he does in this world,*
> *He comes again from that world*
> *To this world of action.*

So the man who desires.

Now the man who does not desire.—He who is without desire, who is freed from desire, whose desire is satisfied, whose desire is the Soul—his breaths do not depart. Being very Brahman, he goes to Brahman.

(from *Brihad Āranyaka*, IV:4:5-6, in Hume, pp. 140-41)

Accordingly, those who are of pleasant conduct here—the prospect is, indeed, that they will enter a pleasant womb, either the womb of a Brahman, or the womb of a Kshatriya, or the womb of a Vaishya. But those who are of stinking conduct here—the prospect is, indeed, that they will enter a stinking womb, either the womb of a dog, or the womb of a swine, or the womb of an outcaste (*candāla*).

(from *Chāndogya*, V:10:7, in Hume, p. 233)

By the delusions of imagination, touch, and sight,
And by eating, drinking, and impregnation there is birth
    and development of the self.
According unto his deeds (*karma*) the embodied one successively
Assumes forms in various conditions.

(from *Śvetāśvatara*, V:11-12, in Hume, p. 407)

EMANCIPATION
FROM KARMA

In some of the *Upanishads* the problem of emancipation
salvation is closely related to the concepts of *karma* and r
birth, and of the statement of the identity of individual se
with the world self. On the one hand, *karma* stresses recu
rence, continual renewal and rebirth; but this very emphas
leads to a discussion of what is reborn and renewed in th
cyclical process. On the other hand, the doctrine of the ide
tity of *ātman* and *brahman* stresses the permanent and u
changing. This seeming contradiction between the two co
cepts was solved by the understanding that the cycle
rebirth is caused by ignorance of the true nature of the Se
and the failure to realize that it never changes or alters. Ema
cipation becomes, therefore, a process of coming to an awar
ness of that state of being that is beyond process, the identit
of *ātman* and *brahman*. To have this intuitive knowledge is t
become immortal, for "knowing All, he becomes All." Whi
in one sense it is true to say that this search is defined i
terms of escape from the cycle of rebirth, on a higher level
is to be understood as the realization of the soul's true nature

The wise one [the Self] is not born, nor dies.
This one has not come from anywhere, has not becom
   anyone.
Unborn, constant, eternal, primeval, this one
Is not slain when the body is slain. . . .
He, however, who has not understanding,
Who is unmindful and ever impure,
Reaches not the goal,
But goes on to reincarnation.
He, however, who has understanding,
Who is mindful and ever pure,
Reaches the goal
From which he is born no more. . . .

When are liberated all the desires that lodge in one's
  heart,
Then a mortal becomes immortal!
Therein he reaches Brahman!
When are cut all the knots of the heart here on earth,
Then a mortal becomes immortal!

(from *Katha*, II, III, and VI, selected verses, in Hume, pp.
349, 352, and 360)

PART TWO

THE GROWTH OF
THE TRADITION

〰〰〰〰

(550 B.C.–300 A.D.)

INTRODUCTION

Few cultural stereotypes are less acceptable than that
which sees Indian civilization as static and unchanging.
While it is true that there is an unquestionable continuity
linking the remote past in an unbroken line with the present, there have been numerous transformations within the
general cultural pattern. These have not involved a rejection of the past or a break with historic traditions, but they
have led to a culture of extraordinary richness and diversity. It was this possibility for inward transformation that
led the modern Indian thinker Sri Aurobindo to speak of
India's "stupendous vitality, her inexhaustible power of
life and joy of life, her almost unimaginable prolific crea-
tiveness." [1]

The sixth century B.C. saw the beginning of one such
period of creativity, and the force of this outburst of energy altered many features of Indian life. To this time belong many of the great achievements of the Indian mind,
and at the end of the age—the first and second centuries
of the Christian era—remarkable changes had taken place
in the social and religious life of India. By that time, almost all the great themes of the tradition can be clearly

[1] Sri Aurobindo, *The Renaissance in India* (Calcutta: Ayra Publishing House, 1946), p. 11.

discerned, and the form and style of the great classical Hindu civilization that reached its zenith after the fourth century A.D have been foreshadowed.

As we have seen, the Vedic Age provided the Hindu tradition with attitudes and values which have in large measure become unquestioned assumptions. One of these was the cluster of ideas around the belief in *karma* and rebirth; another was the acceptance of the divinely-ordained class structure. Related to both of these, and supporting them while being in turn fortified by them, was the concept of *dharma*, one of the most pervasive of all Hindu ideas. In the earliest Vedic literature the concept of an unalterable moral law underlying the universe had made possible the creation of a coherent world-view, and as *dharma* this was transformed into a definition of the duties and obligations of social life. *Dharma* received its most explicit formulations in the great law books that outlined the nature of the social order, especially as it was exemplified in the class structure.

Historically, the period from about 550 B.C. to 300 A.D. is marked by the rise to prominence of two great religious movements, Jainism and Buddhism, and by the emergence of great empires that attempted for the first time to create governmental authorities that would bring most of the area of India under the rule of one dynasty. The center of both the religious and political movements was the area south and north of the Ganges River now known as Bihar. Here Magadha, the first Indian state of which we have any certain knowledge, began a career of expansion shortly after 600 B.C. By the end of the century, under Bimbisāra, it had become the strongest state of North India and it retained this position for over three hundred years. Of the history of South India at this time we know very little, but probably there were no kingdoms as strong as those of the Magadha rulers.

It was during the reign of Bimbisāra that Gautama (died about 483 B.C.), the founder of Buddhism, and Mahāvira (died about 468 B.C.), the founder of Jainism, flourished. Both were members of the warrior class who left their homes in search of salvation. They were also alike in rejecting the Vedic literature as the revealed truth from which there could be no dissent; having gathered followers, they taught doctrines that bear many resemblances to each other. But there is no real evidence that either influenced the other; their lives and teachings must be seen as part of the intellectual ferment that characterized the age. Although both Buddhism and Jainism are closely related to the main Hindu tradition, no attempt will be made to present their doctrines here, except insofar as they illumine certain features of the main cultural movement. The particular emphasis in Jain thought that had a considerable influence on general Indian thinking was the belief that all matter possessed living souls, and that therefore killing and violence of all kinds were evil. The belief in *ahimsa*, or non-killing, became a common belief and was finally given political implications by Mahatma Gandhi in our own time. Buddhism, with its analysis of the human condition as characterized by suffering occasioned by desire or attachment, has had a profound influence on all Indian thought. Its influence is especially seen in art; most of the early examples of Indian sculpture and architecture are Buddhist in origin.

At the end of the fourth century B.C. the Maurya family, under Chandragupta (c. 322 to 298 B.C.), established themselves at Magadha, and they quickly expanded their power over most of North India and into what is now modern Afghanistan. His capital city was at Pātaliputra, a very large city on a tributary of the Ganges. According to Greek visitors, his palace was the most magnificent in the world. Under his grandson, the famous Ashoka (c. 269-232 B.C.), the Mauryan Empire reached its greatest extent, and it was not until the time of Aurangzīb (1658-1707) that one ruler again controlled so much territory in India.

Knowledge of Ashoka's reign comes mainly from the edicts he had carved on rocks and pillars throughout his extensive dominions. These inscriptions were not precisely laws, but rather statements of policy and, in some cases, homilies addressed to his officials. Ashoka's reign had enduring consequences, for he appears to have been the first Indian king to patronize Buddhism in a significant way. Because of this, Buddhism spread not only throughout India but beyond its borders, most notably to Ceylon. This meant that although India was never a Buddhist country in the sense that the majority of the people were Buddhists, the values of Buddhism permeated very deeply the fabric of Indian life. Ashoka gave India an ideology that, even when it was forgotten, still influenced the life of the people.

The downfall of Ashoka's empire in the generation after his death was the result of causes that can be generalized to explain the failure of successive Indian dynasties. Problems of communication, rebellious governors, intrigues within the palace, foreign invasions, all played a part. Various attempts were made by other rulers, including invaders from Central Asia, to create new empires, but none had any lasting success until the Guptas established their dynasty in the fourth century A.D. The history of India from about 150 B.C. to 200 A.D. is marked by invasions and internal turmoil.

During this period of dynastic struggles the Brahmanical religion of the Vedic Age transformed itself into the Hinduism of the later ages. Again it must be stressed that there had never been a period when the Vedas had not been the living scriptures of probably the majority of the people, but partly in response to the challenge of the great heretical movements of Jainism and Buddhism the guardians of the ancient tradition reformulated and redefined many of the old concepts in a new class of religious literature. These were the *dharmashāstra* texts which, by incorporating many practices which had grown up since the completion of the Vedic literature and by reinterpreting Vedic customs which had fallen into disuse, made it possible for the ancient tradition to survive in a changing society. These texts, by providing both meticulous directions for all of the contingencies of life and at the same time, many examples of exceptions to the general rules, became the guide for the ordering of social life. An important feature of these texts is that they underwent revision and change over a long period, thus making it possible for them to reflect changing conditions and needs of society. One of the most famous of the texts, the *Manu Smriti*, for example, probably originated in the third century B.C. but it did not receive its final form until the fourth century A.D.

The growth of theism as an integral part of the Hindu tradition was another important element in the religious life of the period. This theistic movement, taking the form of devotion to a particular god, may have its roots in the worship of the ancient Vedic gods or it may reflect influence from non-Aryan religions of India, but it is probably true that some form of worship in which the devotees looked to a god for help and protection was the most widespread form of religious expression among the common people. Two gods that emerge are of particular importance—Vishnu and Shiva. Henceforth they dominate the religious scene. The *Bhagavad Gītā*, the most famous of the religious works of the period, is associated with Vishnu in that its central figure, Krishna, is later identified as an incarnation of Vishnu. While there is no comparable literary monument to Shiva, his cult was apparently widespread. Here as elsewhere in this period one senses the passionate intensity and surging creativity of Indian life.

CHAPTER IV

THE EXPOSITION
OF LIFE'S DUTIES

*One of the most important aspects of the Hindu tradition
is the emphasis placed on the performance of social duties
and obligations according to carefully formulated codes of
behavior. These codes find their most vivid expression in
three great ideal structures: the four classes, the four
stages of life, and the four ends of man. While it is clear
that these idealized constructions were never fully realized
within Indian society at any time, nevertheless they provided the background for social life, and still exercise a
powerful appeal to all those who live within the Hindu
milieu. Very briefly, what is involved in the three idealiza-
tions is, first of all, that society is grouped by nature and
divine law into four classes; secondly, that each man in
each class passes in his lifetime through four carefully
marked stages; and, thirdly, that there are certain ends of
life which are legitimate and proper for the virtuous man
to pursue. The element common to the three structures is
the assumption that there are fundamental differences in
men that make it necessary for different men to be controlled by norms of behavior appropriate for their station
in life, and that the same standards cannot be made applicable to all men. In every situation the guiding factor is
dharma, that protean word already noted in the introduc-*

tion. This means that man applies to problems of social and moral behavior the understanding of his duty or obligation as a member of a particular group in a particular situation. The resolution of moral decisions does not take place in the context of the individual making choices through private appeal to conscience but rather through a knowledge of what is suitable in the context of one's membership in a group. This ideal has implications for ethical theory and practice which will frequently be illustrated in the selections.

The fundamental social ideal is that of the four-fold division of society, already briefly noted in Chapter II. In the accounts of the division of society into four classes (varna) in the sacred texts it is emphasized that the origin of the class structure is divine, not human, the implication being that the right ordering of society is ultimately a religious, not a secular, concern. In other words, the social law, even in its ordering of the most commonplace concerns, is coterminous with the law of the universe.

The theory was that all people were divided into four classes. The first class were the Brāhmans, the priestly order, the possessors and guardians of the great tradition. No priestly class in any other civilization, perhaps, has ever made such claims for its sanctity as did the Brāhmans; but neither has any other received such willing recognition of that sanctity. Not all Brāhmans were priests, since there were too many of them to be absorbed into ritual functions, and they filled many occupations, most notably in government service. The second class, the kshatriyas, or warriors, supplied the rulers and soldiers, but probably at no time, certainly not after 600 B.C., did the class supply all the soldiers or even all the kings. The vaishyas were the merchants, traders and farmers. These three classes were the "twice-born," signifying that they underwent a religious ceremony of initiation. This was the dividing line between them and the fourth class, the shūdras, to whom were allotted the menial and unpleasant tasks of society. The shūdras had a dharma, however, just as did the twice

born classes. This was not true of those groups completely
outside the class structure, the "outcastes"; they were considered beyond the pale of the laws of class and society.

The actual origin of the class ideal is obscure, although
it reflects a fairly natural and widespread classification of
functions within society. Probably its origin is in the most
primitive levels of Aryan social organization, the product
of a life dependent upon agriculture and the skill of warriors to protect life, with a religion that was characterized
by a complex ritual needing skilled performers. Com-
pounding the difficulty of any discussion of the origin of
the class structure is the fact that it is the statement of an
ideal and not the description of the actual condition of
society; the actual social framework of the Hindu tradition
is the immensely complex web of castes. For Hindu society
what is important in everyday living is not so much the
four great classes as the multitudinous exclusive social
groupings that have proliferated throughout the centuries.
There are thousands of these groups, with boundaries defined by many restrictions, the most important of which
relate to marriage and the eating of food, and, to a lesser
extent, by occupation. The relation of these castes to the
four great classes is much disputed, although the explanation of the sacred texts is definite enough—they are seen as
subdivisions brought about by miscegenation. Historically
the origin of the castes is probably to be found in many
other factors, such as invasions by foreign groups, numerous and quite distinct indigenous peoples, the emphasis of
the religious tradition on ritual purity, and geographic separation. What is important is that the ideal of the four
divinely ordained classes gave religious sanction to the
whole structure of caste and class, and that each caste lives
by its own dharma.

The second great ideal that undergirded the social and
religious structure was the conception of four stages
(āshrams) of life. Just as society as a whole was understood to be divided into classes performing mutually exclusive functions that came together under the general work

ing of dharma, so each individual life was divided into stages that were distinct but in the end produced a harmonious totality. These stages, it should be noted, were taken to be applicable mainly to members of the three "twice-born" classes, and only to men and boys. After initiation, the boy became a celibate student, living in the house of his teacher or guru. Then he married, and observed the obligations and enjoyed the pleasures of the life of a householder. This placing of family life at the heart of the ideal value system is of immense significance for the Hindu tradition, for it means that the most basic of actual groupings within the society is unequivocally invested with all the sanctions that religion can give. The family that is pictured in the texts, and that in fact dominates the Hindu cultural pattern, is the joint family, with all the sons bringing their wives into the parental home. It is that large family unit that is the center of religious rites and all social customs, and its role in preserving and transmitting the values and traditions of the Hindu culture cannot be overemphasized.

Following the fulfillment of his duties as a householder, and having assured the continuance of his family, a man next becomes a hermit in the forest, meditating and studying the scriptures. Then finally comes the fourth stage when, abandoning all earthly ties, he wanders about unhindered by family, home, or possessions. Here, as everywhere, the assumption is that dharma is not the same at every stage of life, just as it is not the same for all men. While it cannot be supposed that this ideal pattern was ever followed by a majority of men, even by all Brāhmans, the values that it enshrines have made a potent appeal throughout Indian history, coloring the imagination and guiding responses to life even when the four stages were not followed in their entirety.

The third ideal construct, the four ends of life, related the religious understanding of the nature of human existence to the conduct of everyday life. The four legitimate ends to be pursued were dharma, or duty; material gain (artha); *the pleasures of physical sense* (kāma); *and salva-tion* (moksha).[1] *Since it was assumed that not only did men differ in their needs and capabilities according to their class but also according to their stage of life, these legitimate ends were defined in terms appropriate for one's particular station. Kāma, physical pleasure, was defined very differently for a Brāhman student, for example, than it was for a mature member of the warrior class. Overarch-ing all the ends was* dharma, *the essential element that made them all work together for the right ordering of society.*

This social understanding of the implication of religion, especially the emphasis on the dharma of class and caste, goes a long way to explain how the old Vedic traditions were not only able to survive but actually to provide sources for change and growth in the vital centuries from 600 B.C. to 300 A.D. That external invasions and internal strife, as well as the rise of Buddhism and Jainism, did not destroy the ancient religious culture is probably due in large measure to the great encompassing social ideals of class, the stages of life, and the ends of man. They permit-ted a wide diversity of expression in a genuinely plural so-ciety but they maintained a coherent framework of actual institutional life and ideal statement.

THE CLASS STRUCTURE

The Statement of the Ideal

The following description of the class structure is taken from the *Manu Smriti,* the famous text that gives detailed descrip-tions of the duties of each class and prescribes penalties for the transgression of the customary laws. The verses given here are preceded by a genealogy of all creation that goes back to

[1] In some texts, only three ends are given, with *dharma* including salvation.

the time when "this universe existed in the shape of darkness," and the "Self-existent . . . appeared with irresistible creative power, dispelling darkness."

But in the beginning he assigned their several names, actions, and conditions to all (created beings), even according to the words of the Veda.

He, the Lord, also created the class of the gods, who are endowed with life, and whose nature is action; and the subtile class of the Sādhyas, and the eternal sacrifice.

But from fire, wind, and the sun he drew forth the threefold eternal Veda, called *Rik*, Yajus, and Sāman, for the due performance of the sacrifice.

Time and the divisions of time, the lunar mansions and the planets, the rivers, the oceans, the mountains, plains, and uneven ground,

Austerity, speech, pleasure, desire, and anger, this whole creation he likewise produced, as he desired to call these beings into existence. . . .

Whatever he assigned to each at the (first) creation, noxiousness or harmlessness, gentleness or ferocity, virtue or sin, truth or falsehood, that clung (afterwards) spontaneously to it.

As at the change of the seasons each season of its own accord assumes its distinctive marks, even so corporeal beings (resume in new births) their (appointed) course of action.

But for the sake of the prosperity of the worlds, he created the Brāhman, the Kshatriya, the Vaishya, and the Shūdra to proceed from his mouth, his arms, his thighs, and his feet. . . .

To Brāhmans he assigned teaching and studying (the Veda), sacrificing for their own benefit and for others, giving and accepting (of alms).

The Kshatriya he commanded to protect the people, to bestow gifts, to offer sacrifices, to study (the Veda), and to abstain from attaching himself to sensual pleasures;

The Vaishya to tend cattle, to bestow gifts, to offer sacrifices, to study (the Veda), to trade, to lend money, and to cultivate land.

One occupation only the lord prescribed to the Shūdra, to serve meekly even these (other) three castes.

(from *Manu Smriti*, I and X, *passim*, in *Sacred Books of the East*, XXV, pp. 12-13, 24)

Mutual Dependence of the Classes

For the Brāhman authors of the religious texts one validation of the class structure was the empirical evidence of a harmonious social structure. A hierarchical system, where each was aware of the boundaries of his duties and obligations, reflected the fundamental order of the universe, and peace and prosperity in this and future existences was assured by obedience to customary laws. This emphasis on the importance of the correct fulfillment of the proper duties of one's class underlies two features of the social codes. On the one hand it explains the high privileges accorded the Brāhman as the keystone of the social structure; on the other, it makes understandable the severity with which breaches of *dharma* were treated. The first selection, which is taken from the great epic poem, the *Mahābhārata*, emphasizes the harmony that results from following one's own *dharma*. The speaker is Bhīsma, one of the great heroic figures of the poem. The second selection is from the *Bhagavad Gītā*; here the consequence of failing to follow one's class obligations is depicted.

Bhīsma said: "I shall discourse on duties that are eternal. The suppression of wrath, truthfulness of speech, justice, forgiveness, begetting children upon one's own wedded wives, purity of conduct, avoidance of quarrel, simplicity, and maintenance of dependents,—these nine duties belong to all the four orders (equally). Those duties, however, which belong exclusively to Brāhmanas, I shall now tell thee! Self-restraint, O king, has been declared to be the first duty of Brāhmanas. Study of the Vedas, and patience in undergoing austerities, (are also their other duties). By practising these two, all their acts are accomplished. If while engaged in the observance of his own duties, without doing any improper act, wealth comes to a peaceful Brāhmana possessed of knowledge, he should then marry and seek to beget children and should also practise charity and perform sacrifices. It has been declared by the wise that wealth thus obtained should be enjoyed by distributing it (among deserving persons and relatives). By his study of the Vedas all the pious acts (laid down for the Brāhmana) are accomplished. Whether he does or does not achieve anything else, if he devotes himself to the study of the Vedas he becomes (by that) known as a Brāhmana or the friend of all creatures. I shall also tell thee, O Bhārata, what the duties are of a Kshatriya. A Kshatriya, O king, should give but not beg, should himself perform sacrifices but not officiate as a priest in the sacrifices of other's. He should never teach (the Vedas) but study (them with a Brāhmana preceptor). He should protect the people. Always exerting himself for the destruction of robbers and wicked people, he should put forth his prowess in battle. Those among Kshatriya rulers who perform great sacrifices, who are possessed of a knowledge of the Vedas, and who gain victories in battle, become foremost of those that acquire many blessed regions hereafter by their merit. Persons conversant with the old scriptures do not applaud that Kshatriya who returns unwounded from battle. This has been declared to be the conduct of a wretched Kshatriya. There is no higher duty for him than the suppression of robbers. Gifts, study, and sacrifices, bring prosperity to kings. Therefore, a king who desires to acquire religous merit should engage in battle. Establishing all his subjects in the observance of their respective duties, a king should cause all of them to do everything according to the dictates of righteousness. Whether he does or does not do any other act, if only he protects ·his subjects, he is regarded to accomplish all religious acts and is called a Kshatriya and the foremost of men. I shall now tell thee, O Yudhishthira, what the eternal duties of the Vaishya are. A Vaishya should make gifts, study the Vedas, perform sacrifices, and acquire wealth by fair means. With proper attention he should also protect and rear all (domestic) animals as a sire protecting his sons. Anything else that he will do will be regarded as improper for him. By protecting the (domestic) animals he would obtain great happiness. The Creator, having created the (domestic) animals, bestowed their care upon the Vaishya. Upon the Brāhmana and the Kshatriya he conferred (the care of) all creatures. I shall tell thee what the Vaishya's profession is and how he is to earn the means of his sustenance. If he keeps (for others) six kine, he may take the milk of one cow as his remuneration; and if he keeps (for others) a hundred kine, he may take a single pair as such fee. If he trades with other's wealth, he may take a seventh part of the profits (as his share). A seventh also is his share in the profits arising from the trade in horns, but he should take a sixteenth if the trade be in hoofs. If he engages in cultivation with seeds supplied by others, he may take a seventh part of the yield. This should be his annual remuneration. A Vaishya should never desire that he should not tend cattle. If a Vaishya desires to tend cattle, no one else should be employed in that task. I should tell thee, O Bhārata, what the duties of a Shudra are. The Creator intended the Shudra to become the servant of the other three orders. For this, the service of the three other classes is the duty of the Shudra. By such service of the other three, a Shudra may obtain great happiness. He should wait upon the three other classes according to their order of seniority. A Shudra should never amass wealth, lest, by his wealth, he makes the numbers of the three superior classes obedient to him. By this he would incur sin. With the king's permission, however, a Shudra, for performing religious acts, may earn wealth. I shall now tell thee the profession he should follow and the means by which he may earn his livelihood. It is said that Shudras should certainly be maintained by the (three) other orders. Worn out umbrellas, turbans, beds and seats, shoes, and fans, should be given to the Shudra servants. Torn clothes, which are no longer fit for wear, should be given away by the regenerate classes unto the Shudra. These are the latter's lawful acquisitions. Men conversant with morality say that if the Shudra approaches any one belonging to the three regenerate orders from desire of doing menial service, the latter should assign him proper work. Unto the sonless Shudra his master should offer the funeral cake. The weak and the old amongst them should be maintained. The Shudra should never abandon his master whatever the nature or degree of the distress into which the latter may fall. If the master loses his wealth, he should with excessive zeal be supported by the Shudra servant. A Shudra cannot have any wealth that is his own. Whatever he possesses belongs lawfully to his master. Sacrifice has been laid down as a duty of the three other orders. It has been ordained for the Shudra also, O Bhārata! A Shudra, however, is not competent to utter *swāhā* and *sadhā* or any other Vedic *mantra*. For this reason, the Shudra, without observing the vows laid down in the Vedas, should worship the gods in minor sacrifices called *Pāka-yajnas.* . . . Sacrifice (as has been already said), O Bhārata, is as much laid down for the Shudra as for the three other classes. Of all sacrifices, devotion has been laid down to be the foremost. Devotion is a high deity. It cleanses all sacrificers.

(from *Mahābhārata* XII:60, *passim*, in P. C. Roy, *The Mahābhārata*)

When a family decays, the immemorial religious laws of that family are destroyed. When the religious laws of the family are destroyed, then lawlessness destroys the whole family. Because lawlessness prevails, the women of the family become corrupted, and when women are corrupt, intermingling of caste follows. Intermingling of caste leads to hell both those who destroy the family as well as the family itself. The ancestors also fall into hell for they are deprived of the offerings of food made to them.

(from *Bhagavad Gītā*, I:40-42)

THE FOUR STAGES OF LIFE

The Student

Following the rites of initiation, of which the visible symbol was the wearing of a sacred cord around the chest, a boy of the three upper classes went to live and study in the house of his teacher. The relationship that developed between pupil and teacher is a constant theme of Indian literature and one of the unifying features of the whole tradition. Respect was given to the teacher that did not differ essentially from that paid to parents, while the pupil's development was regarded as a sacred charge by his teacher. The main subject of study was the memorization of Vedic texts but archery, the science of war, medicine, astrology, and music were all included within the sacred texts. This system of education ensured the transmission of the tradition and meant that a common culture and common language existed throughout India for the members of the upper classes. It also exalted the power and prestige of the teachers, the Brāhmans.

The selection given here is taken from a text prescribing proper norms of behavior written possibly in the fifth century B.C.

He who has been initiated shall dwell as a religious student in the house of his teacher . . .

Twelve years (should be) the shortest time (for his residence with his teacher).

A student who studies the sacred science shall not dwell with anybody else than his teacher.

Now (follow) the rules for the studentship.

He shall obey his teacher, except when ordered to commit crimes which cause loss of caste.

He shall do what is serviceable to his teacher, he shall not contradict him.

He shall always occupy a couch or seat lower than that of his teacher.

He shall not eat food offered at a sacrifice to the gods or the Manes,

Nor pungent condiments, salt, honey, or meat.

He shall not sleep in the day-time.

He shall not use perfumes.

He shall preserve chastity.

He shall not embellish himself by using ointments and the like.

He shall not wash his body with hot water for pleasure. But, if it is soiled by unclean things, he shall clean it with earth or water, in a place where he is not seen by a Guru.

Let him not sport in the water whilst bathing; let him swim motionless like a stick. . . .

Let him not look at dancing.

Let him not go to assemblies for gambling, &c., nor to crowds assembled at festivals.

Let him not be addicted to gossiping.

Let him be discreet.

Let him not do anything for his own pleasure in places which his teacher frequents.

Let him talk with women so much only as his purpose requires.

Let him be forgiving.

Let him restrain his organs from seeking illicit objects.

Let him be untired in fulfilling his duties;

Modest;

Possessed of self-command;

Energetic;

Free from anger;

And free from envy.

Bringing all he obtains to his teacher, he shall go begging with a vessel in the morning and in the evening, and he may beg from everybody except low-caste people unfit for association with Aryas.

(from *Apastamba Dharma Sūtra*, I:1,2,3, and 6, *passim*, in *Sacred Books of the East*, II, pp. 7-8, 10-11.

The Householder and Family Life

As one of the texts points out, the householder is the source of all the other stages of life "because the others do not produce offspring." As the selections given here indicate, the centrality of marriage and the family in the social system was clearly recognized. Three functions of family life were singled out for particular attention: the maintenance of the tradition through the performance of certain rituals that only a householder could perform; begetting of offspring to ensure the continuance of the rites; and the enjoyment of the pleasures of physical love as a legitimate end of human life.

Closely related to the status of the householder was the attitude towards women revealed in the texts. Perhaps no other literature shows such an ambivalence at this point as does the Indian, for on one level woman was seen as a lustful temptress, the occasion of sin for men who would otherwise remain chaste, while on another level, that of wife and mother, she is praised almost to excess. It may be that the literature is the product of a class of men who, valuing asceticism, resented the passions aroused in them by women, or it may be that the complexity of the Indian attitude represents a true understanding of human nature.

Monogamy was the normal marital arrangement, although a man might take a second wife in certain circumstances, as when his first wife was barren. Divorce was impossible for the twice-born castes, since the marriage rite was a sacrament that could not be revoked.

One should first examine the family [of the intended bride or bridegroom], those on the mother's side and on the father's side. . . . One should give his daughter in marriage to a young man endowed with intelligence. One should marry a girl who possesses the characteristics of intelligence, beauty, and good character, and who is free from disease. . . .

(from *Āśvalāyana Grihya Sūtra*, I:5, *passim*, in *Sources of Indian Tradition*, p. 230)

A householder should perform every day a Smriti rite [i.e., a domestic rite prescribed by the Sacred Law, Smriti] on the nuptial fire or on the fire brought in at the time of the partition of ancestral property. He should perform a Vedic rite on the sacred fires.

Having attended to the bodily calls, having performed the purificatory rites, and after having first washed the teeth, a twice-born [Aryan] man should offer the morning prayer.

Having offered oblations to the sacred fires, becoming spiritually composed, he should murmur the sacred verses addressed to the sun god. He should also learn the meaning of the Veda and various sciences. . . .

He should then go to his lord for securing the means of maintenance and progress. Thereafter having bathed he should worship the gods and also offer libations of water to the manes.

He should study according to his capacity the three Vedas, the *Atharva Veda*, the Purānas, together with the Itihāsas [legendary histories], as also the lore relating to the knowledge of the Self, with a view to accomplishing successfully the sacrifice of muttering prayers.

Offering of the food oblation, offerings with the proper utterance, performance of Vedic sacrifices, study of the sacred texts, and honoring of guests—these constitute the five great daily sacrifices dedicated respectively to the spirits, the manes, the gods, the Brahman, and men.

He should offer the food oblation to the spirits [by throwing it in the air] out of the remnant of the food offered to the gods. He should also cast food on the ground for dogs, untouchables, and crows.

Food, as also water, should be offered by the householder to the manes and men day after day. He should continuously carry on his study. He should never cook for himself only.

Children, married daughters living in the father's house, old relatives, pregnant women, sick persons, and girls, as also guests and servants—only after having fed these should the householder and his wife eat the food that has remained. . . .

Having risen before dawn the householder should ponder over what is good for the Self. He should not, as far as possible, neglect his duties in respect of the three ends of man, namely, virtue, material gain, and pleasure, at their proper times.

Learning, religious performances, age, family relations, and wealth—on account of these and in the order mentioned are men honored in society. By means of these, if possessed in profusion, even a shūdra deserves respect in old age.

(from *Yājnavalkya Smriti,* I:97-116, *passim,* in *Sources of Indian Tradition,* pp. 231-32)

I will now propound the eternal laws for a husband and wife who keep to the path of duty, whether they be united or separated.

Day and night must women be kept in dependence by the males of their families, and, if they attach themselves to sensual enjoyments, they must be kept under one's control.

Her father protects her in childhood, her husband protects her in youth, and her sons protect her in old age; a woman is never fit for independence.

Reprehensible is the father who gives not his daughter in marriage at the proper time; reprehensible is the husband who approaches not his wife in due season, and reprehensible is the son who does not protect his mother after her husband has died.

Women must particularly be guarded against evil inclinations, however trifling they may appear; for, if they are not guarded, they will bring sorrow on two families.

Considering that the highest duty of all castes, even weak husbands must strive to guard their wives.

He who carefully guards his wife, preserves the purity of his offspring, virtuous conduct, his family, himself, and his means of acquiring merit. . . .

No man can completely guard women by force; but they can be guarded by the employment of the following expedients:

Let the husband employ his wife in the collection and expenditure of his wealth, in keeping everything clean, in the fulfilment of religious duties, in the preparation of his food, and in looking after the household utensils.

Women, confined in the house under trustworthy and obedient servants, are not well guarded; but those who of their own accord keep guard over themselves, are well guarded.

Drinking spirituous liquor, associating with wicked people, separation from the husband, rambling abroad, sleeping at unseasonable hours, and dwelling in other men's houses, are the six causes of the ruin of women. . . .

Thus has been declared the ever pure popular usage which regulates the relations between husband and wife; hear next the laws concerning children which are the cause of happiness in this world and after death.

Between wives who are destined to bear children, who secure many blessings, who are worthy of worship and irradiate their dwellings, and between the goddesses of fortune who reside in the houses of men, there is no difference whatsoever.

The production of children, the nurture of those born, and the daily life of men, of these matters woman is visibly the cause.

Offspring, the due performance of religious rites, faithful service, highest conjugal happiness and heavenly bliss for the ancestors and oneself, depend on one's wife alone.

She who, controlling her thoughts, speech, and acts, vio-
lates not her duty towards her lord, dwells with him after
death in heaven, and in this world is called by the virtuous
a faithful wife.

(from *Manu Smriti* IX:1-7, 10-13, 25-29, *Sacred Books of the
East*, XXV, pp. 328-29, 332)

The Hermit

Indicative of the movement of life from one position to another that adds to the richness and complexity of the Indian
tradition, the householder turns his back upon family life and
becomes a hermit. In this stage of life he seeks to fulfill his
dharma through performing rituals and studying the scriptures,
particularly the *Upanishads*. He is not entirely cut off from the
world, however, but is available to those who seek his counsel.

Asceticism, which is often associated with the whole of the
Indian tradition, is the appropriate mode of life in this stage.
It is possible that the stress on asceticism as the characteristic
feature of the religious life was an attempt to institutionalize
a growing tendency within Indian society towards renunciation
of the world. For Buddhism and Jainism, the monastic existence was the normal state, and the appeal of these rival faiths
may have seemed a threat to those aspects of the social structure, especially family life, which were so highly valued by the
ancient tradition.

The goal of Indian asceticism is self-control and the acquisition of spiritual power, and it has little relation to the idea
of "mortifying the flesh." That the power gained through austerities of the most rigorous kind was so great that even the
gods grew fearful and sought to prevent the continuance of
the sage's meditation is a very common theme in Indian literature.

When a householder sees his skin wrinkled, and his hair
white, and the sons of his sons, then he may resort to the
forest.

Abandoning all food raised by cultivation, and all his

belongings, he may depart into the forest, either committing his wife to his sons, or accompanied by her.

Taking with him the sacred fire and the implements required for domestic sacrifices, he may go forth from the villages into the forest and reside there, duly controlling his senses.

Let him offer those five great sacrifices according to the rule, with various kinds of pure food fit for ascetics, or with herbs, roots, and fruit.

Let him wear a skin or a tattered garment; let him bathe in the evening or in the morning; and let him always wear his hair in braids, the hair on his body, his beard, and his nails being unclipped.

Let him perform the food offering with such food as he eats, and give alms according to his ability; let him honour those who come to his hermitage with alms consisting of water, roots, and fruit.

Let him be always industrious in privately reciting the Veda; let him be patient of hardships, friendly towards all, of collected mind, ever liberal and never receiver, and compassionate toward all beings. . . .

He should live without a fire, without a house, a silent sage subsisting on roots and fruit. . . .

(from *Manu Smriti* VI:2-8, 25, in *Sacred Books of the East* XXV, pp. 198-200)

The Homeless Wanderer

Having gained the knowledge that led to salvation, the hermit cuts off all earthly ties, even to his hut in the forest, and becomes a homeless wanderer. He no longer performs the rituals, for he has passed beyond needing the results they bring. Desiring neither to live or die, he wanders about until death claims him.

But having thus passed the third part of a man's natural term of life in the forest, he may live as an ascetic during

the fourth part of his existence, after abandoning all a
tachment to worldly objects.

He who after passing from order to order, after offerin
sacrifices and subduing his senses, becomes, tired with gi
ing alms and offerings of food, an ascetic, gains bliss aft
death.

When he has paid the three debts, let him apply h
mind to the attainment of final liberation; he who seeks
without having paid (his debts) sinks downwards.

Having studied the Vedas in accordance with the rul
having begat sons according to the sacred law, and havin
offered sacrifices according to his ability, he may direct h
mind to the attainment of final liberation.

A twice-born man who seeks final liberation, withou
having studied the Vedas, without having begotten son
and without having offered sacrifices, sinks dow
wards. . . .

Departing from his house fully provided with the mear
of purification, let him wander about absolutely silent, an
caring nothing for enjoyments that may be offered t
him.

Let him always wander alone, without any companio
in order to attain final liberation, fully understanding th
the solitary man, who neither forsakes nor is forsake
gains his end.

He shall neither possess a fire, nor a dwelling, he may g
to a village for his food, (he shall be) indifferent to ever
thing, firm of purpose, meditating and concentrating h
mind on Brahman.

A potsherd instead of an alms-bowl, the roots of tre
for a dwelling, coarse worn-out garments, life in solitud
and indifference towards everything, are the marks of on
who has attained liberation.

Let him not desire to die, let him not desire to live; l
him wait for his appointed time, as a servant waits for th
payment of his wages.

Let him put down his foot purified by his sight, let hir

drink water purified by straining with a cloth, let him utter speech purified by truth, let him keep his heart pure.

Let him patiently bear hard words, let him not insult anybody, and let him not become anybody's enemy for the sake of this perishable body.

Against an angry man let him not in return show anger, let him bless when he is cursed, and let him not utter speech, devoid of truth, scattered at the seven gates.

Delighting in what refers to the Soul, sitting in the postures prescribed by the Yoga, independent of external help, entirely abstaining from sensual enjoyments, with himself for his only companion, he shall live in this world, desiring the bliss of final liberation.

(from *Manu Smriti*, VI, *passim*, in *Sacred Books of the East*, XXV, pp. 204-07)

THE RECOGNITION
OF LIFE'S LIMITATIONS

The statement of the ideal expression of the fulfillment of *dharma* through adherence to the proper duties of class and stage of life was adjusted to actual human conditions and possibilities by many discussions within the texts of the appropriate action for a situation when the strict formulas could not be applied. Special provision was made for "times of distress," when a man might have to improvise a moral response. These exceptions to the general rules made the social structure much less rigid in practice than it was in theory.

Among the several occupations the most commendable are, teaching the Veda for a Brâhmana, protecting the people for a Kshatriya, and trade for a Vaishya.

But a Brâhma*n*a, unable to subsist by his peculiar occupations just mentioned, may live according to the law applicable to Kshatriyas; for the latter is next to him in rank

If it be asked, 'How shall it be, if he cannot maintain himself by either of these occupations?' the answer is, he may adopt a Vaishya's mode of life, employing himself in agriculture and rearing cattle.

But a Brâhma*n*a, or a Kshatriya, living by a Vaishya's mode of subsistence, shall carefully avoid the pursuit of agriculture, which causes injury to many beings and depends on others.

Some declare that agriculture is something excellent, but that means of subsistence is blamed by the virtuous; for the wooden implement with iron point injures the earth and the beings living in the earth.

But he who, through a want of means of subsistence gives up the strictness with respect to his duties, may sell in order to increase his wealth, the commodities sold by Vaishyas, making however the following exceptions.

He must avoid selling condiments of all sorts, cooked food and sesamum, stones, salt, cattle, and human beings

All dyed cloth, as well as cloth made of hemp, or flax, or wool, even though they be not dyed, fruit, roots, and medical herbs;

Water, weapons, poison, meat, Soma, and perfumes of all kinds, fresh milk, honey, sour milk, clarified butter, oil wax, sugar, Kusa-grass;

All beasts of the forest, animals with fangs or tusks birds, spirituous liquor, indigo, lac, and all one-hoofed beasts. . . .

A Kshatriya who has fallen into distress, may subsist by all these means; but he must never arrogantly adopt the mode of life prescribed for his betters.

A man of low caste who through covetousness lives by the occupations of a higher one, the king shall deprive of his property and banish.

It is better to discharge one's own appointed duty incompletely than to perform completely that of another for he who lives according to the law of another caste is instantly excluded from his own.

A Vaishya who is unable to subsist by his own duties, may even maintain himself by a Shûdra's mode of life, avoiding however acts forbidden to him, and he should give it up, when he is able to do so.

But a Shûdra, being unable to find service with the twice-born and threatened with the loss of his sons and wife through hunger, may maintain himself by handicrafts.

Let him follow those mechanical occupations and those various practical arts by following which the twice-born are best served.

(from *Manu Smriti* X:80-100, *passim*, in *Sacred Books of the East*, XXV, pp. 420-23)

THE POSSIBILITY
OF GROWTH AND CHANGE

A further indication that the tradition was not static but allowed for growth is shown in the discussions of the sources of *dharma*. One source was scriptural, and while injunctions drawn from the sacred texts would always carry a special sanctity, the distinction made between the two classes of scripture, *shruti*, the works that are revealed, and *smriti*, the works that belong to the tradition, that preserve customary usage, made possible the entry of new ideas and new interpretations. Another source of *dharma* was the prompting of one's conscience, which itself had been formed through obedience to the appropriate obligations and duties. These aspects of *dharma* are touched upon in the following selection.

The whole Veda is the first source of the sacred law, next the tradition and the virtuous conduct of those who know

the Veda further, also the customs of holy men, and finall
self-satisfaction.

Whatever law has been ordained for any person b
Manu, that has been fully declared in the Veda: for tha
sage was omniscient.

But a learned man after fully scrutinising all this witl
the eye of knowledge, should, in accordance with the au
thority of the revealed texts, be intent on the performanc
of his duties.

For that man who obeys the law prescribed in the re
vealed texts and in the sacred tradition, gains fame in thi
world and after death unsurpassable bliss.

But by Shruti (revelation) is meant the Veda, and b
Smriti (tradition) the Institutes of the sacred law: thos
two must not be called into question in any matter, sinc
from those two the sacred law shone forth.

Every twice-born man, who, relying on the Institutes c
dialectics, treats with contempt those two sources of th
law, must be cast out by the virtuous, as an atheist and
scorner of the Veda.

The Veda, the sacred tradition, the customs of virtuou
men, and one's own pleasure, they declare to be visibly th
fourfold means of defining the sacred law.

The knowledge of the sacred law is prescribed for thos
who are not given to the acquisition of wealth and to th
gratification of their desires; to those who seek the know
edge of the sacred law the supreme authority is the revel
tion, Shruti.

But when two sacred texts (Shruti) are conflicting, bot
are held to be law; for both are pronounced by the wise t
be valid law.

(from *Manu Smriti* II:6-14, in *Sacred Books of the Eas*
XXV, pp. 30-32)

LIFE AS SACRAMENT

A potent force in maintaining the tradition was the scheme of sacraments that provided a religious sanction to each important step in life. The following enumeration of the forty sacraments suggests how impressive and solemn rituals bounded human existence with a reminder of the individual's relation to society and the moral order. Many of these are no longer observed, but the chief ones, such as marriage, are still performed according to the ancient rites.

1) The ceremony relating to the conception of the embryo; 2) the ceremony relating to the desired birth of a male child; 3) the parting of the pregnant wife's hair by the husband [to ward off evil spirits]; 4) the ceremony relating to the birth of the child; 5) the naming of the child; 6) the first feeding; 7) the tonsure of the child's head; 8) the initiation; 9-12) the four vows taken in connection with the study of the Veda; 13) the ceremonial bath [graduation]; 14) the union with a mate who could practice dharma together with him [i.e., marriage]; 15-19) the daily performance of the five sacrifices to gods, manes, men, spirits, and the Brahman; 20-26) and the performance of the following sacrifices, that is, of the seven cooked-food sacrifices . . . ; 27-33) the seven kinds of oblation sacrifices . . . ; 34-40) the seven kinds of soma sacrifices . . . these are the forty sacraments.

Now follow the eight good qualities of the soul, namely, compassion to all beings, forbearance, absence of jealousy, tranquillity, goodness, absence of meanness, and absence of covetousness. He who is sanctified by these forty sacraments but is not endowed with the eight good qualities of the soul does not become united with the Brahman, nor does he even reach the abode of the Brahman. On the other hand, he who is, verily, sanctified by a few only of the sacraments but is endowed with the eight good qualities of the soul becomes united with the Brahman, he dwells in the abode of the Brahman.

(from *Gautama Dharma Sūtra*, VIII:14-26, in *Sources of Indian Tradition*, p. 235)

A WIDOW'S
ACT OF DEVOTION

One striking witness to the Hindu conviction that marriage was a sacramental rite that endured beyond death was the custom observed in many areas, particularly in North India, of a widow burning herself on her husband's funeral pyre. The practice was condemned by European travellers as inhuman, but it was regarded by Hindus as an act of the greatest spiritual merit, even though, as this passage shows, they frequently tried to persuade women not to follow their husbands into the flames. This description of the preparation of a Queen about to die, and the attempt of her son to dissuade her, is taken from the account of the reign of Harsha written by the poet Bāna in the seventh century A.D. The woman who died on her husband's funeral pyre was known as a *satī*, meaning a "virtuous woman," and this word is often applied to the act itself. Not all Indian widows cremated themselves with their husbands; the action seems to have been really widespread only among the upper classes. It was common, however, from the eighth century, and was not suppressed until the nineteenth century.

It is not, my dear, [the Queen said to her son, who was seeking to persuade her not to enter the fire], that you are unloved, without noble qualities, or deserving to be abandoned. With my very bosom's milk you drank up my heart. If at this hour my regard is not towards you, it is that my lord's great condescenscion comes between us. Furthermore, dear son, I am not ever craving for the sight of another lord. I am the lady of a great house, born of a stainless ancestry, one whose virtue is her dower. Have you forgotten that I am the lioness mate of a great spirit, who like a lion had his delight in a hundred battles? Daughter, spouse, mother of heroes, how otherwise could such a woman as I, whose price was valour, act? This hand has been clasped by even such a hero, thy father, a chief among princes, peer of Bharata and other great kings. Upon this head have the subservient wives of countless feudatories poured coronation water from golden ewers. This forehead, in winning the honourable fillet of chief-queen, has enjoyed a thing scarce accessible to desire. These breasts have worn robes swayed by the wind of fans waved by captive wives of foes; they have been sucked by sons like you. Upon the heads of rival wives have these feet been set; they have been adored with diamond-wreaths of diadems by the bending matrons of a whole capital. Thus every limb has fulfilled its mission: I have spent my store of good works, what more should I look to? I would die while still unwidowed. I cannot endure, like the widowed Rati, to make unavailing lamentations for a burnt husband. Going before, like the dust of your father's feet, to announce his coming to the heavens, I shall be high esteemed of the hero-loving spouses of the gods. Nay, what will the smoke-bannered one burn of me, who am already on fire with the recent sight of his heart-rending pains? Not to die, but to live at such a time would be unfeeling. Compared with the flame of wifely sorrow, whose fuel is imperishable love, fire itself is chilly cold. How suits it to be parsimonious of a life light as a bit of rotten straw, when that life's lord, majestic as Kailāsa, is passing away? Even should I live, yet after the mortal sin of slighting the king's death the joys, my son, of my son's rule will touch me not. In those that are consumed by grief felicity is ominous, accursed, and unavailing. Not in the body, dear son, but in the glory of loyal widows would I

abide on earth. Therefore dishonour me no more, I be
seech you, beloved son, with opposition to my heart's
desire.

So saying she fell at his feet. But the prince hastily drew
them away, and bending down, held her in both his arms
and raised her prostrate form. Pondering the inevitable
ness of grief, deeming that act to be the better part befit
ting a lady of rank, recognizing her fixed resolution, he
stood in silence with downcast looks.

True is it that, even when made timorous by affection, a
noble nature resigns itself to what accords with place and
time. Having embraced her son and kissed his head, the
queen went forth on foot from the women's quarter, and
though the heavens, filled with the citizens' lamentations
seemed to block her path, proceeded to the Sarasvatī'
banks. Then, having worshipped the fire with the bloom
ing red lotus posies of a woman's timorous glances, she
plunged into it, as the moon's form enters the adorable
sun.

(from Bāna, *Harsacarita*, in E. B. Cowell and F. W. Thomas
pp. 153-55)

CHAPTER V

THE MAINTENANCE OF
THE SOCIAL FABRIC

〜〜〜〜〜

The importance of the great social ideals—class, stages of life, the ends of man—were discussed in the previous chapter; in the selections in this chapter the significance of political ideas within the tradition will be explored. One feature that emerges at once is that while the texts make a formal distinction between the study of morals (dharma-shāstra) and the art of government (arthashāstra), in practice no real separation was made. This was so partly because of the deeply ingrained belief that the social order was a divine construction, and partly because of what may be called the horizontal and vertical divisions of human life within the Hindu system. The horizontal structure was that of class, with duties defined in terms of one's particular station in life, leading to a way of life that tended to be self-contained. To lead a good life within this framework meant the fulfilling of functions that were both secular and religious, and the texts make little distinction between instructions on the conduct of business and on the per-formance of the sacrifices. These horizontal divisions of life, with their tendency to stratify society, were cut across by vertical social divisions—such as the stages of life and the legitimate ends of man—that worked against a com-pletely rigid social order.

In such a society a fusion of spiritual and temporal power would seem inevitable, but priest-kings did not arise in Indian history. Instead, the ordering of society took place through a mutual exaltation of the powers and functions of the priestly and warrior classes. Since the authors of the texts were priests it is not surprising that the superiority of this class is emphasized, but it is significant that temporal power is rarely claimed. The admission of the temporal rights of rulers involved, however, the acceptance by kings of the responsibility of maintaining the laws of class. The king was not thought of as a law-giver; his task was the preservation of existing orders to prevent "the confusion of caste and class." State power entered ordinary life only when the internal regulations of groups broke down, and the assumption was that the ruler acted to restore a relationship, not to take an active part in creating the social order.

This view of the ruler's function was enormously important for the development of Hindu civilization, for it meant that life within the social units could become almost autonomous. Rulers were generally content, as long as taxes were paid, to leave the people to their own devices. This meant that dynasties could rise and fall without touching the fabric of social life. But this did not mean a static society, for particularly with the rise of the great Mauryan Empire new political practices and concepts received religious sanction and became part of the general tradition. One of the most significant of these was an increased emphasis on the divinity of the king. Here as elsewhere it should be noted that "king" in the tradition becomes a kind of short-hand designation for all the functions of political power, and "government" would often be a more accurate term.

The clearest expression of the emphasis on royal prerogative is given in the work associated with Kautilya, the minister of Chandragupta Maurya, known as the Arthashāstra, or "Treatise on Material Gain." This book exalts the power of the king and extends government control to lmost every aspect of life. Here Kautilya seems to be in onflict with the tendency, noted above, for Indian social roups to lead an autonomous existence, without intererence by the king. It might be argued, however, that he attempt to control all social relationships does not onflict with the laws of class and caste, but merely makes hem more explicit by emphasizing the king's role in society. Even Kautilya's assertion that material advantage is he chief end of life, since the others depend upon it, can e understood as an elaboration of the usual statement of he duty of kings to maintain the whole social order.

Another important source for the political thought of he period is the great series of edicts carved on rocks and illars by the Emperor Ashoka (c. 269-232 B.C.). Behind he edicts, with their many fervent appeals for righteousess, can be seen the authority of a king willing to compel is people to be virtuous insofar as this is possible.

Other sources drawn upon in this chapter to illustrate he understanding of the role of the king within the Iindu tradition are the Mahābhārata, the great epic oem, and the Manu Smriti, the statement of ideal law lready frequently drawn upon. All of these sources underine Kautilya's sentiment that "the king shall never allow eople to swerve from their duties . . . for whoever upolds his own duty, following the rules of class . . . will urely be happy both here and hereafter" (I:3).

KINGSHIP AS A REMEDY
FOR AN EVIL SOCIETY

n the twelfth book of the *Mahābhārata* there are numerous iscussions of duties and functions of kings. These are genrally cast in the form of dialogues between Bhīsma, the elder tatesman of the Kuru clan, and Yudhishthira, the oldest of

the five brothers who are struggling to regain the throne whic
is rightfully theirs. In the selection given here, Bhīshma
asked a crucial question: why does a king, who is merely
man, have the right to dominate other human beings? Huma
history, he suggests by way of answer, is rightly understod
only when one realizes the vast cycles through which huma
existence has passed. The greatest of these cycles is almo
unimaginably long—billions of years—but the four smalle
cycles are of immediate concern to man. Each of these cycl
is marked by a decline in virtue; the one in which we are li
ing marks the nadir of human virtue. In every cycle the rule
are the embodiment of the proper *dharma* or values for t
time, and in this age, the characteristic of kings is that th
are protectors of the laws of class and caste. Their instrume
for fulfilling this function is punishment, and "the science
chastisement" occupies a large place in the political thoug
of the age. But as the passage suggests, sternness alone w
not enough; it had to be combined with justice. In the sear
for a suitable ruler to become the founder of the true line
kings, it was not until the birth of Prithi, the seventh in t
order of succession, that a ruler was found who fulfilled t
requirements.

Yudhishtira asked, "Subject like others to the same kin
of grief and joy, . . . resembling others in birth an
death, in fact, similar to others in respect of all the att
butes of humanity, for what reason does one man, t
king, govern the rest of the world numbering many m
possessed of great intelligence and bravery? . . . The
cannot but be a grave reason for this since the whole wor
bows down to one man as to a god!" . . .

Bhīshma said, "Listen in detail how sovereignty fi
began in the Krita age. At first there was no sovereign
no king, no chastisement, and no chastiser. All men us
to protect one another righteously. As they thus lived,
Bhārata, righteously protecting one another, they fou
the task (after sometime), to be painful. Error then beg
to assail their hearts. Having become subject to error, t
perceptions of men, O prince, came to be clouded, an

hence their virtue began to decline. When their perceptions were dimmed and when men became subject to error, all of them became covetous, O chief of the Bhāratas!
And because men sought to obtain objects which they did
not possess, another passion called lust (of acquisition)
got hold of them. When they became subject to lust, another passion, named wrath, soon soiled them. Once subject to wrath, they lost all consideration of what should be
done and what should not. Unrestrained sexual indulgence
set in. Men began to utter what they chose. All distinctions between food that is clean and unclean and between
virtue and vice disappeared. When this confusion set in
amongst men, the Vedas disappeared. Upon the disappearance of the Vedas, righteousness was lost. When both
the Vedas and righteousness were lost, the gods were possessed by fear. Overcome with fear, O tiger among men,
they sought the protection of Brahman. Having gratified
the divine Grandsire of the universe, the gods, afflicted
with grief, said unto him, with joined hands;—O god, the
eternal Vedas have been afflicted in the world of men by
covetousness and error! For this, we have been struck with
fear. Through loss of the Vedas, O Supreme Lord, righteousness also has been lost! For this, O Lord of the three
worlds, we are about to descend to the level of human
beings! In consequence, however, of the cessation of all
pious rites among men, great distress will be our lot. Do
thou then, O Grandsire, think of that which would benefit
us, so that the universe, created by thy power, may not
meet with destruction!—Thus addressed, the Self-born
and divine Lord said unto them,—I shall think of what
will do good to all! Ye foremost of gods, let your fears be
dispelled!—The Grandsire then composed by his own intelligence a treatise consisting of a hundred thousand les-
sons. In it were treated the subjects of Virtue, Profit, and
Pleasure. The Self-born designated them as the three ends
of man. The diverse means of acquisition, the desire for
diverse kinds of wealth, the methods of agriculture and
other operations that form the chief source of revenue,

and the various means for producing and applying illu
sions, the methods by which stagnant water is rendere
foul, were laid down in it. All those means, O tiger amon
kings, by which men might be prevented from deviatin
from the path of righteousness and honesty, were all d
scribed in it. Having composed that highly beneficial tre
tise, the divine Lord cheerfully said unto the deities havin
Indra for their head, these words:—For the good of th
world and for establishing the three ends of man (Virtu
Profit, and Pleasure), I have composed this science repr
senting the very essence of speech! Assisted by chastis
ment, this science will protect the world. Dealing rewar
and punishments, this science will operate among me
And because men are led (to the acquisition of the ol
jects of their existence) by chastisement, or, in other word
chastisement leads or governs every thing, therefore wi
this science be known in the three worlds as *Dandani*
(science of chastisement). . . .

(from *Mahābhārata*, XII:59, *passim* in P. C. Roy, X, p
180-87)

THE DANGER OF ANARCHY

Some writers have seen in the horror of anarchy which chara
terizes ancient Indian thought a reflection of social disord
that followed the breakup of the Mauryan Empire, but wha
ever the cause, the emphasis is very plain. In the natural sta
of society, it is said, "the law of the fish" is dominant—tl
big one eats the smaller. According to legend, the peop
promised Manu, the mythical lawgiver pictured here as tl
first king, that they would give him a share of their produ
in return for protection. Kingship is thus the result of a "soci
contract," although the aim of the relationship—the prote
tion of the laws of class—is part of the framework of the ur
verse.

Yudhishthira said,—'Thou hast said what the duties are of the four modes of life and of the four orders. Tell me now, O grandsire, what are the principal duties of a kingdom.'

Bhīshma said,—'The (election and) coronation of a king is the first duty of a kingdom. A kingdom in which anarchy prevails becomes weak and is soon afflicted by robbers. In kingdoms torn by anarchy, righteousness cannot dwell. The inhabitants devour one another. An anarchy is the worst possible of states. The *Shrutis* declare that in crowning a king, it is Indra that is crowned (in the person of the king). A person who is desirous of prosperity should worship the king as he should worship Indra himself. No one should dwell in kingdoms torn by anarchy. Agni does not convey (to the gods) the libations that are poured upon him in kingdoms where anarchy prevails. If a powerful king approaches kingdoms weakened by anarchy, from desire of annexing them to his dominions, the people should go forward and receive the invader with respect. Such conduct would be consistent with wise counsels. There is no evil greater than anarchy. If the powerful invader be inclined to equity, everything will be right. If, on the other hand, he be enraged, he may exterminate all. That cow which cannot be easily milked has to suffer much torture. On the other hand, that cow which is capable of being easily milked, has not to suffer any torture whatever. The wood that bends easily does not require to be heated. The tree that bends easily, has not to suffer any torture (at the hands of the gardener). Guided by these instances, O hero, men should bend before those that are powerful. The man that bends his head to a powerful person really bends his head to Indra. For these reasons, men desirous of prosperity should (elect and) crown some person as their king. They who live in countries where anarchy prevails cannot enjoy their wealth and wives. During times of anarchy, the sinful man derives great pleasure by robbing the wealth of other people. When, however, his (ill-got) wealth is snatched by others, he wishes for a king. It is

evident, therefore, that in times of anarchy the ver
wicked even cannot be happy. The wealth of one
snatched away by two. That of those two is snatched awa
by many acting together. He who is not a slave is made
slave. Women, again, are forcibly abducted. For these re
sons the gods created kings for protecting the people.
there were no king on Earth for wielding the rod of cha
tisement, the strong would then have preyed on the wea
after the manner of fishes in the water. It hath been hear
by us that men, in days of old, in consequence of anarch
met with destruction, devouring one another like strong
fishes devouring the weaker ones in the water. . . .

'Thus, O Yudhishthira, those men on Earth who desir
prosperity should first elect and crown a king for the pr
tection of all! Like disciples humbling themselves in th
presence of preceptors or the gods in the presence of In
dra, all men should humble themselves before the king
One that 'is honored by his own people becomes an obje
of regard with his foes also, while one that is disregarde
by his own is overridden by foes. If the king be overridde
by his foes, all his subjects become unhappy. Therefor
umbrellas and vehicles and outward ornaments, an
viands, and drinks, and mansions, and seats, and beds, an
all utensils for use and show, should be assigned to th
king. By such means the king will succeed in dischargin
his duties of protection (the better) and become irresist
ble. . . .

'In the absence of royal protection, all things, inspire
with fear and anxiety and becoming senseless and utterin
cries of woe, would meet with destruction in no time. N
sacrifices extending for a year and completed with presen
according to the ordinances would occur if the king di
not exercise the duty of protection. In the absence of roy
protection Brāhmanas would never study the four Veda
or undergo austerities or be cleansed by knowledge an
rigid vows. In the absence of royal protection, the slayer
a person guilty of the slaughter of a Brāhmana would n
obtain any reward; on the other hand, the person guilty

Brāhmanicide would enjoy perfect immunity. In the absence of royal protection, men would snatch other people's wealth from their very hands, and all wholesome barriers would be swept away, and everybody, inspired with fear, would seek safety in flight. In the absence of royal protection, all kinds of injustice would set in; an intermixture of castes would take place; and famine would ravage the kingdom. In consequence again of royal protection, men can everywhere sleep fearlessly and at their ease without shutting their houses and doors with bolts and bars. Nobody would bear the evil speeches of others, far less actual assaults, if the king did not righteously protect the Earth. If the king exercises the duty of protection, women decked with every ornament may fearlessly wander everywhere without male relatives to attend upon them. Men become righteous and without injuring serve one another because the king exercises the duty of protection. In consequence of royal protection the members of the three orders are enabled to perform high sacrifices and devote themselves to the acquisition of learning with attention. The world depends upon agriculture and trade and is protected by the Vedas. All these again are duly protected by the king exercising his principal duty. Since the king, taking a heavy load upon himself, protects his subjects with the aid of a mighty force, it is for this that the people are able to live in happiness. Who is there that will not worship him in whose existence the people exist and in whose destruction the people are destroyed? That person who does what is agreeable and beneficial to the king and who bears (a share of) the burthen of kingly duties that strike every caste with fear, conquers both this and the other world. That man who even thinks of doing an injury to the king, without doubt meets with grief here and goes to hell hereafter. No one should disregard the king by taking him for a man, for he is really a high divinity in human form.'

(from *Mahābhārata*, XII:67, *passim*, as in P. C. Roy, X, pp. 215-17)

WAR AND PEACE

In dealing with political problems, the ancient Indian writers
tended to solve them either by constructing a mythological
framework, as in the previous passage, or by analyzing all possibilities in a system of minute classifications, as in the following selection from Kautilya's *Arthashāstra*, the most famous
work on statecraft. The assumption underlying the argument
of the passage is that war is the natural occupation of kings.
One possible result of this aspect of the tradition may have
been that refusal to recognize the sovereignty of other kings
led to a constant state of war. Another result may have
been that the common people regarded war as the concern of
the king and his fighting men, and lived out their lives unmoved by the strife around them. This was probably what
Megasthenes, the Greek ambassador to the Mauryan court,
had in mind when he wrote that during a battle "the tillers
of the soil . . . are undisturbed . . . for the combatants
make carnage of each other, but allow those engaged in hus-
bandry to remain quite unmolested."

If a king thinks:
"That by making peace with one, I can work out my
own resources, and by waging war with another, I can destroy the works of my enemy," then he may adopt that
double policy and improve his resources. . . .
When the advantages derivable from peace and war are
of equal character, one should prefer peace; for disadvan-
tages, such as the loss of power and wealth, sojourning,
and sin, are ever attending upon war.
The same holds good in the case of neutrality and war.
Of the two (forms of policy), double policy and alliance, double policy (*i.e.* making peace with one and waging war with another) is preferable; for whoever adopts
the double policy enriches himself, being ever attentive to
his own works, whereas an allied king has to help his ally at
his own expense.

One shall make an alliance with a king who is stronger than one's neighbouring enemy; in the absence of such a king, one should ingratiate oneself with one's neighbouring enemy, either by supplying money or army or by ceding a part of one's territory and by keeping oneself aloof; for there can be no greater evil to kings than alliance with a king of considerable power, unless one is actually attacked by one's enemy.

A powerless king should behave as a conquered king (towards his immediate enemy); but when he finds that the time of his own ascendancy is at hand, due to a fatal disease, internal troubles, increase of enemies, or a friend's calamities that are vexing his enemy, then under the pretence of performing some expiatory rites to avert the danger of his enemy, he may get out (of the enemy's court); or if he is in his own territory, he should not go to see his suffering enemy; or if he is near to his enemy, he may murder the enemy when opportunity affords itself.

A king who is situated between two powerful kings shall seek protection from the stronger of the two; or from one of them on whom he can rely; or he may make peace with both of them on equal terms. Then he may begin to set one of them against the other by telling each that the other is a tyrant causing utter ruin to himself, and thus cause dissension between them. When they are divided, he may put down each separately by secret or covert means. Or, throwing himself under the protection of any two immediate kings of considerable power, he may defend himself against an immediate enemy. Or, having made an alliance with a chief in a stronghold, he may adopt the double policy (*i.e.* make peace with one of the two kings and wage war with another). Or, he may adapt himself to circumstances, depending upon the causes of peace and war in order. Or, he may make friendship with traitors, enemies, and wild chiefs who are conspiring against both the kings. Or, pretending to be a close friend of one of them, he may strike the other at the latter's weak point by employing enemies and wild tribes. Or, having made friendship with

both, he may form a Circle of States. Or, he may make an
alliance with the Madhyama or the neutral king; and with
this help he may put down one of them or both. Or when
hurt by both, he may seek protection from a king of righteous character among the Madhyama king, the neutral
king, and their friends or equals, or from any other king
whose subjects are do disposed as to increase his happiness
and peace, with whose help he may be able to recover his
lost position, with whom his ancestors were in close intimacy or blood relationship, and in whose kingdom he can
find a number of powerful friends.

Of two powerful kings who are on amicable terms with
each other, a king shall make alliance with one of them
who likes him and whom he likes; this is the best way of
making alliance.

(from Kautilya, *Arthaśāstra* VII:1, in Shamasastry, pp. 296-
297)

ASHOKA'S VISION
OF TRUE CONQUEST

One of the most persistent desires of Indian rulers was to become a "Universal Emperor," a semi-divine figure who would
conquer the whole world. Imbued with this ideal, many rulers
sought to extend their power over all of India. One of the few
who nearly succeeded was Ashoka (c. 269-232 B.C.), who,
having inherited a vast empire, sought to extend it still farther.
But, according to tradition, he was filled with horror in the
moment of conquest at the cost of his victory, and accepted
the teachings of Buddha, with their emphasis on peace, as his
guide.

The record of Ashoka's attempts to spread the Rule of
Righteousness is contained in the edicts he had engraved on
pillars and rocks. His insistence that he was the father and

protector of his people is in keeping with traditional theories of Indian kingship, and he sought to use the machinery of the state to encourage virtuous living. As these selections from the Edicts suggest, Ashoka was especially anxious to end the killing of animals and to encourage his officials to administer strict justice. His injunction to his people to practice religious tolerance is especially noteworthy. It is possible that this emphasis reflects to some extent his recognition that the Brāhman priesthood resented his support of Buddhism, which was the religion of a minority of the population.

When the king, Beloved of the Gods and of Gracious Mien, had been consecrated eight years Kalinga was conquered, 150,000 people were deported, 100,000 were killed, and many times that number died. But after the conquest of Kalinga, the Beloved of the Gods began to follow Righteousness (Dharma), to love Righteousness, and to give instruction in Righteousness. Now the Beloved of the Gods regrets the conquest of Kalinga, for when an independent country is conquered people are killed, they die, or are deported, and that the Beloved of the Gods finds very painful and grievous. And this he finds even more grievous—that all the inhabitants—brāhmans, ascetics, and other sectarians, and householders who are obedient to superiors, parents, and elders, who treat friends, acquaintances, companions, relatives, slaves, and servants with respect, and are firm in their faith—all suffer violence, murder, and separation from their loved ones. Even those who are fortunate enough not to have lost those near and dear to them are afflicted at the misfortunes of friends, acquaintances, companions, and relatives. The participation of all men in common suffering is grievous to the Beloved of the Gods. Moreover there is no land, except that of the Greeks, where groups of brāhmans and ascetics are not found, or where men are not members of one sect or another. So now, even if the number of those

killed and captured in the conquest of Kalinga had been
hundred or a thousand times less, it would be grievous t
the Beloved of the Gods. The Beloved of the Gods wi
forgive as far as he can, and he even conciliates the fore
tribes of his dominions; but he warns them that there :
power even in the remorse of the Beloved of the God
and he tells them to reform, lest they be killed.

For all beings the Beloved of the Gods desires securit
self-control, calm of mind, and gentleness. The Beloved c
the Gods considers that the greatest victory is the victor
of Righteousness; and this he has won here (in India) an
even five hundred leagues beyond his frontiers in th
realm of the Greek king Antiochus, and beyond Antiochu
among the four kings Ptolemy, Antigonus, Magas, and A
exander. Even where the envoys of the Beloved of th
Gods have not been sent men hear of the way in which h
follows and teaches Righteousness, and they too follow :
and will follow it. Thus he achieves a universal conques
and conquest always gives a feeling of pleasure; yet it is bu
a slight pleasure, for the Beloved of the Gods only looks o
that which concerns the next life as of great importance.

I have had this inscription of Righteousness engrave
that all my sons and grandsons may not seek to gain ne
victories, that in whatever victories they may gain the
may prefer forgiveness and light punishment, that the
may consider the only [valid] victory the victory of Righ
eousness, which is of value both in this world and the nex
and that all their pleasure may be in Righteousness. . .

(from the Thirteenth Rock Edict in *Sources of Indian Trad
tion*, pp. 146-47)

Here no animal is to be killed for sacrifice, and no festiva
are to be held, for the king finds much evil in festival
except for certain festivals which he considers good.

Formerly in the Beloved of the God's kitchen severa
hundred thousand animals were killed daily for food; bu
now at the time of writing only three are killed—two pea

cocks and a deer, though the deer not regularly. Even these three animals will not be killed in future.

(from the First Rock Edict in *Sources of Indian Tradition*, p. 148)

The Beloved of the Gods . . . honors members of all sects, whether ascetics or householders, by gifts and various honors. But he does not consider gifts and honors as important as the furtherance of the essential message of all sects. This essential message varies from sect to sect, but it has one common basis, that one should so control one's tongue as not to honor one's own sect or disparage another's on the wrong occasions; for on certain occasions one should do so only mildly, and indeed on other occasions one should honor other men's sects. By doing this one strengthens one's own sect and helps the others, while by doing otherwise one harms one's own sect and does a disservice to the others. Whoever honors his own sect and disparages another man's, whether from blind loyalty or with the intention of showing his own sect in a favorable light, does his own sect the greatest possible harm. Concord is best, with each hearing and respecting the other's teachings. It is the wish of the Beloved of the Gods that members of all sects should be learned and should teach virtue. . . . Many officials are busied in this matter . . . and the result is the progress of my own sect and the illumination of Righteousness.

(from the Twelfth Rock Edict in *Sources of Indian Tradition*, p. 151)

In the past kings sought to make the people progress in Righteousness but they did not progress. . . . And I asked myself how I might uplift them through progress in Righteousness. . . . Thus I have decided to have them instructed in Righteousness, and to issue ordinances of Righteousness, so that by hearing them the people might

conform, advance in the progress of Righteousness, and
themselves make great progress. . . . For that purpose
many officials are employed among the people to instruct
them in Righteousness and to explain it to them. . . .

Moreover I have had banyan trees planted on the road
to give shade to man and beast; I have planted mango
groves, and I have had ponds dug and shelters erected
along the roads at every eight kos. Everywhere I have had
wells dug for the benefit of man and beast. But this benefit
is but small, for in many ways the kings of olden time have
worked for the welfare of the world; but what I have done
has been done that men may conform to Righteousness.

(from the Seventh Pillar Edict in *Sources of Indian Tradition*
p. 152)

CHAPTER VI

THE SEARCH FOR

SALVATION

~~~~~~~~~

During the period that we have characterized as the Age of
Growth, the older Vedic religion was reinterpreted and, to
some extent, transformed, but the sacred texts remained
the source of revealed truth. At the same time, certain
other ideas had become so firmly fixed in the tradition that
they were the unquestioned assumptions of almost all
schools of thought. The most fundamental of these, the
doctrine of karma, the idea that each act carried with it a
necessary result, and belief in the transmigration of the
soul, as we have seen, had already been accepted when
the Upanishads were written, and with the passing of
time they had been woven more deeply into the fabric of
Indian life. It is against the background of these assumptions, as well as of the ancient Vedic inheritance, that the
religious developments of the Age of Growth took place.

One of the most important features of the religious life
of the period was the rise of sects or cults which have remained ever since an essential feature of Hinduism. These
sects were marked by two features which were of great significance for the spiritual life of India. One was bhakti, an
attitude of devotion and adoration towards some particular god; the other was an emphasis on the grace of this
deity in freely granting salvation to his devotees. The

deities that were the object of devotion seem, in general, to have been of two kinds: either folk heroes who were deified (or, conceivably, deities who were made culture heroes), or personifications of some natural force. Krishna and Rama are examples of the first class, Shiva of the second, although Krishna and Rama are not strictly comparable to Shiva, since they are regarded as incarnations of Vishnu. In any case, it is around Vishnu, in one of his incarnations, or Shiva that the sectarian cults are mainly centered. Both deities were widely worshipped in some form by about 300 A.D., and it is quite possible that by then most of the people would have classed themselves as followers of one or the other. Thus the distinction between the Vaishnavite, or follower of Vishnu, and the Shaivite, became a basic feature of Hinduism.

The devotees of Vishnu picture their deity, either in his own person or in that of his incarnations, as beneficent and loving. Symbols denoting light and the life-giving sun are frequently associated with him, and his grace in offering salvation to his followers is stressed. This aspect of the Vishnu cult is prominent in the Bhagavad Gītā, the greatest literary monument of the cults that emphasized worship of an individual god. This famous work forms a part of the Mahābhārata, but is probably a separate composition. It exalts Krishna as supreme deity, but endeavors to bring all of the main trends of religious experience into a harmonious whole. Partly because it offers something to seekers of all kinds, partly because it synthesizes the ethical and religious insights of the Hindu tradition into a coherent statement, the Gītā has played an important role in the life of India.

Shiva is almost certainly one of the most ancient of Indian gods, dating back before the physical and spiritual conquest of India by the Aryans. Images found at the site of the prehistoric Indus Valley civilization bear a striking resemblance to later representations of Shiva, and his cult is strongest in South India, the area where Aryan influence were latest in coming. He is a god of fertility and power but he is also pictured as an ascetic, covered with ashes and with snakes garlanded around his neck. Most frequently worshipped through a phallic symbol, a reminder of his origin as a god of fertility, he is also the Lord of the Dance, maintaining the cosmic order through his energy and power.

A characteristic feature of the Hindu tradition, the use of images in worship, is associated with the rise to prominence of the great cults. Images of the gods seem to have been unknown in Vedic times, but probably the emphasis on devotion offered to one particular deity fostered the use of plastic representations. Whatever the cause, images of all kinds became one of the most obvious marks of Hinduism, with carving becoming one of the most highly developed of the arts. The religious life of the people was thus nourished on a visual statement unmatched, perhaps, in the history of any civilization.

The Buddhist and Jain movements which flourished in the centuries when Vaishnavism and Shaivism were also taking hold can only be mentioned in passing, although they influenced the Hindu tradition at many points. The interpenetration of the various movements was an extremely complex process, which, because of the lack of detailed historical data, cannot be analyzed with any certainty. The use of images in Buddhism, for example, might seem to be a clear case of the influence of the sectarian cults, but the very widespread and early use of images by Buddhism suggests the possibility that the influence was the other way around.

MAN'S TRUE NATURE

As we have already seen, for Indian religion salvation is understood in terms of the fundamental beliefs in *karma* and rebirth. On one level, the search for salvation is related to an attempt to improve one's *karma*, the fruit of one's actions, in order to improve one's future existence; on another and higher level, salvation is understood as the finding of a mode of existence that is beyond the changing flux of time and circumstance. This concept was directly linked to the ancient message of the *Upanishads* that there is an identity between man's spirit and the universal spirit, and that salvation consisted in an intuitive realization of this truth. To come to this state of knowledge is to realize man's true nature.

A description of man's nature is placed near the beginning of the *Bhagavad Gītā*, where Arjuna, the great warrior, is filled with horror at the consequences that will follow from the fratricidal war in which he is engaged. Krishna, who is acting as his charioteer, insists that the first prerequisite for facing this and all other problems is an understanding of the true nature of human existence. Krishna's statement is one of the *Bhagavad Gītā's* most famous passages.

The Blessed Lord said:

You grieve for those who should not be mourned, and yet you speak words of wisdom! The learned do not grieve for the dead or for the living.

Never, indeed, was there a time when I was not, nor when you were not, nor these lords of men. Never, too, will there be a time, hereafter, when we shall not be.

As in this body, there are for the embodied one [i.e., the soul] childhood, youth, and old age, even so there is the taking on of another body. The wise sage is not perplexed thereby.

Contacts of the sense-organs, O son of Kuntī, give rise to cold and heat, and pleasure and pain. They come and go, and are not permanent. Bear with them, O Bhārata.

That man, whom these [sense-contacts] do not trouble, O chief of men, to whom pleasure and pain are alike, who is wise—he becomes eligible for immortality.

For the nonexistent there is no coming into existence; nor is there passing into nonexistence for the existent. The ultimate nature of these two is perceived by the seers of truth.

Know that to be indestructible by which all this is pervaded. Of this imperishable one, no one can bring about destruction.

These bodies of the eternal embodied one, who is indestructible and incomprehensible, are said to have an end. Therefore fight, O Bhārata.

He who regards him [i.e., the soul] as a slayer, and he who regards him as slain—both of them do not know the truth; for this one neither slays nor is slain.

He is not born, nor does he die at any time; nor, having once come to be will he again come not to be. He is unborn, eternal, permanent, and primeval; he is not slain when the body is slain.

Whoever knows him to be indestructible and eternal, unborn and immutable—how and whom can such a man, O son of Prithā, cause to be slain or slay?

Just as a man, having cast off old garments, puts on other, new ones, even so does the embodied one, having cast off old bodies, take on other, new ones.

Weapons do not cleave him, fire does not burn him; nor does water drench him, nor the wind dry him up.

He is uncleavable, he is unburnable, he is undrenchable, as also undryable. He is eternal, all-pervading, stable, immovable, existing from time immemorial.

He is said to be unmanifest, unthinkable, and unchangeable. Therefore, knowing him as such, you should not grieve [for him].

And even if you regard him as being perpetually born and as perpetually dying, even then, O long-armed one, you should not grieve for him.

For, to one who is born death is certain and certain is birth to one who has died. Therefore in connection with a thing that is inevitable you should not grieve. . . .

Unmanifest in their beginnings are beings, manifest in the middle stage, O Bhārata, and unmanifest, again, in their ends. For what then should there be any lamentation?

Someone perceives him as a marvel; similarly, another speaks of him as a marvel; another, again, hears of him

as a marvel; and, even after hearing of him, no one
knows him.

The embodied one within the body of everyone, O
Bhārata, is ever unslayable. Therefore, you should not
grieve for any being. . . .

When one renounces all the desires which have arisen in
the mind, O son of Prithā, and when he himself is content within his own Self, then is he called a man of
steadfast wisdom.

He whose mind is unperturbed in the midst of sorrow,
and who entertains no desires amid pleasures; he from
whom passion, fear, and anger have fled away—he is
called a sage of steadfast intellect.

He who feels no attachment toward anything; who, having
encountered the various good or evil things, neither re-
joices nor loathes—his wisdom is steadfast.

When one draws in, on every side, the sense-organs from
the objects of sense as a tortoise draws in its limbs from
every side—then his wisdom becomes steadfast.

(from *Bhagavad Gītā*, II:11-30, 55-59, in *Sources of Indian
Tradition*, pp. 284-85, 298)

The Way of Salvation: Duty

Having stated the goal, Krishna proceeds to show how it may
be obtained. His definition of the end of life as a state beyond
any attachment, including concern for the results of action,
raises the problem of how action can be performed without
motivation, that is, without being involved in its result. He
gives the answer in terms of performance of *dharma*, the duties
appropriate to one's particular class. This fulfillment of one's
obligations as defined by life is known as *karma yoga*, the
discipline of action, but it must be carefully distinguished from
what is known in western thought as "salvation by works."
Karma yoga, the way of obedience to the demands imposed by
a particular existence, is a necessity for all those who seek to
escape from the involvement in the fruits of actions, or, in
other words, in rebirth.

Not by nonperformance of actions does a man attain freedom from action; nor by mere renunciation of actions does he attain his spiritual goal.

For no one, indeed, can remain, for even a single moment, unengaged in activity, since everyone, being powerless, is made to act by the dispositions of matter.

Whoever having restrained his organs of action still continues to brood over the objects of senses—he, the deluded one, is called a hypocrite.

But he who, having controlled the sense-organs by means of the mind, O Arjuna, follows without attachment the path of action by means of the organs of action—he excels.

Do you do your allotted work, for action is superior to nonaction. Even the normal functioning of your body cannot be accomplished through actionlessness.

Except for the action done for sacrifice, all men are under the bondage of action. Therefore, O son of Kunti, do you undertake action for that purpose, becoming free from all attachment. . . .

But the man whose delight is in the Self alone, who is content with the Self, who is satisfied only within the Self—for him there exists nothing that needs to be done.

He, verily, has in this world no purpose to be served by action done nor any purpose whatsoever to be served by action abnegated. Similarly, he does not depend on any beings for having his purpose served.

Therefore, without attachment, always do the work that has to be done, for a man doing his work without attachment attains to the highest goal. . . .

Better is one's own dharma [class duties] which one may be able to fulfill but imperfectly, than the dharma of others which is more easily accomplished. Better is death in the fulfillment of one's own dharma. To adopt the dharma of others is perilous. . . .

The fourfold class system was created by Me in accordance with the varying dispositions and the actions [resulting

from them]. Though I am its creator, know Me, who
am immutable, to be a non-doer.

Actions do not cling to Me, for I have no yearning for
their fruit. He who knows Me thus [and himself acts in
that spirit] is not bound by actions.

So knowing was action done even by men of old who
sought liberation. Therefore do the same action [i.e.
your class duties] which was done by the ancients in
ancient times.

What is action? What is inaction?—as to this even the
wise sages are confounded. I will expound action to you
knowing which you will be liberated from evil.

One has to realize what is action; similarly, one has to realize what is wrong action; and one has also to realize
what is inaction. Inscrutable, indeed, is the way of
action.

He who sees inaction in action and action in inaction, he is
discerning among men, expert in the technique of
karma-yoga, the doer of the entire action [enjoined by
his dharma].

He whose undertakings are all devoid of motivating desires
and purposes and whose actions are consumed by the
fire of knowledge—him the wise call a man of learning.

Renouncing all attachment to the fruits of actions, ever
content, independent—such a person even if engaged in
action, does not do anything whatever.

(from *Bhagavad Gītā*, III:3-9, 17-19, IV:13-20, in *Sources of
Indian Tradition*, pp. 286-87, 289)

The Way of Salvation: Knowledge

The second way commended by Krishna for a realization of
the true nature of man is the path of knowledge. This does
not mean the gaining of information or even of wisdom—
although it includes knowledge of the scriptures and the teachings of the sages—but rather the acquisition of truth that

comes through meditation. In the following selection both the fruits and techniques of this way, or *yoga*, are strikingly delineated.

To him who has subjugated his self by his self, his self is a friend; but to him who has not restrained his self, his own self behaves inimically, like an enemy. The self of one who has subjugated his self and is tranquil, is absolutely concentrated on itself, in the midst of cold and heat, pleasure and pain, as well as honour and dishonour. The devotee whose self is contented with knowledge and experience, who is unmoved, who has restrained his senses, and to whom a sod, a stone, and gold are alike, is said to be devoted. And he is esteemed highest, who thinks alike about well-wishers, friends, and enemies, and those who are indifferent, and those who take part with both sides, and those who are objects of hatred, and relatives, as well as about the good and the sinful. A devotee should constantly devote his self to abstraction, remaining in a secret place, alone, with his mind and self restrained, without expectations, and without belongings. Fixing his seat firmly in a clean place, not too high nor too low, and covered over with a sheet of cloth, a deerskin, and blades of Kusa grass,—and there seated on that seat, fixing his mind exclusively on one point, with the workings of·the mind and senses restraincd, he should practice devotion for purity of self. Holding his body, head, and neck even and unmoved, remaining steady, looking at the tip of his own nose, and not looking about in all directions, with a tranquil self, devoid of fear, and adhering to the rules of chastity, he should restrain his mind, and concentrate it on me, and sit down engaged in devotion, regarding me as his final goal. Thus constantly devoting his self to abstraction, a devotee whose mind is restrained, attains that tranquillity which culminates in final emancipation, and assimilation with me. Devotion is not his, O Arjuna! who eats too much, nor his who eats not at all; not his who is addicted to too much sleep, nor his who is ever awake. That devotion which destroys all misery is his, who takes due food and exercise, who toils duly in all works, and who sleeps and awakes in due time. When a man's mind well restrained becomes steady upon the self alone, then he being indifferent to all objects of desire, is said to be devoted. As a light standing in a windless place flickers not, that is declared to be the parallel for a devotee, whose mind is restrained, and who devotes his self to abstraction.

(from *Bhagavad Gītā*, VI:7-19, in *Sacred Books of the East,* VIII, pp. 68-69)

The Way of Salvation: Devotion

Throughout all the discussions of the ways of salvation in the *Bhagavad Gītā* is the implicit assumption that transcending and completing the disciplines of work and knowledge is the way of devotion to Krishna as Supreme Lord. Through surrender to him, men find the final end they seek—the realization of their true self. It is this emphasis on devotion that has made the *Gītā* the scripture that appeals most directly to the heart of the Indian people. The verses given here describe the glorious vision of Krishna that comes to Arjuna, overwhelming his senses with the splendor and power of the god who has sought through his love and mercy to bring him to a realization of the truth.

ARJUNA:

Fain would I see,
As thou Thyself declar'st it, Sovereign Lord!
The likeness of that glory of Thy Form
Wholly revealed. O Thou Divinest One!
If this can be, if I may bear the sight,
Make Thyself visible, Lord of all prayers!
Show me Thy very self, the Eternal God!

KRISHNA:

Gaze, then, thou Son of Prithâ! I manifest for thee
Those hundred thousand thousand shapes that clothe
my Mystery:
I show thee all my semblances, infinite, rich, divine,
My changeful hues, my countless forms. See! in this face
of mine . . .
Wonders unnumbered, Indian Prince! revealed to none
save thee.
Behold! this is the Universe!—Look! what is live and
dead
I gather all in one—in Me! Gaze, as thy lips have said,
On GOD ETERNAL, VERY GOD! See ME! see what thou
prayest!

.   .   .   .

Thou canst not!—nor, with human eyes, Arjuna! ever
mayest!
Therefore I give thee sense divine. Have other eyes, new
light!
And, look! This is My glory, unveiled to mortal sight!

ARJUNA:

I mark Thee strike the skies
With front in wondrous wise
Huge, rainbow-painted, glittering; and thy
mouth
Opened, and orbs which see
All things, whatever be,
In all Thy worlds, east, west, and north and
south.

O Eyes of God! O Head!
My strength of soul is fled,
Gone is heart's force, rebuked is mind's desire!
When I behold Thee so,
With awful brows a-glow,
With burning glance, and lips lighted with fire,

Fierce as those flames which shall
Consume, at close of all,
Earth, Heaven! Ah me! I see no Earth and
Heaven!
Thee, Lord of Lords! I see,
Thee only—only Thee!
Ah! let Thy mercy unto me be given! . . .

How, in the wide worlds three
Should any equal be?
Shall any other share Thy majesty?

Therefore, with body bent
And reverent intent,
I praise, and serve, and seek Thee, asking grace.
As father to a son,
As friend to friend, as one
Who loveth to his lover, turn Thy face

In gentleness on me!
Good is it I did see
This unknown marvel of Thy Form! But fear
Mingles with joy! Retake,
Dear Lord! for pity's sake
Thine earthly shape, which earthly eyes may bear!

Be merciful, and show
The visage that I know;
Let me regard Thee, as of yore, arrayed
With disc and forehead-gem,
With mace and anadem,
Thou who sustainest all things! Undismayed

Let me once more behold
The form I loved of old,
Thou of the thousand arms and countless eyes!
My frightened heart is fain
To see restored again
The Charioteer, my Krishna's kind disguise. . . .

KRISHNA:
 Yea! it was wonderful and terrible
 To view me as thou didst, dear Prince! The gods
 Dread and desire continually to view!
 Yet not by Vedas, nor from sacrifice,
 Nor penance, nor gift-giving, nor with prayer
 Shall any so behold, as thou hast seen!
 Only by fullest service, perfect faith,
 And uttermost surrender am I known
 And seen, and entered into, Indian Prince!
 Who doeth all for Me; who findeth Me
 In all; adoreth always; loveth all
 Which I have made, and Me, for Love's sole end,
 That man, Arjuna! unto Me doth wend.

(from *Bhagavad Gītā*, XI, selected verses, as in Sir Edwin
Arnold, *The Song Celestial*)

INCARNATION: THE RESPONSE
TO HUMAN NEED

One of the most vital aspects of the Hindu tradition is the
belief in the numerous incarnations of the great divinities,
especially of Vishnu. The *Bhagavad Gītā* presents this in a
striking manner with the assertion that whenever the world
is threatened by disorder then Krishna appears to restore order
to human affairs. While in the *Gītā* itself it is not explicitly
stated that Krishna is an incarnation of Vishnu, later religious
thought interpreted him as such and around him gathered an
enormous literature describing his loving care for mankind.

KRISHNA:
 Manifold the renewals of my birth
 Have been, Arjuna! and of thy births, too!
 But mine I know, and thine thou knowest not,

O Slayer of thy Foes! Albeit I be
Unborn, undying, indestructible,
The Lord of all things living; not the less—
By Maya, by my magic which I stamp
On floating Nature-forms, the primal vast—
I come, and go, and come. When Righteousness
Declines, O Bharata! when Wickedness
Is strong, I rise, from age to age, and take
Visible shape, and move a man with men,
Succoring the good, thrusting the evil back,
And setting Virtue on her seat again.
Who knows the truth touching my births on earth
And my divine work, when he quits the flesh
Puts on its load no more, falls no more down
To earthly birth: to Me he comes, dear Prince!

(from *Bhagavad Gītā*, IV:5-9, in Arnold, *The Song Celestial*)

ADORATION OF SHIVA

While the early devotees of Shiva did not leave a literary
monument comparable to the *Bhagavad Gītā*, it is quite certain that he is one of the most ancient of the gods of the
Indian people. One indication of this, apart from the existence
of images from the Indus Valley civilization that bear a striking resemblance to Shiva, are the references in one of the
later *Upanishads*, *Śvetāśvatara*. There Shiva seems to be identified with Rudra, the storm-god of the Vedic hymns. The hymn
given here shows how closely theism, especially in terms of
worship of one supreme God, was related to the great tradition.

The One spreader of the net, who rules with his ruling
    powers,
Who rules all the worlds with his ruling powers,
The one who alone stands in their arising and in their con-
    tinued existence—

They who know That, become immortal.
For truly, Rudra (the Terrible) is the One—they stand
    not for a second—
Who rules all the worlds with his ruling powers.
He stands opposite creatures. He, the Protector,
After creating all beings, merges them together at the end
    of time.
Having an eye on every side and a face on every side,
Having an arm on every side and a foot on every side,
The One God forges together with hands, with wings,
Creating the heaven and the earth.
He who is the source and origin of the gods,
The ruler of all, Rudra, the great seer,
Who of old created the Golden Germ,
May He endow us with clear intellect!
The form of thine, O Rudra, which is kindly (*śiva*),
Unterrifying, revealing no evil—
With that most benign form to us
Appear, O dweller among the mountains!
O dweller among the mountains, the arrow
Which thou holdest in thy hand to throw
Make kindly (*śiva*), O mountain protector!
Injure not man or beast!
Higher than this is Brahma. The Supreme, the Great,
Hidden in all things, body by body,
The One embracer of the universe—
By knowing Him as Lord men become immortal.
I know this mighty Person
Of the color of the sun, beyond darkness.
Only by knowing Him does one pass over death.
There is no other path for going there.
Than whom there is naught else higher,
Than whom there is naught smaller, naught greater,
The One stands like a tree established in heaven.
By Him, the Person, this whole world is filled.
    That which is beyond this world
    Is without form and without ill.
They who know That, become immortal;

But others go only to sorrow.
Who is the face, the head, the neck of all,
Who dwells in the heart of all things,
All-pervading is He, and bountiful;
Therefore omnipresent, and kindly (*śiva*).
A mighty lord is the Person,
The instigator of the highest being
Unto the purest attainment,
The ruler, a light imperishable!
A Person of the measure of a thumb is the inner soul,
Ever seated in the heart of creatures.
He is framed by the heart, by the thought, by the mind.
They who know That, become immortal.

  The Person has a thousand heads,
  A thousand eyes, a thousand feet;
  He surrounds the earth on all sides,
  And stands ten fingers' breadth beyond.
  The Person, in truth, this whole world is,
  Whate'er has been and whate'er will be;
  Also ruler of immortality,
  [And] whatever grows up by food.
  It has a hand and foot on every side,
  On every side an eye and head and face,
  It has an ear everywhere in the world.
  It stands encompassing all.

(from *Śvetāśvatara Upanishad*, III:1-16, in Hume, pp. 399-
401)

THE GREAT HERESIES
OF THE TRADITION

All great religious traditions give rise to movements that are
closely related in fundamental ideas and value structures to
the parent stock but which historically have stood in opposi-

tion to the main lines of the development. Within the general context of Indian civilization, Buddhism and Jainism were both formidable rivals for the allegiance of the people and both had a far-reaching influence on many aspects of the Hindu tradition, but all that can be attempted here, however, is to indicate two important emphases of the great heretical movements that arose in the sixth century B.C. The first selection is traditionally regarded as the first sermon of Gautama, or Buddha, the Enlightened One. Here is sounded a note that comes to be associated, not very accurately, with the Hindu tradition itself: the supposition that the characteristic mark of the human condition is misery. According to this diagnosis, the suffering of mankind is caused by attachment, by the error of supposing that there is anything—including the Self —that is permanent in this world of perpetual change. The remedy was the Middle Way, a refusal to be concerned with anything that did not serve to cut the bonds of attachments of all kinds.

The second selection expresses the important Jain doctrine that all matter is possessed of life which differs in quality but not in kind in different objects. The logical extension of this belief was that no form of life should be injured in any way. The emphasis is perhaps not so much on compassion for all life as for the fundamental vision of an integrated universe. There is also the suggestion that the passion involved in killing and the taking of life binds one to existence. This Jain doctrine undoubtedly played a part in the general Indian belief in nonviolence.

Buddha's First Sermon

Thus I have heard. Once the Lord was at Vārānasī, at the deer park called Isipatana. There he addressed the five monks:

There are two ends not to be served by a wanderer. What are these two? The pursuit of desires and of the pleasure which springs from desire, which is base, common, leading to rebirth, ignoble, and unprofitable; and the pursuit of pain and hardship, which is grievous, ignoble, and unprofitable. The Middle Way of the Tathāgata avoids both these ends. It is enlightened, it brings clear vision, it makes for wisdom, and leads to peace, insight, enlightenment, and Nirvāna. What is the Middle Way? . . . It is the Noble Eightfold Path—Right Views, Right Resolve, Right Speech, Right Conduct, Right Livelihood, Right Effort, Right Mindfulness, and Right Concentration. This is the Middle Way. . . .

And this is the Noble Truth of Sorrow. Birth is sorrow, age is sorrow, disease is sorrow, death is sorrow; contact with the unpleasant is sorrow, separation from the pleasant is sorrow, every wish unfulfilled is sorrow—in short all the five components of individuality are sorrow.

And this is the Noble Truth of the Arising of Sorrow. It arises from craving, which leads to rebirth, which brings delight and passion, and seeks pleasure now here, now there—the craving for sensual pleasure, the craving for continued life, the craving for power.

And this is the Noble Truth of the Stopping of Sorrow. It is the complete stopping of that craving, so that no passion remains, leaving it, being emancipated from it, being released from it, giving no place to it.

And this is the Noble Truth of the Way which Leads to the Stopping of Sorrow. It is the Noble Eightfold Path—Right Views, Right Resolve, Right Speech, Right Conduct, Right Livelihood, Right Effort, Right Mindfulness, and Right Concentration.

(from *Samyutta Nikāya*, V:421 ff., in *Sources of Indian Tradition*, pp. 101-02)

The Jain Vision of Life

From clubs and knives, stakes and maces, breaking my limbs,
An infinite number of times I have suffered without hope.
By keen-edged razors, by knives and shears,
Many times I have been drawn and quartered, torn apart and skinned.

Helpless in snares and traps, a deer,
I have been caught and bound and fastened, and often I
have been killed.
A helpless fish, I have been caught with hooks and nets;
An infinite number of times I have been killed and
scraped, split and gutted.
A bird, I have been caught by hawks or trapped in nets,
Or held fast by birdlime, and I have been killed an infinite
number of times.
A tree, with axes and adzes by the carpenters
An infinite number of times I have been felled, stripped of
my bark, cut up, and sawn into planks.
As iron, with hammer and tongs by blacksmiths
An infinite number of times I have been struck and
beaten, split and filed. . . .
Ever afraid, trembling, in pain and suffering,
I have felt the utmost sorrow and agony. . . .
In every kind of existence I have suffered
Pains which have scarcely known reprieve for a moment.

(from *Uttarādhyayana*, XIX, selections, in *Sources of Indian Tradition*, pp. 59-60)

CHAPTER VII

THE UNIVERSE OF
THE GREAT EPICS

∽∽∽∽∽∽

The culture and civilization that had been developing in India for nearly two thousand years is reflected in two great poems, the Mahābhārata and the Rāmāyana, that are different in texture and theme from the religious texts. These two works are usually referred to as epics, but the implied comparison with the Odyssey and Iliad is not altogether apt. Simply in terms of authorship, the Mahābhārata is the product of many hands, and hundreds of years must have elapsed between the first and the last compositions. The original materials have been so worked over that it is now quite impossible to separate any kernel and show it to be the most ancient. At the same time, despite the continuous reworking of the poem, the heterogeneous elements have been woven into an extraordinarily complex structure with all the parts related. But the most important difference between the Indian epics and their western counterparts is the place the Mahābhārata and the Rāmāyana have held for two millennia in the life of the Indian people. While probably originally secular in origin, insofar as that term has any meaning within the Indian tradition, by about 200 A.D. both poems had become scripture, accepted as smriti, the part of the texts which are regarded as dependent upon tradition, not divine revela-

tion, for their truth. The vast storehouse of myths, legends, and moral teaching has provided the Indian people with the material for artistic productions of every kind as well as coloring every aspect of their lives. They have thus given Indian society a basis of common ideas and ideals as well as a common treasury of stories known to all. This inheritance from the epics cannot be overstressed in any attempt to explain the unity and endurance of Hindu life. Although the peoples of India differ widely in language and race, they share a history that is half human, half divine, but that has been lived out on Indian soil.

The Mahābhārata tells the story of the great war that took place for the control of the kingdom of the Kurus, an area near modern Delhi. The occasion of the war was a struggle for the succession between two branches of the family. The succession had devolved on Dhritarāshtra, but since he was blind his brother Pāndu ruled in his place. When Pāndu, because of a curse, had to go into exile, he left his five sons in Dhritarāshtra's care, with the expectation that the oldest, Yudhishthira, would succeed. The other four brothers—Arjuna, Nakula, Bhīma, and Sahadeva—all play important parts in the story, but Arjuna is in many ways the hero of the poem. Civil war began when Dhritarāshtra's hundred sons, led by the oldest, Duryodhana, refused to give up the kingdom. The long story that follows is filled with many digressions and embellishments, but the rivalry of the cousins is the central theme, and it provides the unifying thread for the introduction of the most diverse materials, including lengthy discussions on statecraft.

The Rāmāyana, ascribed to Sage Valmīki, tells the story of how Rāma, heir apparent to the kingdom of Ayodhya, went into exile with his wife, Sītā, and his brother Lakshman, because of the promise made by his father to his stepmother to let her son succeed to the throne. The heart of the poem is the capture of Sītā by Rāvan, the demon king of Ceylon, and the long struggle to free her, with the assistance of Hanumān and his fellow monkeys, provides op-

portunity for stirring battle scenes as well as praise for Rāma's and Sītā's incomparable virtue.

In the selections given here no attempt has been made to tell the long and complex story, but only to indicate the way in which the epics reinforce the values that are particularly prized within the Hindu tradition. Throughout the selections there are continual reminders of the themes already mentioned—the duties of class, the role of a king and the nature of a true marital relationship.

THE MAHĀBHĀRATA:
THE FOUNDING OF
THE ROYAL LINE

The central theme of the *Mahābhārata* is the great war between the sons of the two royal brothers, Dhritarāshtra and Pāndu, and the following selection traces the strange origin of the hundred sons of the one and of the five sons of the other. The story is told in the form of a dialogue between a descendant of the family and a great sage. Interwoven into the narrative are many familiar elements of the Hindu tradition: the importance of sons, the character of the gods, the power of asceticism, and the nature of kingship. All these form a complex pattern of grotesque fantasy and historical possibility that takes the reader into a self-contained universe quite different from the ordinary structure of reality. No doubt part of the secret of the appeal of the stories of the great poem to the people of India is the success of the authors in creating a new order of life, where the people are recognizably human but the conventions of action and behavior are not those familiar in everyday life.

Janamejaya asked: 'O best of Brahmanas, how did Ghandhari have a hundred sons? And how were the five sons of Pandu born of the Gods?'

Vaisampayana continued: 'Bhishma, the grandfather of the Kurus, heard that Ghandhari, the daughter of King Suvala, had obtained as a boon from Hari a promise that she should have a hundred sons. Bhishma sent to ask for her as a wife to Dhritarashtra, but Suvala hesitated because of Dhritarashtra's blindness. Eventually he consented, and the chaste Ghandhari agreed; but she blindfolded herself so that she should not be different from her husband. Her brother Sakuni brought her to the Kurus by whom she was received with great honour. Ghandhari, after her marriage, pleased everyone with her behaviour. . . . After Ghandhari conceived, she bore the burden for two years. But she was so beside herself with suffering because of the load in her womb that she struck herself and thereupon was delivered of a ball of hard flesh. She was about to destroy it when Dwaipayana appeared before her. She said: "O Rishi, you granted me the boon of a hundred sons. See what I have!"

'The Rishi told her to sprinkle the ball with water and bring a hundred pots of clarified butter. The ball was divided into a hundred parts the size of a thumb and each was put into a pot, and the pots were left for two years.

'The first to be born was Duryodhana, who began to cry and bray like an ass; and at the sound vultures and crows also began to utter cries, winds began to blow and fires broke out. . . .

'At once jackals and other beasts began to howl, and hearing these frightful omens the wise Vidura said: "It is evident that this your son shall be the destroyer of your race. The prosperity of all depends on his being abandoned. If you keep him calamities will surely follow. O King, you will still have ninety-nine sons; if you wish for the good of your race and of the world, cast this child away. It has been said that for the sake of a family one member should be cast off; for the sake of a village, a family; for the sake of a country, a village; and for the sake of a soul the whole world!"

'But Dhritarashtra had not the heart to do so.

'After Duryodhana the other ninety-nine sons were bo
in succession; also a daughter named Dussala.'

Janamejaya said: 'O tongue of Brahma, now that y
have told me about the birth of the hundred sons and o
daughter of Dhritarashtra, I wish to hear how the Pa
davas, the sons of Pandu, were born.'

Vaisampayana said: Among the Yadavas was a ki
named Sura, who had a beautiful daughter named Prith
It happened that Pritha once pleased the terrible Bra
mana, Durvasa, by the way she carried out her duties. T
sage, having foreknowledge that Pandu, her future h
band, would not be able to have children, imparted to l
a mantra, whereby she could summon what God s
wished, to give her sons.

'But instead of waiting as she should have done, she, c
of curiosity, wished to see if the mantra would work, a
though a maiden, she invoked Surya, the Sun God, who
once appeared. She was overcome with confusion, but
approached and asked her: "O black-eyed one, what
you wish?"

'Pritha said: "O Bharata, a Brahmana gave me t
mantra and I used it only to test its power. I ask yc
forgiveness. A woman, whatever her offence, deserves to
forgiven."

'Surya said: "I know all that Durvasa has said. Do r
be afraid, but grant me the happiness of embracing y
And you know that my embraces are always fruitful. H
ing summoned me you are bound to fulfil the purpose
the summons, otherwise you will be guilty of a grave si

'He talked with her for a long time in order to allay I
anxiety, but from fear of her relatives she would not cc
sent. At length he said: "O Princess, I promise that y
shall not suffer on my account," and so saying he took h
At once a son, Karna, was born from their union, enca
in natural armour and wearing ear-rings. As soon as he w
born Surya restored her virginity, and ascended to heav
But she, from shame, threw Karna into a river; he w
however, rescued by Radha and her husband, who broug

im up. Later on Indra, to benefit his son Arjuna, asked Karna for his armour; Karna agreed and was given in return a dart with power to kill one person, whether God, man, or Rakshasa.

'Although the large-eyed Pritha, daughter of Kuntibo-ha, was beautiful and accomplished, no king had asked for her, so her father invited kings and princes from many countries to visit him. And when they were all seated he made his daughter select a husband from among them. The intelligent Pritha entered the hall and looking down on that great gathering, her eyes rested on Pandu, proud as a lion, with the strength of a bull. At once she began to tremble with emotion; then, walking modestly, she went to him and placed the marriage garland round his neck. Seeing that she had made her choice, the rest of the princes and kings returned to their homes on elephants and horses and in chariots.

'After the marriage ceremonies Pandu returned to his capital with Pritha, his queen.

'In due course, according to custom, Pandu chose a second wife, Madri, the daughter of the King of Madra. And on an auspicious day, he married her. For some time, he gave himself up to his wives and to the enjoyment of them and of their company.

'He then determined to subdue the robber tribes and the kings who had in the past taken the Kuru lands; and with the permission of Bhishma and his elders set out. He consumed all who came against him, so that the kings of the world paid tribute to him.

'Pandu, one day, while hunting on the slopes of Hima-vat saw in the forest a huge stag coupling with his doe. Letting fly five arrows, Pandu pierced both the deer. They fell to the ground and the stag began to weep bitterly, like a man. For he was no deer, but the son of a great Rishi, and had been enjoying his wife in the form of a deer.

'He spoke to Pandu and said: "O King, even wicked men do not do this that you have done. You belong to a virtuous race. How is it then that you have forgotten your

self and done such a cruel deed?" Pandu replied: "Whe
kings go out to hunt deer they kill them as they do the
enemies when chasing them. Even Rishis hunt deer ar
sacrifice them to the Gods. Why do you reproach me?"

'The deer said: "Virtuous kings do not attack their en
mies when they are unprepared, but first declare war. I o
not blame you for killing deer, but to kill any creature i
the act of copulation is a great sin. When male and fema
join together it is agreeable to every creature; it is ordaine
by the Gods, and is productive of good to all. You shoul
have waited until the act had been completed. You you
self have known the pleasures of sexual union, and you ar
also acquainted with morality. I am a Muni, existing o
fruits and roots, and I have lived in peace with all. Som
times I assume the form of a deer and roam through th
woods with my mate. We had gone to a secluded spot i
the forest and you came upon us and killed us. For this
shall curse you—not for killing a Brahmana (for you wer
not aware of this), but for killing a deer at such a time. S
then, when you wish to have your wives, and you join wit
them, as soon as you do this you shall go to the world o
Spirits, and your wife shall follow you. As you brough
grief to me whilst I was enjoying happiness, so shall th
same happen to you."

'So saying, the deer died, and Pandu was dismayed an
sorrowful. He wept bitterly, and said: "Oh, the Gods hav
forsaken me. There is only one thing for me to do. I wi
give up my kingdom, my family, my friends; I will shav
my head and wander alone over the earth and by endurin
severe penances free myself from all my sins. I shall see
nothing, neither will I mock anyone nor knit my brows a
them. I will not harm the four orders of life—beasts, bird
worms and plants, but devote myself to the good of a
creatures. I shall not desire either to live or to die, an
shall regard impartially those who do me good or ill."

'Looking at his wives and sighing, he bade them go t
his people and tell them what he intended to do. But the
begged him to let them stay with him. So he delivered h

wels and robes to his attendants, ordering them to return
Hastinapura.

'Pandu, after reflection, called Pritha and said to her:
Strive to raise sons for me in this time of distress. You
now that on account of my evil act I cannot have chil-
ren, but the self-born Manu has said that a man who
annot beget children on his wife may have them through
er by other men."

'Pritha said: "Do not speak like this. No man in the
orld is superior to you. Embrace me, let us have children,
nd I will die with you. Death is a friend to a woman
ithout a husband."

'Pandu replied: "What you say is true. But I will tell
ou about the customs of old which were lauded by the
reat Rishis. In former times women were not kept at
ome dependent on husbands and relatives. They went
bout freely; nor did they keep to their husbands, and for
his they were not regarded as wicked. And so it is today
mong the Northern Kurus. The custom of a woman hav-
g but one husband is quite recent. The Vedas have de-
lared that a wife should obey her husband; and so, O
oman of faultless beauty, joining my palms I place them
n your head as an act of propitiation. I ask you to raise
ons for me, for only thus shall I be able to tread the
ath that is reserved for those blest with children."

'Pritha said: "You know that in my youth, I was granted
boon by the Rishi—a mantra for invoking the Gods to
elp me. O foremost of men, tell me which of the Celes-
ials I shall summon. I await your commands."

'Pandu replied: "First summon the God of Justice, the
most virtuous of the Celestials. The son he begets on you
hall be the first among the Kurus." '

Vaisampayana continued: 'In due time Pritha summoned the God of Justice, who appeared seated in his re-
plendent chariot. Smiling he asked,: "O Pritha, what do
ou wish of me?" Pritha, also smiling, said: "I wish you to
ive me a son!" The God joyfully granted her request, and
rom the union was born an excellent child, and a voice

from the skies said: "This child shall be the first of m
and the most virtuous, and he shall rule the earth. T
first-born of Pandu shall be called Yudhisthira."

'Pandu again spoke to Pritha: "The wise have said th
a Kshatriya must be endowed with great physical streng
Therefore ask for such a son." Thus commanded, Prit
summoned Vayu, the mighty God of the winds, who car
to her riding on a deer. "What do you wish, O Pritha?"
asked. Smiling modestly, she said: "Give me, O Celest
Being, a son of great strength and large limbs, capable
humbling the pride of anyone." Vayu then possessed he
and when the child was born, a voice said: "This chi
shall be called Bhima, of mighty arms and fierce energy
And so it was. And once, while he was asleep on her lap
tiger frightened his mother, so that she leapt up, and t
child falling on to a great rock, the rock was smashed in
a hundred pieces. On the very day that Bhima was bon
Duryodhana also was born.

'After the birth of Bhima, Pandu began to consider he
he might have a son who would achieve great fam
"Everything in the world," he thought, "depends on d
tiny and effort. But destiny cannot be actualised witho
timely effort. Indra is the chief of the Gods, of immeas
able might and glory. If I gratify him I shall obtain a s
who shall be capable of overcoming men and Rakshasa

'He then stood on one leg for a whole year, his mi
fixed in meditation. At last Indra, gratified, said: "I w
give you a son who will be celebrated over the three worl
and who will cherish the welfare of Brahmanas, men ar
cows. He will be the despair of the wicked and the delig
of the good—the embodiment of Kshatriya virtues."

'Pandu told all this to Pritha, who went away and i
voked Sakra Indra, the ruler of the Gods, who came to h
and got a child on her. As soon as the child was born,
voice loud and deep as the clouds, filling the welkin, sai
"This child, O Pritha, shall be equal in energy to Siva hin
self; he shall increase your joy and uphold the prosperity
the Kuru race; he shall overcome the enemies of the Go

and become famous in his own generation and those that succeed him." '

Vaisampayana continued: 'After the birth of Pandu's sons and the hundred sons of Dhritarashtra, Pandu's second wife, Madri, said to him: "O sinless one, I do not complain that Pritha, though inferior to me in birth, is above me as your first wife; neither do I grudge Ghandhari her hundred sons, but it grieves me that I have no children of my own. I do not like to ask Pritha if she would object to my having children, but I beg you to ask her for me."

'Pandu replied: "O Madri, I have often thought about this. Now that you tell me you wish for children I will approach Pritha and I know she will not refuse." When Pandu spoke to Pritha about Madri's wish for children, she agreed to use the mantra, and said to Madri, "Which of the Gods do you wish to be the father of your children? Tell me, and I will invoke him." Madri, after reflecting, thought of the twin Aswins. They came to her, and by them she had twin sons, Nakula and Sahadeva; and a voice was heard saying: "These children shall transcend in energy and beauty even their fathers, the Aswins."

'The eldest of Pritha's sons was Yudhisthira, the second Bhimasena, the third Arjuna; of Madri's, the first-born twin was Nakula and the next Sahadeva, and they all grew up in beauty, accomplishments and courage equal almost to the Gods.

'When Pandu saw his five handsome sons growing up in the forest on the slopes of the mountain, he felt his sexual force returning, and one day, accompanied by Madri, he went out to wander in the woods. It was the time of Spring, the season that causes unrest in all born creatures. Flowers bloomed everywhere filling the woods with gentle perfume, and the pools were full of lotus-blossoms. Pandu in the midst of all this sat down to rest with the youthful Madri, gazing at her beauty; and his desire for her flared up like a forest fire. Unable to restrain himself, he put his arms around her, while she, knowing that his death would be the result, endeavoured to restrain him. But intoxicated

with desire, and as if he wished to put an end to his life, h
united himself to her, and no sooner was this done tha
his life left him, in accordance with the Rishi's curs
Madri, clasping the body of her lord, began to weep. The
she went to Pritha and told her what had happene
Pritha at first reproached her; but afterwards said that sh
at least was fortunate in that she had seen Pandu's fac
for a moment, suffused with happiness. They disputed a
to which of them should ascend the funeral pyre, eac
wishing to be the one. At last it was agreed that Mad
should do so. The body of Pandu, having been brougl
back to Hastinapura, was anointed with fragrant ointmer
and sandal paste, and dressed in a white dress. When
was placed on the pyre, Madri ascended and lay beside h
lord. A torch was put to the wood, and both the dead an
the living were soon burnt to ashes.

(from *Mahābhārata*, Adi Parva, as selected by S. C. Not
The Mahābhārata, pp. 54-67.

THE RĀMĀYANA:
THE DEFENCE OF DHARMA

The *Rāmāyana* tells how Rama, most perfect of princes, wa
banished from his kingdom for fourteen years because h
father, King Dasratha, made a vow to his stepmother, Kaikey
that he would grant her whatever she asked. When Kaikat
asked that Rāma should be banished and her own son, Bharat
should become heir, all of the main characters—the Kin§
Rāma, Bharata—were confronted with problems of conflictin
loyalties. Perhaps even more important than the working ou
of the story are the statements on ideal conduct that follo
as these problems are resolved. In the following selection a
of Rāma's friends, including his father and finally even hi
stepmother, urge him to disregard the vow, but Rāma insist
that his primary duty is as a son, and that the word his fathe

has spoken must be fulfilled, even though it means hardship for the kingdom. Rāma's arguments provide a valuable insight into the inner meaning of Hindu ethics.

The princes surrounded by relatives and friends passed the night sorrowing. The day having dawned, the brothers observed the fire sacrifice and performed the repetition of silent prayer on the banks of the river Mandakini, then entering the hermitage of Rama, they sat in profound silence, no one uttering a word, a great peace prevailing over all.

At length, Shri Bharata, in the midst of his friends, broke the silence and thus addressed Shri Rama: "O My Brother, our illustrious sovereign conferred the kingdom on me to satisfy my mother and fulfil the obligation of his former boons and my mother having given this kingdom to me, I now offer it to thee, enjoy it without hindrance. When the dam bursts in the rainy season, none can stem the tide, similarly none but thee can protect this vast dominion. O King, as an ass cannot equal the pace of a horse, nor an ordinary bird's flight that of an eagle, so am I unable to rule the kingdom without thee. . . .

The people hearing Shri Bharata's words applauded them saying, "Well said!" "Well said!"

Then the compassionate Rama perceiving Bharata afflicted and lamenting, consoled him saying: "O Bharata, man is not free, time drags him hither and thither. All objects perish, all individualised souls must depart when their merit is exhausted; sons, friends, wives, all who live must die one day. Hoarding and spending, prosperity and destitution, meeting and parting, life and death are all akin. When the ripe fruit falls, we are not surprised, thus a man being born should not fear when death claims him. . . .

"I cannot disregard the commands of my illustrious father, he is worthy to be obeyed by thee and me, being our parent and our ruler. O Son of Raghu, I shall, therefore,

obey his will and dwell in the forest. O Chief of Me
those who desire felicity in a future state, and who a
virtuous and benevolent should obey their elders. O Gre
One, bear in mind the behests of our father, a lover
truth, and return to the capital to rule over the kingdom

Rama, the lover of his people, having spoken, cease
then the pious Bharata answered Rama, putting forth pe
suasive arguments of righteous purport, saying: "O Lor
who is there in this world like thee? Adversity does n
move thee, nor does any agreeable thing touch thee. A
look on thee as their superior, yet thou seekest counsel
thine elders!

"The man to whom the living and dead are one ar
who is indifferent as to what he possesses or loses, for wh
reason should he grieve? O Lord, those who like the
know, as thou dost, what is the nature of the soul and i
essence, are not moved in the hour of distress!

"O Prince of Raghu, like the gods, thou art magnar
mous, thou art ever forbearing and faithful to thy vow
Thou art wise, thou knowest and seest all! Thou art awa
of the motives of men's actions and the cause of the
abandoning them, therefore, that distress which is insu
portable to others, does not, in any wise, disturb thee."

Having spoken thus, Bharata continued: "O Rama, I
gracious to me, though during my absence in a strang
land, my mother committed those sins which cause m
affliction. I am bound by the ties of duty, else would I ha
slain my wicked mother. What is evil and what is good
known to me, descended as I am from the righteous Kir
Dasaratha, therefore I am unable to act contrary to virtu
I cannot speak evil in the assembly of my pious and age
father, who has passed away, and where is a man to I
found so wholly acquainted with the law of righteousne
as was the king, yet what person familiar with the mor
law, would commit so great a wrong prompted by the d
sire to please a woman? There is an ancient saying that,
the approach of death, man loses the power of judgmen
The king has verily justified this adage to the whole worl

Through fear of Queen Kaikeyi's wrath or her threat of self-imposed destruction, or through mental agitation, the king may have acted thus without consulting his subjects, but thou art not bound by such a deed. He who imputes the transgressions of his father to righteous motives is not considered a good son; as heir to the king, reveal not the errors of thy sire, but conceal this unjust deed from the world.

"O Hero, it is thy duty to save my mother Kaikeyi, my father, my relatives and myself from the consequences of this action condemned by all. O Brother, remember thy duty as a warrior and reflect on the outcome of thy sojourn in the forest as an ascetic, but do thou also consider the good of thy people. It becomes thee not to undertake this course of action. The first duty of a warrior is to be installed so that he may be able to protect his people. Say, why should a man giving up that which is an established duty, embrace that which is wretched, cheerless, visionary and undefined? If, O Blessed One, thou desirest to undertake this mortification, why dost thou not seek it through the arduous labour of ruling the four castes? It is said that the duty of the householder is the highest dharma, then, why dost thou abandon it?

"O Lord, hear me; I am but thy child in respect of learning, age and state, how should I be able to govern the kingdom? I, a child, void of understanding and virtue and in rank also thine inferior; how should I be able to live without thee much less rule in thy stead? Therefore, O Raghava, O Thou Virtuous One, do thou, with thy relatives govern the kingdom without opposition and acquire merit! The great sage, the Holy Vasishtha, is here present with the ministers and priests, permit thyself to be crowned and return with us to Ayodhya!

"As Indra, having conquered his foes, entered heaven attended by the Maruts, do thou enter Ayodhya, thereby discharging thy duties to the gods, the sages, and thine ancestors, gratifying the ambitions of thy friends! Regard me as thy servant and command me! O Noble One, let thy

friends to-day rejoice at thine enthronement and let th
evil doers flee to the uttermost ends of the earth! O Chie
of Men, wash away the taint of my mother's guilt and de
liver our great parent from this heinous sin. With my hea
bent in submission, I entreat thee; as Shri Vishnu show
his compassion to all beings, do thou show mercy to us
Shouldst thou however reject my prayer and go hence t
some other forest, then will I follow thee there!"

Shri Rama, thus entreated by Shri Bharata, who ha
placed his head at the feet of his brother in humility, stil
remained steadfast in his vow and did not waver or con
sent to return to Ayodhya. Beholding the constancy o
Shri Rama, all present rejoiced to see him so faithful to hi
vow, yet bewailed his determination not to return to th
capital.

(from Valmiki, *Rāmāyana*, translated by Hari Prasad Shastr
pp. 382-88)

PART THREE

THE FLOWERING OF
THE TRADITION

〰〰〰〰

(300-1200 A.D.)

INTRODUCTION

The fourth and fifth centuries A.D. are usually referred to as the Classical Age because the achievements in art and literature during these centuries provided the standards of excellence against which the more ancient as well as the later products of the culture are judged. This tendency to impose a style and form upon the imagination ultimately became a stultifying legacy, but for centuries it served to channel the exuberant streams of Indian creativity into an art that was both disciplined and vital. While it is obviously impossible to give terminal dates to this process of artistic and intellectual growth, political changes as well as observable cultural traits suggest those chosen for the selections in the section. The fourth century saw the establishment of the powerful Gupta dynasty (c. 320-540 A.D.), and by 1200 A.D. the Islamic invaders from the northwest had begun through their political hegemony to alter the direction of Indian social development.

The rise of the Gupta dynasty can be seen as a manifestation of the impulse to political unification, which is one of the characteristic motifs of Indian history. Like the Mauryan Empire of five centuries before, it was based on Magadha in modern Bihar, and gradually extended its control over most of North India. During the two hundred years that the Guptas maintained their power India quite possibly enjoyed the greatest period of material prosperity in its history, and this physical wellbeing, combined with political stability and self-confidence, is undoubtedly re flected in the flowering of art and culture. And as a corol lary, the fall of the Empire in the sixth century must have hastened a decline in cultural achievement.

Poetry and drama were two areas of particular accom plishment during the Gupta Empire, and in general both appear to have been composed for a sophisticated, courtly audience. By this time Sanskrit had become a highly devel oped language, with a very scientific grammatical struc ture, and the poets, both in lyric and dramatic poetry, made full use of all its potentialities. While the Indian theater may have had its remote origins in temple rituals, in the hands of the dramatists of the Gupta period it mir rored the brilliant secular society that patronized it. An interesting feature of this poetic drama is that it does no know tragedy in the European understanding of the term and the happy ending demanded by literary convention indicates, on one level, the emphasis and taste of the soci ety. On a deeper level, the absence of tragedy is explain able in terms of the basic Indian belief in *karma*, with it insistence that man is responsible for the good or evil tha befalls him. There is little place for the assertion of human will against any forces outside and beyond human control.

Perhaps the same temperament that demanded happy endings also accounts for the extraordinary vitality and en ergy shown in the painting and sculpture of the period. One particular feature of this vitality, the strongly sensu ous and erotic element, has frequently been interpreted in a religious sense, as representing the longing of the soul fo union with the divine, but this seems to be a forced inter pretation. It is more likely that it is a reflection of the ar tists'—and the society's—awareness of the close relation ship of the vitality of the imagination to the process of growth and change in nature.

Other areas of culture where there was considerable ac

vance in this period were medicine, astronomy, and mathematics. While the modern Western tendency is to classify such fields as science, and to separate them from other cultural movements, in ancient India they were closely identified with religious concerns. For this reason alone it is difficult to identify ideas that are strictly comparable to Greek and Western science, but the difficulty is compounded by the fact that no one with the requisite breadth of scientific, religious, and linguistic skills has given his attention to the study of this aspect of the Hindu tradition. It is clear, nevertheless, that during the Gupta period Indians possessed mathematical concepts unknown to the Western world at that time. The most notable of these discoveries was the decimal system, a knowledge of which passed to Europe through the Arabs. Indian knowledge of medicine also seems to have been very advanced, as were surgical techniques. It was astronomy, however, that received the most attention in the texts. This interest had an extremely practical basis in the very highly developed practice of astrology, which occupies a unique place in the Hindu tradition. All the great events of life, such as marriage, were conducted in strict conformity with astrological data, and while this aspect of the tradition is one that arouses little sympathy in the outside observer it is important to recognize the extraordinary complexity of the study. It is probably no exaggeration to say that the precision needed in the study of horoscopes is comparable to that used in modern scientific reasoning.

In terms of literary works and of great movements the religious achievements of the era were perhaps less striking than in the preceding period, but as a time of synthesis the importance of the Gupta age cannot be overemphasized. Just as in the arts the imagination was disciplined into forms that have remained canonical for Indian taste, so in religion the disparate forms of experience were absorbed into the structure of orthodoxy. The resulting synthesis was not a new religion, since the *Vedas* still remained as the fundamental texts and the position of the

Brāhman priesthood was unchallenged, but the old rituals were largely replaced by forms of worship that emphasized devotion to a particular deity. Closely related to this was the use of images to represent the gods and the erection of temples as the center of their worship.

The synthesis of the devotional cults with the older Brahmanical tradition found literary expression in the Purānas. The word itself means "ancient," but the reference is not so much to the age of the books themselves as to the subjects they deal with—the origins and history of the gods, the creation of the world, the genealogies of kings. The Purānas are regarded as scripture, and it is through them that the legends and stories of the tradition have reached the common people. The almost endless variety of Indian religious experience that is given a place in them provides opportunity for the most varied temperaments to find something congenial, thus making it possible to bring the skeptical agnostic and the passionate theist, the profound philosopher and the illiterate peasant, under one encompassing roof.

The religious synthesis was strengthened, perhaps made possible, by philosophical developments that reached their height after the fourth century A.D. Philosophical speculation had, of course, a much more ancient beginning than this, but apparently the systemization and codification of the traditional "six systems" of Indian philosophy took place at this time. These systems are not philosophical statements comparable to Western models, nor are they really comparable to each other, but taken as a whole they provided an impressive intellectual framework for the Hindu tradition.

The great cultural, religious, and philosophical movements of the Classical Age coalesced to give Hinduism its distinctive characteristics. So deeply were these interwoven into the fabric of the social structure that the shocks administered to Indian life by the invasion of the Muslims in the eleventh and twelfth centuries did not destroy the essential unity that had been created.

CHAPTER VIII

THE LITERARY
REFLECTION

~~~~~~~~~

Nowhere was the flowering of the Hindu tradition more conspicuous than in the literary arts, and in distinction to other ages of Indian civilization the particular glories of the period were secular, not sacred, works. Although this division can be made only with great qualification, since even the most secular of Indian works are integrated within a religious framework, nevertheless there is a great body of literature that served primarily to entertain and delight without apparently seeking to penetrate very deeply into the human condition.

For a variety of reasons the literary classics of India, as distinct from the religious texts, have not made a great impression upon Western readers. This is partly due to fundamental problems in aesthetics, since the canons of taste are very different, but translation difficulties have also contributed to the failure of Sanskrit literature to make a wide appeal. Not only does much of its charm depend upon sound, but within the tradition a value was placed on displays of ingenuity and virtuosity that are foreign to Western, especially English, literary conventions. Furthermore, the precision of Sanskrit vocabulary and grammar imposes restrictions on translators that have prevented the classics' being rendered into lively, modern English.

Yet if translation from the great age of Sanskrit literature cannot adequately convey its beauty, it can show a
pattern of life and the way that artists handled the materials that were available to them. The poets and dramatists
moved within the conventions of their tradition and neither questioned nor defended its values, but rather accepted them as the framework of the universe. This means
that there is remarkably little tension within the literature,
no striving to exalt personal will, no denunciation of fate
or of the gods. Instead, the great works of the period present a picture of man at peace with himself and with his
society.

The following selections illustrate various familiar
themes—the pains and pleasures of passionate human
love, the virtues and vices of women, the greatness of
kings, the beauty of nature, and, on a somewhat different
level, the need for worldly wisdom. While the treatment
of these themes is frequently idealized, the values and beliefs of the tradition stand out in clear relief, and while the
passages cannot convey much of the power of the originals
they serve to embody some aspects of the life of the Hindu
tradition.

The Pleasures of Love

One of the recognized ends of life within the Hindu tradition
was the enjoyment of physical love, and the poets were fond
of depicting the stirring of passionate emotion. One of the
most famous of these love scenes is contained in the play
Shakuntalā, where Kālidās, the greatest of Indian dramatists,
describes with great delicacy the meeting of King Dushyanta
and Shakuntalā, who is a hermit's daughter. As the scene
opens, the King, who has been hunting in the forest, hears
Shakuntalā complaining to her two companions that her dress
is becoming too tight for her. Through such statements, and
by combining references to nature with images of sexual desire—the vine clasping the tree, the opening flower, the bee

drinking nectar—the author creates a mood of expectancy and longing. The continuity between the life of man and that of the natural world suggested here is an important theme in Indian literature.

KING

This youthful form, whose bosom's swelling charms
By the bark's knotted tissue are concealed,
Like some fair bud close folded in its sheath,
Gives not to view the blooming of its beauty.
But what am I saying? In real truth, this bark-dress,
though ill-suited to her figure, sets it off like an ornament.

The lotus with mean plants entwined
Is not a whit less brilliant: dusky spots
Heighten the lustre of the cold-rayed moon:
This lovely maiden in her dress of bark
Seems all the lovelier. Yet the meanest garb
Gives to true beauty fresh attractiveness.

SHAKUNTALĀ   [*Looking before her.*

That Keshara-tree beckons to me with its young shoots, which, as the breeze waves them to and fro, appear like slender fingers. I will go and attend to it.

[*Walks towards it.*

PRIYAMVADĀ

Dear Shakuntalā, please rest in that attitude one moment.

SHAKUNTALĀ

Why so?

PRIYAMVADĀ

The Keshara-tree, whilst your graceful form bends about its stem, appears as if it were wedded to some lovely twining creeper.

SHAKUNTALĀ

Ah! saucy girl, you are most appropriately named Priyamvadā ("Speaker of flattering things").

KING

What Priyamvadā says, though complimentary, is nevertheless true. Verily,
Her ruddy lip vies with the opening bud;
Her graceful arms are as the twining stalks;
And her whole form is radiant with the glow
Of youthful beauty, as the tree with bloom.

ANASŪYĀ

. See, dear Shakuntalā, here is the young jasmine, which you named "the Moonlight of the Grove," the self-elected wife of the mango-tree. Have you forgotten it?

SHAKUNTALĀ

Rather will I forget myself. [*Approaching the plant and looking at it.*] How delightful is the season when the jasmine-creeper and the mango-tree seem thus to unite in mutual embraces! The fresh blossoms of the jasmine resemble the bloom of a young bride, and the newly-formed shoots of the mango appear to make it her natural protector. [*Continues gazing at it.*

PRIYAMVADĀ   [*Smiling.*

Do you know, my Anasūyā, why Shakuntalā gazes so intently at the jasmine?

ANASŪYĀ

No, indeed, I cannot imagine. I pray thee tell me.

PRIYAMVADĀ

She is wishing that as the jasmine is united to a suitable tree, so, in like manner, she may obtain a husband worthy of her.

SHAKUNTALĀ

Speak for yourself, girl; this is the thought in your own mind. [*Continues watering the flowers.*

KING

Would that my union with her were permissible! and yet I hardly dare hope that the maiden is sprung from a caste different from that of the Head of the hermitage. But away with doubt:

> That she is free to wed a warrior-king
> My heart attests. For, in conflicting doubts,
> The secret promptings of the good man's soul
> Are an unerring index of the truth.

However, come what may, I will ascertain the fact.

SHAKUNTALĀ [*In a flurry.*

Ah! a bee, disturbed by the sprinkling of the water, has left the young jasmine, and is trying to settle on my face. [*Attempts to drive it away.*

KING [*Gazing at her ardently.*

Beautiful! there is something charming even in her repulse.

> Where'er the bee his eager onset plies,
> Now here, now there, she darts her kindling eyes:
> What love hath yet to teach, fear teaches now,
> The furtive glances and the frowning brow.
> [*In a tone of envy.*
> Ah happy bee! how boldly dost thou try
> To steal the lustre from her sparkling eye;
> And in thy circling movements hover near,
> To murmur tender secrets in her ear;
> Or, as she coyly waves her hand, to sip
> Voluptuous nectar from her lower lip!
> While rising doubts my heart's fond hopes destroy,
> Thou dost the fulness of her charms enjoy.

(from Kālidās, *Shakuntalā*, translated by Monier Williams, pp. 14-17)

The Pain of Love

Bhavabhūti, a playwright who lived early in the eighth century A.D., wrote of the pains, as well as the pleasures, of love. In the following scene from *Mālati and Mādhava* the hero is telling his friends of his first sight of the beautiful Mālati. The emphasis of the play on the distress that comes from separation from one's beloved, and the anguish one feels as one longs to be reunited with her, is a common motif of Indian drama.

MĀDH. Led by her maidens to collect the flowers
  That thickly hung on my o'ershadowing tree,
  She neared the spot. Ah! then too plain I noted
  The signs of passion, for some happy youth
  Long entertained, the lovely maid revealed.
  As slender as the lotus stalk her shape;
  Her pallid cheeks, like unstained ivory,
  Rivalled the beauty of the spotless moon;
  And still her prompt compliance with the wishes
  Of her attendant damsels showed herself
  Indifferent to all. I scarce had gazed
  Upon her, but my eye felt new delight,
  As bathed with nectar, and she drew my heart
  As pow'rfully as attracts the magnet gem
  The unresisting ore, at once towards her.
  That heart, though causeless be its sudden passion,
  Is fixed on her for ever, chance what may,
  And though my portion be henceforth despair.
  The goddess destiny decrees at pleasure
  The good or ill of all created beings.

MAK. Nay, Mādhava, this cannot be, believe me,
  Without some cause. Behold! all nature's sympathies
  Spring not from outward form, but inward virtue.
  The lotus buds not till the sun has risen;
  Nor melts the moon-gem till it feels the moon.

What then ensued?

MĀDH. When her fair train beheld me, they exchanged
Expressive looks and smiles, and each to each,
As if they knew me, murmured—This is he!
The music of their tinkling zones was stilled,
Repressed the silver echo of their anklets
Sharp clanging to their undulating motion.
Hushed was the melody their bracelets made,
Whilst their fair lotus palms, in sportive mood,
Were beating measure to their merriment.
Silent they stood, and with extended fingers,
As if they said, "The fates have favoured us,
Lady, behold *him* here!" . . .

MAK. Proceed, my friend.

MĀDH. What words shall picture what those looks con-
      veyed;
The lore of love those lotus eyes revealed?
What firmness could resist the honest warmth
Of nature's mute expressiveness, nor fall
Before those orbs, that now like opening buds,
Beneath the creeper of the tremulous brow
Expansive bloomed, and now retiring shrunk
But half-averted from the answering gaze,
Then dropped the veiling lashes o'er their bright-
      ness?
I felt their influence, and those looks of love,
Beaming with mild timidity, and moist
With sweet abandonment, bore off my heart—
Nay plucked it from my bosom by the roots
All pierced with wounds.
Incredulous of my happiness, I sought
To mark her passion, nor display my own,
Though every limb partook the fond emotion.
Thence I resumed my task, and wove my wreath,
Seeming intent, till she at length withdrew
Attended by her maidens and a guard
Of eunuchs armed with staves and javelins.
A stately elephant received the princess

And bore her towards the city. Whilst they moved
As winds the lily on its slender stalk,
So turned her head towards the grove of *Kāma*
    (the God of Love),
And from her delicate lids she shot retiring
Glances, with venom and ambrosia tipped.
My breast received the shafts. A mingled flame
And deathly chillness, since alternate spread
Throughout my form, and doom me to such agony
Words cannot paint, the world has never witnessed
Perception dimly pictures present objects,
And past perceptions fade from recollection!
Vain were the lunar ray or gelid stream
To cool my body's fever, whilst my mind
Whirls in perpetual round, and knows not rest.

(from Bhavabhūti, *Mālati and Mādhava*, trans. by H. H. Wilson, *The Theatre of the Hindus*, II, pp. 22-24)

The Perils of Love

Bhartrihari, a poet who is said to have lived in the seventh
century, wrote a cycle of one-stanza poems in which he displayed to a remarkable degree the ambiguous attitude to
women and love so often found in the Hindu tradition. He
feels, almost simultaneously, the attractions of physical love
as well as of asceticism. Possibly he is suggesting that these
are two ways of life, and one must choose one or the other,
or he may be saying that both ways of life make such a powerful appeal that there is no use trying to separate them. Like
Kalidās, he blends images from nature with symbols of erotic
desire to create his effects.

No doubt sensual pleasures lead to no good result, and
prevent us from properly renouncing the world. People
may think and speak thus, but there is nevertheless something powerful and, indeed, indefinable, in sensuality,
something that can even agitate the souls of those who

have turned away from the world to devote themselves to meditation and the search for truth.

You, for your part, have found consolation in studying the divine Vedic writings, while we, on the other hand, are the disciples of poets whose words are always pleasing. You will therefore hold that there is nothing better on this earth than doing good to others, while we shall maintain that there is nothing better than lotus-eyed, beautiful women. . . .

It would have been an easy matter to pay for our passage over the ocean of existence if there had been no women with beautiful eyes to hinder our progress.

No one in this world, O king, has ever succeeded in crossing his ocean of desires. Of what use to us are abundant riches if we must let our youth slip away from us without the enjoyment of our wives whom we adore? Let us therefore hasten to our homes so that we may be able to reach them before the beauty of our loved ones has been withered by the approach of age. . . .

What greater calamity can a man suffer in this world than his own youth, which is at once the abiding-place of passion, the cause of dreadful agonies in hell, the seed of ignorance, the gatherings of clouds that hide the moon of knowledge, the great friend of the God of Love, and the chain that binds together innumerable sins.

Fortunate indeed is the person who can retain the mastery of his senses at the critical period of his youth—youth, this waterer of the tree of love, the rapid-flowing stream of sexual enjoyment, the dear friend of the God of Love, the full moon of the chakor-like eyes of women, and the treasury of happiness and wealth.

"Beautiful woman. What a divine expression! What a magnificent form!" cries the man who is blinded by passion; or, perhaps, "What a breast! What eye-brows!" In this way the sight of a beautiful woman delights him. He feels intoxicated with an excessive joy, and yet he may know very well that she is a woman whose impurity is known to the whole world.

How can we go on loving women when the thought of
her warms our hearts, the sight of her intoxicates us, and a
touch of her nearly drives us mad?

A woman is indeed the very incarnation of the purest
ambrosia so long as we have her within sight; but no
sooner is she beyond the range of our vision than she becomes worse even than poison.

Whatever young woman we may have in mind she is
neither ambrosia nor poison—if she loves us she will be
like an ambrosial creeper embracing us with its tendrils
but if she is indifferent she is like a poisonous plant.

A whirlpool of uncertainty, a palace of pride, a prison of
punishment, a storehouse of sin, a fraud in a hundred
different respects, an obstacle placed for us before the
gates of paradise, the field of deceit, a basket of illusion
the open throat of hell: such are some of the features of
women, who change nectar into poison and are as a chair
by which man is attached to the chariot of folly.

It is certain enough that the face of a woman is not
made up of the moon, that her eyes are not twin lotuses
and that her limbs are not really gold. Why, alas, have
poets been led to deceive us in this manner? Men are capable of distinguishing; but nevertheless, deceived by the
poets, they none the less adore those fawn-eyed women
even though they know well enough that their bodies are
composed of nothing more than skin, flesh, and
bone. . . .

We behold a young girl with a lotus-eyed face resembling the splendour of the moon, and we remark the ambrosia on her lips. Too soon this face, like a rotten piece of
fruit, will lose all its flavour, and will begin to taste like
bitter poison.

A young woman is like a river; for the lines of her body
resemble the waves; her breasts represent the ducks swim-
ming on the surface, the nymphs are seen in the brilliant
colours of her face: but the bed of the river is dangerous
its course is difficult to perceive and leads rapidly to the

ocean; so let men turn aside from it if they do not wish to be drowned.

(from Bhartṛihari, *Sṛingāra Sataka*, stanzas 51-52, 68-77, 79-80, trans. by J. M. Kennedy)

A WIFE'S DEVOTION

By way of contrast to the passionate, demanding love of a young girl, the dramatists frequently picture the devotion offered by a wife to her husband. In the selection given here Shakuntalā is being advised by her father on the proper deportment of a wife, and, as one of the characters suggests, his words are a compendium of what the tradition understands to be the duties of a faithful wife. In this case the advice is made more meaningful to the audience by their knowledge that when Shakuntalā arrives at the palace of her husband he will reject her, denying that she is his wife and that he is the father of her child.

KANWA

Listen, then, my daughter. When thou reachest thy
husband's palace, and art admitted into his family,
    Honour thy betters; ever be respectful
    To those above thee; and, should others share
    Thy husband's love, ne'er yield thyself a prey
    To jealousy; but ever be a friend,
    A loving friend, to those who rival thee
    In his affections. Should thy wedded lord
    Treat thee with harshness, thou must never be
    Harsh in return, but patient and submissive.
    Be to thy menials courteous, and to all
    Placed under thee, considerate and kind:
    Be never self-indulgent, but avoid
    Excess in pleasure; and, when fortune smiles,

Be not puffed up. Thus to thy husband's house
Wilt thou a blessing prove, and not a curse.
What thinks Gautamī of this advice?

GAUTAMĪ

An excellent compendium, truly, of every wife's duties!
Lay it well to heart, my daughter.

KANWA

Come, my beloved child, one parting embrace for me
and for thy companions, and then we leave thee. . . .
Soon shall thy lord prefer thee to the rank
Of his own consort; and unnumbered cares
Befitting his imperial dignity
Shall constantly engross thee. Then the bliss
Of bearing him a son—a noble boy,
Bright as the day-star—shall transport thy soul
With new delights, and little shalt thou reck
Of the light sorrow that afflicts thee now
At parting from thy father and thy friends.

(from Kālidās, *Shakuntalā*, in Monier Williams, p. 100)

DIVINE AND HUMAN LOVE

Of all the legends about the gods, none has had a more
creative effect on the Indian imagination than the stories of
Krishna and his love for the milkmaids. While in modern
times there has been a tendency to allegorize these incidents,
with the milkmaids understood as the desire of the soul for
God, and Krishna's response symbolizing the generous response of God's love, it seems likely that originally the stories
were meant to be taken fairly literally. The Krishna who dallied
with endless beautiful maidens while his mistress Rādhā waited
for him consumed by passion can be understood as completing, not contradicting, the austere Krishna of the *Bhagavad
Gītā*. This aspect of Krishna's personality found its greatest

literary expression in the *Gītā Govinda*, a long poem written in Sanskrit by Jayadeva in the twelfth century. While this poem may appear to be a celebration of the joys and pains of physical desire, it is in fact widely sung as a religious lyric in praise of Krishna. Hari, lord, here refers to Krishna.

Sandal and garment of yellow and lotus garlands upon his body of blue,
In his dance the jewels of his ears in movement dangling over his smiling cheeks.
Hari here disports himself with charming women given to love!
The wife of a certain herdsman sings as Hari sounds a tune of love
Embracing him the while with all the force of her full and swelling breasts.
Hari here disports himself with charming women given to love!
Another artless woman looks with ardour on Krishna's lotus face
Where passion arose through restless motion of playful eyes with sidelong glances.
Hari here disports himself with charming women given to love!
Another comes with beautiful hips, making as if to whisper a word,
And drawing close to his ear the adorable Krishna she kisses upon the cheek.
Hari here disports himself with charming women given to love!
Another on the bank of the Jamna, when Krishna goes to a bamboo thicket,
Pulls at his garment to draw him back, so eager is she for amorous play.
Hari here disports himself with charming women given to love!
Hari praises another woman, lost with him in the dance of love,

The dance where the sweet low flute is heard in th
clamour of bangles on hands that clap.
Hari here disports himself with charming women given t
love!
He embraces one woman, he kisses another, and fondl
another beautiful one,
He looks at another one lovely with smiles, and starts i
pursuit of another woman.
Hari here disports himself with charming women given t
love!
May all prosperity spread from this, Shri Jayadeva's fame
and delightful
Song of wonderful Keshava's secret play in the forest
Vrindāvana!
Hari here disports himself with charming women given t
love! . . .
With his limbs, tender and dark like rows of clumps
blue lotus flowers,
By herd-girls surrounded, who embrace at pleasure, ar
part of his body,
Friend, in spring beautiful Hari plays like Love's own se
Conducting the love sport, with love for all, bringing d
light into being.

(from Jayadeva, *Gītā Govinda*, trans. by George Keyt)

THE CELEBRATION OF
A PRINCE'S BIRTH

The life of India during the classical age is reflected in t
works of Bāna, the chronicler of the deeds of the Emper
Harsha (606-647 A.D.), who restored the political unity
India for a short time in the seventh century. Bāna's descri
tions frequently have a vivid mastery of detail that must ov

a good deal to actual observation of court life. One such passage is the account of the celebrations that followed the birth of Harsha. The lack of all restraints, which is in sharp contrast to the usual decorum of Indian life, is reminiscent of modern celebrations of such festivals as Holi. The exuberance shown in the scenes described here is quite in keeping, however, with the vitality and passion of much Hindu literature and art of the time.

Then the festal jubilation gradually blossomed forth. Here young people, of ancient noble houses and unused to dancing, showed by frolics their love for the king. There drunken slave women allured the favourites, while the monarch himself looked on with a secret smile. In one place respectable old feudatories were, much to his amusement, clasping the necks of the intoxicated bawds of the capital in a furious dance. In another place naughty slave boys, set on by a glance from the sovereign, betrayed in songs the secret amours of the ministers of state. Elsewhere wanton water-girls raised a laugh by embracing aged ascetics. Elsewhere again in the eagerness of ardent rivalry throngs of slaves carried on a war of foul language. In another place chamberlains knowing nothing of dancing were, to the entertainment of the maids, violently forced to dance by the king's women. The festival showed mountains of flower heaps, rum-booths like shower-baths, a hoarfrost of camphor dust, a booming of drums like Shiva's laugh, a hubbub like the ocean-churning, vortexes of dancing rings, a horripilation of rays from jewelled ornaments, a very tiara of sandal forehead marks, a never ceasing propagation of echoes, an endless efflorescence of tokens of favour.

Young men frolicked in thousands, prancing, like Kāmboja steeds, with garlands of flowers hanging upon their shoulders, leaping with dancing eyes like spotted antelopes, rending the earth with furious stamps. . . . Scarce

could the earth sustain the tramp of troubadours dancin
to time. Smash went the pearls in the ornaments of th
young princes slapping each other in their play. Re
powder crimsoned the earth in every part. . . . The hea
ens gleamed with clouds of perfume powder. . . . Ye
lowed with scattered scent dust, the daylight glowed, a
though Brahmā's lotus, ground by the rocking world, ha
stained it with clouds of pollen from its filaments. Me
tripped over heaps of pearls that fell from necklace
broken in collisions.

In this place and in that harlot-women danced to th
accompaniment of instrumental music. Tambourines wer
slowly, slowly thumped; reeds sweetly piped, cymbals tir
kled, string drums were belaboured, the low gourd lut
sang, gently boomed the *kāhalas* with their brazen sound
ing boxes, while all the time a subdued clapping pro
ceeded. Even the clank of jingling anklets kept time pac
by pace, as if intelligent, with the clapping. Whisperin
softly, like cuckoos, in low passionate tones, they sang th
words of vulgar mimes, ambrosia to their lovers' ear
Wreaths were about their brows, and chaplets round the
ears, upon their foreheads sandal marks. With upraise
creeper-like arms, vocal with rows of bracelets, the
seemed to embrace the very sun. Like Kashmir colts, the
leapt all aglow with saffron stains. Great garlands of ama
ranth hung down upon their round hips, as if they wer
ablaze with passion's flame. Their faces, marked with row
of vermilion spots, seemed to wear the rubric of the edic
plates of Love, whose ordinances none may resist. Dust
were they with camphor and perfumes scattered in hand
fuls, like roads frequented by the desires of youth. Lik
women chamberlains of a children's festival, they lashe
the young folk with great wreaths of flowers. With tossin
forehead marks and earrings they swayed like creepers c
Love's sandal tree. Like waves of passion's flood, the
gleamed all resonant with the cries of anklets adding musi
to their steps. As to what was proper to be said or not, the
were as void of discrimination as the childish play of ha

piness. While the rapid booming of the drums thrilled through their lithe frames, they cast off flower pollen. All day their faces were, like red lotuses, abloom; by night they slept no more than night lotuses. As if possessed, they were surrounded by throngs of princes. Like endearments, they stole away the heart; like songs, they kindled the flame of desire; like the symptoms of stoutness, they gave rise to joy. Adding passionateness to passion itself, a glow to love, a joy to joy, a dancing motion to dancing, festivity to festival, in ogling they seemed to drink with the white (shells) of their eyes, in scolding to imprison in cages of rays from their nails, in gestures of anger to lash with curling eyebrows, in making love to pour a rain of all (sweet) feelings, in deftly moving to scatter transformations.

In other places, where under the terror of chamberlains' wands the people had made room, the king's wives essayed the dance, a brilliant throng with a forest of white parasols held above them, as if they were wood nymphs roaming beneath trees of paradise. Some, wrapt in loose shawls hanging from both shoulders, swayed as if mounted on play swings. Some, with wavy robes torn by the edge of golden armlets, were like rivers lined by crossing ruddy-geese. Others, whose bright side glances were bounded by earrings entangled in tufts of white waving chowries, were like pools with swans plucking at forests of blue lotuses. Others, from whose tripping feet trickled a dew of lac-reddened sweat that besprinkled the palace swans, resembled moonlight nights when the twilight casts a glow upon the moon's disk. Others, with brows curved in derision at the contortions of chamberlains bending beneath golden girdles placed about their necks, seemed love-nets with outstretched arms for toils.

All womankind being thus set dancing, the earth, crimsoned by trickling lac from their feet, seemed rosy with the flush of love. Their round gleaming bosoms made the festival like a mass of auspicious pitchers. Their tossing arms caused the world to seem nought but rings of lotus roots. Their sparkling playful smiles created as it were a season

all of lightning flashes. The days seemed dappled by the
light of dancing eyes. Brilliant ear chaplets of flowers cast a
green tint upon a daylight seemingly of parrots' tails. Dark
hanging sprays of braided hair shed a blackness as of collyr-
ium on the prospect. Uplifted tendril-like hands made all
creation gleam like one red lotus-bed. The radiance of
rainbow-tinted gems infused a colour of jays' wings into
the sunlight. Echoing with clusters of tinkling ornaments,
the heavens seemed nought but clanging bells. Even old
ladies shouted like maniacs. Old men even lost all shame,
as though bewitched. The wise forgot themselves, as if intoxicated. Even hermits' hearts were all agog for a dance
The king gave away all his fortune. Heaps of wealth were
plundered by the folk on every side.

(from Bāna, *Harsacarita*, trans. by E. B. Cowell and F. W
Thomas, pp. 112-15)

THE SCIENCE OF PLEASURE

A distinctive mark of the Hindu tradition is the tendency to
analyze and classify every aspect of human experience. One
of the products of this is the *Kāmasūtra*, or *Aphorisms on
Love*, by Vātsyāyana (c. 400 A.D.). The *Kāmasūtra* has an
undeserved reputation in the West as a pornographic work
but it is in fact a rather pedantic classification of such things
as ways of making love, the skills needed by a courtesan (in
cluding such rather surprising ones as metallurgy and archi
tecture), and the daily routine of the cultured man-about
town. The following account of the way a young man should
spend his time obviously bears little relation to the ordinary
world, but it remains an ideal never quite forgotten by young
men within the tradition.

After acquisition of learning, a person should with the
help of the material resources obtained by him through

gifts from others, personal gain, commerce or service, marry and set up a home, and then follow the ways of the man of taste and culture (*nāgaraka*).

He may make his abode, in accordance with the calling chosen by him, in a city, in a commercial center, or a town; any of these that he chooses should be inhabited by good people.

There he should make for himself a house, with water nearby, having a garden, provided with separate apartments for different activities, and having two retiring rooms.

In the retiring room in the forepart of the house, there shall be a fine couch, with two pillows, pliant at the center, having a pure white sheet; there shall be by its side another couch of lesser height [for lying down]; at the head, there shall be a wicker-seat [for doing his prayers] and a platform for the sandal paste left over after the night's use, a garland, a box for wax and scents, peelings of pomegranate fruit [a mouth deodorant] and betel leaves; a spittoon on the ground; a lute hanging on a bracket on the wall, a painting-board and box of colors, some books and garlands of flowers; not far away on the floor, different kinds of seats; a dice-board; outside the room, cages for the birds kept for playing with, and at a remote end [outside], things for private use.

In the garden a swing, well covered and under the shade of a tree, as also an earthen platform strewn with the falling flowers of the garden. Such is to be the layout of his residence.

He must get up early in the morning, answer the calls of nature, wash his teeth, smear his body with just a little fragrant paste, inhale fragrant smoke, wear some flower, just give the lips a rub with wax and red juice, look at his face in the mirror, chew betel leaves along with some mouth deodorants, and then attend to his work.

Every day he must bathe; every second day, have a massage; every third day, apply unguents to his legs; every fourth day have a partial shave and clipping of the nails;

every fifth or tenth day a more complete shave; he mus
frequently wipe off the perspiration in the armpit; have hi
food in the forenoon and afternoon.

After eating [in the forenoon] comes playing with pa
rots and myna birds and making them talk; and indulgin
in cock and ram fights and in other artistic activities; als
attending to the work he has with his friends and compan
ions. Then a little nap. In the forenoon still, he dresse
and goes out for social calls and for enjoyment of the com
pany of others. In the evening he enjoys music and dance
At the end of it, in his own apartments, decorated an
fragrant with smoke, he awaits, along with his companions
his beloved who has given him an engagement, or els
sends her a message and himself goes out to meet her
. . . Such is the daily routine.

He should arrange excursions in parties for attendin
festivals, salons for enjoying literature and art, drinkin
parties, excursions to parks, and group games. Once a for
night or month, on the day sacred to particular deities, th
actors and dancers attached to the temple of Sarasvat
[the Goddess of learning] gather and present shows [fo
the cultured citizens of the place]; or visiting actors an
musicians from other places present their programs in th
Sarasvatī temple.

(from Vātsyāyana, Kamasūtra, in Sources of Indian Trad
tion, pp. 260-61)

CAUTION AND COMMONSENSE

Over against the tendency within the Hindu tradition to g
to extremes must be set an emphasis on moderation and con
monsense found in much of the literature. The best know
repository of such advice is the Panchatantra, a collection o
stories whose ostensible purpose is to teach wisdom to kin
but which must have always been intended for a wider aud

nce. The original of this work is lost, but many versions were irculated. The one from which the story given below has been aken, the *Hitopadesha*, dates from the twelfth century in its resent form. The stories were interlocked within a compliated framework of other stories, sometimes without any very bvious connection. The story used here, for example, of the Tiger and the Traveller, is told by Speckle-neck, King of the Pigeons, as a warning to be on guard against people who make enerous offers. The story begins with a fowler setting a net or trapping pigeons.

Thus, replied Speckle-neck: I was pecking about one day n the Deccan forest, and saw an old tiger sitting newly bathed on the bank of a pool, like a Brahman, and with oly kuskus-grass in his paws.

"Ho! ho! ye travellers," he kept calling out, "take this golden bangle!"

Presently a covetous fellow passed by and heard him.

"Ah!" thought he, "this is a bit of luck—but I must not isk my neck for it either.

'Good things come not out of bad things; wisely leave a longed-for ill.
Nectar being mixed with poison serves no purpose but to kill.

'But all gain is got by risk, so I will see into it at least;" hen he called out, "Where is thy bangle?"

The Tiger stretched forth his paw and exhibited it.

"Hem!" said the Traveller, "can I trust such a fierce brute as thou art?"

"Listen," replied the Tiger, "once, in the days of my cubhood, I know I was very wicked. I killed cows, Brahmans, and men without number—and I lost my wife and children for it—and haven't kith or kin left. But lately I met a virtuous man who counselled me to practise the duty of almsgiving—and, as thou seest, I am strict at ablutions and alms. Besides, I am old, and my nails and fangs are gone—so who would mistrust me? and I have so far

conquered selfishness, that I keep the golden bangle fc
whoso comes. Thou seemest poor! I will give it thee. Is i
not said,

"*Give to poor men, son of Kūntī—on the wealthy wast*
  not wealth;
Good are simples for the sick man, good for nought t
  him in health.

"Wade over the pool, therefore, and take the bangle."

Thereupon the covetous Traveller determined to trus
him, and waded into the pool, where he soon found him
self plunged in mud, and unable to move.

"Ho! ho!" says the Tiger, "art thou stuck in a slough
stay, I will fetch thee out!"

So saying he approached the wretched man and seize
him—who meanwhile bitterly reflected—

"*Be his Scripture-learning wondrous, yet the cheat will b*
  a cheat;
Be her pasture ne'er so bitter, yet the cow's milk will b
  sweet."

And on that verse, too—

"*Trust not water, trust not weapons; trust not clawed nc*
  horned things;
Neither give thy soul to women, nor thy life to Sons c
  Kings."

And those others—

"*Look! the Moon, the silver roamer, from whose splen*
  dour darkness flies.
With his starry cohorts marching, like a crowned kin
  through the skies.
All the grandeur, all the glory, vanish in the Dragon
  jaw;
What is written on the forehead, that will be, an
  nothing more."

Here his meditations were cut short by the Tiger devouring him. And that, said Speckle-neck, is why we counselled caution.

(from *Hitopadeśa*, trans. by Sir Edward Arnold, *The Book of
Good Counsels*, pp. 9-11)

CHAPTER IX

THE PHILOSOPHIC
STATEMENT OF
THE TRADITION

~~~~~~~~~

*During the centuries when numerous expressions of rel
gious aspiration added to the richness of the Hindu trad
tion, various systems of philosophy attempted to give ord
and coherence to the intellectual ferment of the time. E
the end of the fourth century A.D. six of these had come t
be regarded as orthodox, in contrast to those that we
connected with Buddhism and Jainism. Philosophy is pe
haps not quite the right word for these systems, since the
main function was to help men find salvation, not to di
cuss the kinds of problems that have interested philos
phers in the West. But neither would it be correct to d
scribe them as theologies, for although they are considere
to be valid statements of truths contained in the scri
tures, some of them have little concern with any questio
relating to God. The basis of their orthodoxy is an accep
ance of the common assumptions of the tradition—beli
in karma, rebirth, and dharma—and a general agreemen
that the acquisition of knowledge, however defined, w
the means whereby man was freed from bondage to ign
rance. Because of ignorance, the Self, the permanent e
tity, is clouded by the passions and impurities of life, an
as a modern Indian philosopher points out, all the system
agree that "the summum bonum of life is attained whe*

all impurities are removed and the pure nature of the Self is thoroughly and permanently apprehended and all other extraneous connections with it are absolutely dissociated." [1]

The six systems, then, were ways of dealing with ignorance, using different methods, different approaches to the problem, and different definitions of such terms as Self, knowledge, and ignorance. In the following selections three of the systems—Nyāya, Vaisheshika, and Mīmāmsā —are treated in a very cursory manner, partly because of their subject matter, but mainly because the language used in the writings of these schools was so technical that it is meaningful only with an extended commentary. The other three systems—Yoga, Sānkhya, and Vedānta—are treated more fully because not only did they all occupy an important place in the past but they also had a general influence on the development of Hindu religious thought. Two of them, Yoga and Vedānta, are still central to the tradition.

It is worthwhile pointing out that while there was general acceptance within India—even by such heretical groups as Jains and Buddhists—of the basic beliefs of karma, transmigration, and the demands of dharma, there were, nevertheless, those who rejected the whole framework of conventional assumptions. A reference to the views of one dissenting school, known as Lokāyata or Cārvāka, is probably seen in the first selection, indicating the existence of radical dissent within the Hindu tradition. On the whole, however, thoroughgoing denial of the great assumptions of the general philosophical position was rare and does not seem to have played any very creative role in Indian life.

The Basis of Logical Thinking: Nyāya

The principal aim of the Nyāya system was to clarify the means for obtaining knowledge. These means, it taught, were

[1] S. N. Dasgupta, *A History of Indian Philosophy* (Cambridge: 1922), I, 75.

perception, inference, comparison, and the verbal testimony
of a reliable person or of the scriptures, and their correct use
was seen as an indispensable step towards salvation. The teachings of the Nyāya school, like those of all the other schools,
were preserved in the form of *sūtras*, very short, aphoristic
summaries of the main points of the system. Since these sūtras
were scarcely intelligible by themselves, they were commented
upon by scholars, and it is these commentaries that became
the foundation documents of different schools of interpretation. The selection given here shows the arguments that were
used by the school to prove the existence and rebirth of the
soul. While the sūtra itself may date from the first century
B.C., the commentary (in brackets) is by Vātsyāyana, who
probably lived in the sixth century A.D.

A sense is not soul because we can apprehend an object
through both sight and touch.

("Previously I saw the jar and now I touch it:" such expressions will be meaningless if "I" is not different from
eye which cannot touch and from skin which cannot see.
In other words, the "I" or soul is distinct from the senses.)

This is, some say, not so because there is a fixed relation
between the senses and their objects.

(Colour, for instance, is an exclusive object of the eye,
sound of the ear, smell of the nose, and so on. It is the eye
that, according to the objectors, apprehends colour, and
there is no necessity for assuming a soul distinct from the
eye for the purpose of explaining the apprehension of colour.) . . .

If the body were soul there should be release from sin
as soon as the body was burnt.

(If a person has no soul beyond his body he should be
freed from sins when the body is destroyed. But in reality
sins pursue him in his subsequent lives. Hence the body is
not soul.)

There would, says an objector, be no sin even if the
body endowed with a soul were burnt for the soul is
eternal.

(In the previous aphorism it was shown that the commission of sins would be impossible if we supposed the body to be the soul. In the present aphorism it is argued by an objector that we should be incapable of committing sins even on the supposition of the soul being distinct from our body, for such a soul is eternal and cannot be killed.)

In reply we say that it is not so because we are capable of killing the body which is the site of operations of the soul.

(Though the soul is indestructible we can kill the body which is the seat of its sensations. Hence we are not incapable of committing sins by killing or murder. Moreover, if we do not admit a permanent soul beyond our frail body we shall be confronted by many absurdities such as "loss of merited action" and "gain of unmerited action." A man who has committed a certain sin may not suffer its consequences in this life and unless there is a soul continuing to his next life he will not suffer them at all. This is a "loss of merited action." Again, we often find a man suffering the consequences of action which he never did in this life. This would be a "gain of unmerited action" unless we believed that his soul did the action in his previous life.) . . .

The soul is to be admitted on account of joy, fear and grief arising in a child from the memory of things previously experienced. . . .

A child's desire for milk in this life is caused by the practice of his having drunk it in the previous life.

Some deny the above by saying that a new-born child approaches the breast of his mother just as an iron approaches a loadstone (without any cause).

This is, we reply, not so because there is no approach towards any other thing.

We find that none is born without desire.

Some say that the soul is not eternal because it may be produced along with desire as other things are produced along with their qualities.

This is, we reply, not so because the desire in a new-born child is caused by the ideas left in his soul by the things he enjoyed in his previous lives.

(The desire implies that the soul existed in the previou
lives or, in other words, the soul is eternal.)

(from *Nyāyā Sūtras of Gotama*, Book III, selections, in *Sacre*
Books of the Hindus, VIII, pp. 63-64, 68-69)

The Atomic Nature of Reality: Vaisheshika

The Vaisheshika school was concerned with analyzing th
qualities that distinguish one particular object from anothe
and one of its contributions was an elaborate theory of th
nature of reality. It taught that the universe was compose
of atoms so minute that they had no extension in space
These atoms were eternal, without beginning or end. Th
relevance of this theory to religious thought was that, accor
ing to the followers of the school, it made possible a tru
understanding of the soul and the pathway to saving know
edge. The selection given here is from commentaries on th
sūtras of Kanāda, one of the early exponents of the Vaishe
shika philosophy. The original sūtra is indicated by quotatio
marks. The dating of this material, as of most ancient India
literary work, is quite uncertain, but the origins of the schoo
are probably to be found somewhere between the sixth an
fourth centuries B.C.

THE EFFECT IS THE MARK (OF THE EXISTENCE)
OF THE ULTIMATE ATOM

According to the sūtram of Gautama: "From the evolved i
the production of the evolved, on the evidence of experi
ence by perception." Now the inter-relation of parts an
wholes is perceived. If it were unlimited, there would b
no difference in size or measurement between Moun
Meru and a grain of mustard seed; for they would be with
out distinction, both being originated by infinite parts
Nor can it be said that the difference will be caused by th
difference of the size of each part and of the aggregation o
parts; for without a difference of number, these also woul
be impossible. If it be said that *pralaya*, or destruction o

e creation, may be the limit of the series of parts and
oles, we reply that the final thing having no parts, *pra-*
a itself would be impossible, for it is only disjunction and
struction of parts which can destroy substances. Nor is
junction the limit, for it is impossible for it to have only
e substratum. Therefore, a substance without parts
st be the limit and this is the ultimate atom. A mote is
t the limit; for being a visible substance, it possesses
gnitude, and is composed of more substances than one;
gnitude, as the cause of visual perception, presupposes,
is dependent upon, multiplicity of substance; else there
uld be no magnitude even, and what then would be
use? Nor are the constituent parts of the mote atoms, for
must infer that they also, as originative of a substance
ssessing magnitude, are composed of parts, like thread
d like potsherd. Therefore, whatever substance is an
ect, is composed of parts, and whatever substance is
mposed of parts, is an effect. So that from whichever
rt the nature of being an effect goes away, from it goes
ay also the nature of being made up of parts. This is the
of of indivisible ultimate atoms. So it has been said by
asatadeva, "Earth is two-fold, eternal and non-eternal."

(IT IS) AN ERROR (TO SUPPOSE THAT
THE ULTIMATE ATOM IS NOT ETERNAL)

may be objected as follows: The ultimate atom is not
rnal, since it is corporeal or ponderable, like a water-pot.
nilarly, the possession of colour, the possession of taste,
., may be, one by one, adduced as so many reasons. . . .
ain, the non-eternality of the atom follows also from
e inference which establishes transiency, the inference,
it is, that all that exists is momentary. . . . To meet
ese objections he says: Every inference which has for its
bject the non-eternality of the atom is ignorance, that is,
is of the form of error, since it springs from a fallacy.
is fallacy is occasionally obstruction or opposition to the
of which comprehends the subject; always the absence
 the characteristic of being pervaded (or being the

mark), due to want of evidence preventive of its existen
in the counter-argument; . . . sometimes unproof by
self; and others which should be learned from the kindr
system (the Nyāya system).

(from *The Vaiśeṣika Sūtras of Kanāda*, trans. by Nanda
Sinha, in *Sacred Books of the Hindus*, VI, pp. 146-48)

Proof of the Sacred Texts: Mīmāmsā

The Mīmāmsā system was built upon the logic of the Nyā
school but gave particular emphasis to the importance of
testimony of the *Vedas* as a source of true knowledge. T
practitioners of this school taught that the *Vedas* were eter
and without an author. Coupled with this uncompromis
assertion of the *Vedas* as absolute truth went a denial of
role of a deity as creator. This rejection of theism by a religi
system is an indication of how careful one must be in tra
ferring religious terms and concepts from one tradition to
other.

The selection given here is from a commentary written
the eighth century A.D. by Kumārila on the work of Jaimi
the greatest figure in the school of Mīmāmsā. Kumārila's ar
ment would probably not convince anyone who did not acc
all of his presuppositions, but this kind of reasoning played
important part in establishing the intellectual validity of H
duism over against the teachings of the Buddhists and otl
heretics.

Obj:—Finding the Vedic assertions to be similar to or
nary assertions, we have a general idea of the Veda havi
an author; and this becomes specified by the names 'Kath
&c., given to he different sections of the Veda. . . .

Reply:—Inasmuch as we have neither any rememb
ance of an author nor any need of any such,—no autho
wanted for the Veda; and since the ideas of particular
thorship depend upon the general notion (of such auth
ship), no names can point to any authors of the Veda

Inasmuch as the names "Katha," &c., may be explained as signifying the fact of certain portions of the Veda being explained by such people,—these names cannot necessarily point to an author; specially as the affix (in the word "Katha") is also laid down as denoting the fact of being *expounded* (by Katha).

And thus *Name*, being weaker than Direct Assertion and the rest, cannot set aside the facts based upon these latter. And further, inasmuch as this (Name) is a part of the Veda, it can never possibly set aside the whole of the Veda (by pointing to the fact of its having an author).

Or these ("Katha," &c.) may be taken as conventional names, given, without any reason, to particular sections of the Veda. And the fact of these names (appearing with regard to certain sections of the Veda) being only similar in *sound*, the same words (as signifying the fact of being composed by Katha, &c.) is not to be denied on pain of any punishment (*i.e.*, there is no law which lays down that the two do not resemble in sound only).

Even though the explanation of the Veda is common to all persons (and not restricted particularly to Katha alone), yet the name may be given to certain sections of the Veda, simply on the ground of the possibility (of its being explained by Katha). . . .

The names "Katha," &c., indicating the fact of Katha, &c., being the explainers, are not such as to restrict the explicability of those sections of the Veda to those teachers alone, inasmuch as all that the name does is to show that the section of the Veda has been explained by that particular teacher *also* among others,—just as the mother of Dittha and Kapittha is called "Dittha's mother" (which does not mean that the person is not the mother of Kapittha, but that she is also the mother of Dittha, among others).

The fact that, even though the relation of the section with all teachers is the same, yet it is named after one of them only, is due to the fact that such naming is not a qualification of the agent (*i.e.*, the Teacher) and as such it is not necessary to repeat it with regard to all the Teachers); hence the naming (in accordance with Teachers) being (a qualification) for the sake of another (*i.e.* the Sections of the Veda), the mention of only one of them is necessary.

(Even if the name "Katha" were taken as implying the authorship of Katha with regard to the Veda, then too) it is only an already existing cause (in the shape of Katha) that is signified (by the name "Katha"); and it does not signify the production of something previously non-existent.

And (as for the meaning of Vedic sections according to the name of only one Teacher, it is similar to the case where) a certain sacred place, though visited by many people, is named in accordance with only one of its visitors (such as "Somatīrtha," &c.).

And if the name "Katha" be not due to human agency, then it cannot indicate non-eternality; and if it be due to human agency, then how can its truthfulness be ascertained? . . .

The Veda naturally abandons the denotation of non-eternal meanings,—inasmuch as such denotation is found to be impossible with regard to the Veda, by considering alternatives of eternality and non-eternality with regard to it. Because if the Veda be eternal its denotation cannot but be eternal; and if it be non-eternal (caused), then it can have no validity (which is not possible, as we have already proved the validity of the Veda); and as for the theory that the Veda consists of assertions of intoxicated (and senseless) people, this theory has been already rejected above—(and as such the validity and hence the eternality of the Veda cannot be doubted).

Thus up to this place, we have established by arguments, the fact of the Veda being the means of arriving at the right notion of "Dharmā."

After this (in the succeeding three *pādas*), after having divided the Veda into its three sections, we shall explain what is the meaning (and purpose) of each of these sections.

(from Kumārila, *Ślokavārtika*, Aphorisms XXVII to XXXII, trans. by G. N. Jha)

The Dualism of Matter and Spirit: Sānkhya

According to the Sānkhya system there are two eternal principles in the universe, matter (*prakriti*) and spirit (*purusha*). The Sānkhya school did not posit any creator for these entities, but simply regarded them as self-existent, without beginning or end. Matter is made up of three *gunas* or "strands," known as *sattva* (purity), *rajas* (passion), and *tamas* (darkness). It is the movement of these three strands and their combination in different proportions that create the visible universe. A preponderance of *sattva*, for example, gives things the qualities of lightness and truth, while *rajas* makes for activity and violence and *tamas* produces darkness and stupidity. The working or evolution of these strands is caused by spirit—although just how this action takes place is not clear. The result of the interaction of spirit and matter is the disturbance of the equilibrium that would exist otherwise, and out of disequilibrium comes the cosmos with all its pains and evils, the greatest of which is rebirth. Salvation consists, therefore, in withdrawing spirit from its involvement with matter and restoring the primeval balance when both principles maintained their static being. In this dualism of matter and spirit there is, it should be noted, no suggestion that matter is in any sense evil, but only that matter and spirit are intrinsically different things and, therefore, should not be confused.

Salvation for the Sānkhya system involves the use of knowledge to restore the balance of matter and spirit and to prevent the continued operation of the *gunas*. The gods are not denied, but they have no essential place within the scheme; man quite literally works out his own salvation. While Sānkhya is no longer important as a separate school its general ideas, especially the conception of *gunas*, were widely accepted by other systems. The metaphysical basis of the *Bhagavad Gītā*, for example, is very similar to the Sānkhya understanding of the world.

The selection given here is taken from a writing dated around the fourth century A.D.

Owing to man being assailed by all the kinds of misery, there arises the desire in him to know the means for the removal of such misery. Such an inquiry into the cause of the removal of misery is not rendered useless because there are known and ready remedies, for such remedies are neither invariably nor completely effective. Like those worldly remedies are those that one knows from the scriptures [namely, the performance of Vedic sacrifices to attain the joyous status of heaven]; for that scriptural remedy is impure as sacrifices involve injury [to animals], and its fruits are both perishable and liable to be excelled by other kinds of pleasure. Therefore a remedy which is the opposite of these [the seen one of the world and the heard one of the scriptures] is more beneficial; and that remedy is to be had by knowledge, the discrimination of the manifest material creation, its unmanifest cause [the object], and the presiding sentient spirit [the subject].

Primordial Matter is not an effect [modification]; the intellect, etc., seven in number, are both cause and effect; there are sixteen categories which are only effects; the spirit is neither cause nor effect.

The categories of knowledge are known from means of correct knowledge and in Sānkhya, three sources of valid knowledge are accepted: perception, inference, and valid testimony; all other means of correct knowledge are included in these three. Perception is the determination of objects by their contact with the respective senses perceiving them. Inference is of three kinds, and it results from the knowledge of a characteristic feature and of an object invariably accompanied by that feature. Valid testimony is what one hears from a reliable authority. Perception provides knowledge of sensible objects. Of things beyond the senses, knowledge is had through inference based on analogy; and those that are completely beyond the senses and cannot be established even through that process of inference are ascertained through valid testimony. A thing may not be perceived because of too great distance, of too much proximity, injury to the senses, inattention of mind, smallness or subtlety, an intervening object, suppression by another, or merging in a similar thing.

Primordial matter is not perceived because it is too subtle, not because it does not exist; for it is known from its products [the phenomenal world]. And those products are intellect, etc.; products born of primordial matter are, in their characteristics, partly like it and partly unlike it.

The effect already exists in the cause for the following reasons: what is nonexistent cannot be produced; for producing a thing, a specific material cause is resorted to; everything is not produced by everything; a specific material cause capable of producing a specific product alone produces that effect; there is such a thing as a particular cause for a particular effect.

The evolved [i.e., the product] has the following characteristics: it has been caused, it is noneternal, nonpervasive, attended by movement, manifold, resting on another, an attribute of its source in which it finally merges, endowed with parts, and depending on another for its existence. The nonevolved [i.e., the cause, primordial matter] is the opposite of all this. But the evolved and the unevolved [primordial matter] have these common properties: they are composed of three dispositions [gunas]; they are nondiscriminating and nonsentient; they are object; they are common; and their nature is to evolve. The spirit is opposed in its qualities both to one and to the other.

The three dispositions: they are of the form of pleasure, pain, and dejection; their purposes are illumination, activation, and checking; they function by prevailing over one another, resorting to one another, engendering one another, and acting in cooperation with one another. They are purity [sattva], passion [rajas], and darkness [tamas]. Purity is light, revealing and desirable; passion is stimulating and active; darkness is dense and obscuring; their har-

monious functioning is directed by unity of purpose, as in
the case of a lamp [in which the ingredients, fire, oil, and
wick, conjointly function for the one purpose of producing
light]. . . .

The properties like absence of discriminatory knowledge
can be proved to exist in the evolved by reason of the latter
being composed of the three dispositions and by the absence of this threefold composition of its opposite, namely
the spirit. The existence of an unevolved primary cause is
proved by the fact that the effect has the same properties
as the cause.

The unevolved exists as the primordial cause because the
diverse evolutes are all attended by limitations, because
common features subsist through all of them [arguing inheritance from a common cause], because the evolved has
come into being as the result of the potentiality of a cause,
because the distinction of cause and effect apply to the
entire world without exception.

The unevolved acts [evolves] through its three dispositions [purity, etc.] and through them conjointly, changing
like water according to the difference pertaining to each of
those dispositions.

As all aggregates imply one different from themselves
whom they subserve, as that for whom they are intended
should differ from their own nature, namely, being composed of three dispositions, etc., as such objects should
have one as their presiding authority, as objects imply an
enjoyer, and as there is seen through evolution a striving
for liberation, there exists the spirit. The plurality of spirits
is proven because of the specified nature of birth, death,
and faculties in respect of each person, because of the absence of simultaneous activity on the part of all, and because of the diversity of the nature of three dispositions in
different beings. By the same reason of differences from
the unevolved [primordial matter] which is composed of
the three dispositions, the spirit is proved to be only a
spectator, distinct and unaffected, endowed with cognition
but free of agency.

Hence, as a result of union with the spirit, the evolved though nonsentient, yet appears to be sentient; and on its part, the spirit, too, though the dispositions of matter alone act, appears to act but is really indifferent. It is for the sake of enlightenment of the spirit and the eventual withdrawal from primordial matter [i.e., liberation of the spirit from matter] that the two come together, even as the lame and the blind come together for mutual benefit; creation proceeds from this union.

From primordial matter proceeds intellect; from it ego; from that the group of sixteen [the five subtle elements governing sound, touch, form, taste, and smell, the five senses of knowledge, the five of action, and the mind which is the internal sense presiding over the other ten senses]; from the five [subtle elements] among those sixteen, the five gross elements [ether, air, fire, water, and earth].

The intellect is of the form of determination; its sublime [purity-dominated] forms are virtue, knowledge, dispassion, and mastery; the opposites of these [darkness-dominated vice, ignorance, passion, and powerlessness] represent its forms in delusion.

Ego is of the form of identification; from it proceed twofold creation, the group of eleven [senses] and the five subtle elements. . . .

The subtle elements are not of any specific character; from these five, the five gross elements of matter proceed and these gross elements have specified characters, peaceful, violent, and dormant [according to the relative preponderance of any of the three gunas]. These three specified forms have again a threefold manifestation [in living beings]; the subtle body, the gross body born of parents, together with the gross elements; the subtle ones endure through transmigration], the gross ones are perishable.

. . . According to the exigencies of the causes—virtue, vice, etc.—and the resultant higher or lower births, the subtle body prompted by the purpose of the spirit (viz. its liberation) makes its appearance like an actor in different

guises, thanks to the capacity of the primary cause (prakriti) to manifest diverse forms. . . .

By virtue one progresses toward higher forms of embodied existence; by vice, one goes down toward lower
forms; by knowledge liberation is gained and by its opposite bondage; by nonattachment to mundane objects, one
reaches the state of merging in primordial matter; from
desire impelled by passion further transmigration results;
unimpeded movement is gained through the attainment
of mastery and from its opposite, the opposite of free
movement. . . .

In this transmigratory journey, the sentient spirit experiences the misery due to old age and death till such time as
the subtle body also falls away; hence, in the very nature of
existence, everything is misery. . . .

Therefore, surely, no spirit is bound, none is released,
none transmigrates; primordial matter, taking different
forms, transmigrates, binds herself and releases herself. By
her own seven forms [virtue and vice, ignorance, detachment and attachment, mastery and the lack of it], matter
binds herself; and for the purpose of the spirit, she herself
with one of her forms, namely knowledge, causes release.

(from Īshvarakrishna, *Sānkhya Kārikās*, I:33-69, *passim*, in
Sources of Indian Tradition, pp. 308-14)

The Way of Discipline: Yoga

The name of the fifth orthodox system of philosophy—Yoga—
is one of the most familiar of Indian religious terms, but its
fame has tended to mask the real nature of its position. In
the present context "disciplined activity" seems to give the
sense intended by its usage in the basic text of the school, the
Yogasūtra of Patanjali. The dates of this work are quite uncertain, with some scholars assigning it to the second century
B.C. and others to the fourth century A.D., but the surviving
commentaries all seem to come from a time subsequent to the
later date.

According to Patanjali, the aim of Yoga is to gain control of both physical and mental processes. The metaphysical basis of the system is very similar to that of the Sānkhya school, and the purpose of control is to end the activity of the strands or *gunas*. Unlike Sānkhya, however, the Yoga system accepts the idea of a supreme first cause as the originator of both spirit and matter. The yogic practitioner seeks through a careful process of spiritual exercises to reach a state of "isolation," of the complete separation of spirit from matter. When this is achieved the spirit is free from change and motion.

This selection describes the methods to be followed by the disciple, and while they are expressed in the telegraphic language common to the sūtra form, their meaning is relatively clear.

1. Purificatory action, study, and making God the motive of action, constitute the *yoga* of action.
2. This is for the bringing about of trance and for the purpose of attenuating afflictions.
3. The afflictions are ignorance, egoism, attachment, aversion, and love of life.
4. Ignorance is the field for the others, whether dormant, tenuous, alternated, or fully operative.
5. Ignorance is the taking of the temporal, the impure, the painful, and the not-self to be the eternal, the pure, the pleasurable, and the self.
6. Egoism is the belief that the power of seeing and the power by which one sees is a single essence.
7. Attachment is the attraction to pleasure.
8. Aversion is the repulsion from pain.
9. Flowing on by its own potency, established even in the wise, is love of life.
10. These afflictions may be overcome by their opposites.
11. Their activities are destroyed by meditation.
12. The vehicle of actions has its origin in afflictions, and is experienced in visible and invisible births.
13. It ripens into life-state, life-time, and life-experience, if the root exists.

14. They have pleasure or pain as the fruit, by reason of virtue or vice.

15. By reason of the pains of change, anxiety, and habituation, and by reason of the contrariety of the functionings of the "qualities," all indeed is pain to the discriminating.

16. But future pain is avoidable.

17. The conjunction of the knower and the knowable is the cause of avoidable pain. . . .

23. Conjunction is that which brings about the recognition of the natures of the power of owning and the capacity of being owned.

24. Ignorance is its effective cause.

25. Removal (of bondage) is the disappearance of conjunction on account of the disappearance of ignorance, and that is the absolute freedom of the knower.

26. The means of removing ignorance is through knowledge that discriminates between the soul and the objects of sense. . . .

28. On the destruction of impurity by the sustained practice of the accessories of *yoga*, the light of wisdom reaches up to discriminative knowledge.

29. Restraint, observance, posture, regulation of breath, abstraction (of the senses), concentration, meditation, and trance are the eight accessories of *yoga*.

30. Of these, the restraints are: abstinence from injury (*ahimsā*), veracity, abstinence from theft, continence, and abstinence from avariciousness.

31. They are the great vow, universal, and unlimited by origin, space, time, and circumstance.

32. The observances are cleanliness, contentment, austerity, study, and the making of the Lord the motive of all action. . . .

35. In the presence of one who has given up causing injury all hostility is given up.

36. When one is confirmed in veracity, actions and their consequences depend upon him.

7. When one is confirmed in the habit of not stealing, all treasures come to him.

8. Continence being confirmed, vigour is obtained.

9. Non-covetousness being confirmed, knowledge of the succession of births is obtained.

10. By cleanliness is meant disgust with one's body, and cessation of contact with others.

11. And with the mind becoming pure, come purity, singleness of mind, control of the senses, and fitness for the knowledge of the self.

12. By contentment, comes the acquisition of extreme happiness.

13. By purificatory action, come the removal of impurity and the attainments of the physical body and the senses.

14. By study comes communion with the desired deity.

15. The attainment of trance comes by making God the motive of all actions.

16. Posture is steady and easy. . . .

17. Regulation of breath is the stoppage of the inhaling and exhaling movements of breath. . . .

18. Then the mind is fit for concentration (*dhāranā*).

19. Abstraction (of the senses) (*pratyāhāra*) is that by which the senses do not come into contact with their objects and follow as it were the nature of the mind.

20. Thence the senses are under the highest control.

From Patanjali, *Yogasūtra*, Chapter II, trans. by Rama Prasad (*Sacred Books of the Hindus*, IV, revised)

Non-Dualism: The Vedānta of Shankara

The most important of all the systems of philosophy is Vedānta, which means "the end of the *Vedas*." The term is properly used for the *Vedānta Sūtra*, a text written some time after the fourth century B.C. that summarized the teachings of the *Upanishads* in very terse statements. Many commentaries

were written on these brief aphorisms, but by far the most ?
mous is that of Shankara, a South Indian who lived about tl
end of the eighth century. His interpretation has so dominat«
Indian intellectual life, and has become so well-known in tl
West, that his work has become almost synonymous wi
Vedānta, although other very different interpretations we
made by scholars of great intellectual distinction. Shankarª
achievement in creating a great synthesis of knowledge h
often been compared to that of St. Thomas Aquinas, but
is properly used for the Vedānta Sūtra, a text written some tin
of Indian thought since his time has been much more per«
sive than that of Aquinas on the West. One measure of tl
influence is that it is very difficult for anyone—either Hindu
non-Hindu—to read Indian religious texts without unco
sciously seeing them through the general interpretation giv«
by Shankara.

Shankara's main concern was the nature of the relationsh
between the individual Self (ātman) and the Universal S«
(brahman). His general position was that these were cor
pletely identical, and that all appearances of plurality and d
ference arose from a false interpretation of the data present«
by the mind and senses. In any ultimate understanding, he i
sisted, the only reality was brahman.

In putting forward this interpretation Shankara had to me«
a number of obvious difficulties. One was the great variety
teachings contained in the scriptures, particularly the Upa
ishads, and since Shankara was completely committed to tl
truth of the sacred texts he had to meet each seeming cont«
diction between his teaching and the scriptures. He also h;
to meet the logical arguments of his opponents, especially tl
Buddhists, who met him on his own ground. And, above a
he had to explain the commonsense perception of a plural ur
verse, where men are in fact aware of themselves as individu;
and of different forms of matter external to themselves.

Shankara's broad answer to the objections to his system w
to posit the concept of higher and lower knowledge, and
argue that statements were "true" depending upon the level
experience attained by the person discussing them. The cor
monsense perception of plurality, for example, was perfect
true for the man who had not reached the stage of understan
ing that reality was one. In the same way, the gods of popul
Hinduism were necessary for worship by those who believ«

in them, but on a higher level of spiritual attainment they had no meaning. With the knowledge of the identity of *ātman* and *brahman*, or the Self and Universal Self, all the plurality of the world of lower knowledge simply vanished; plurality did not exist for the enlightened man any more than a knowledge of the unity of being existed for the man who lived in the realm of the lower knowledge. Shankara was not making any value judgment between higher and lower knowledge, suggesting that one was good and the other bad; what he was doing, he would have insisted, was describing the universe as it actually existed, and using this knowledge for the purposes of salvation.

The aim of Shankara's system, then, was the same as that of all the other great philosophical statements—the attainment of salvation, or more accurately, perhaps, of liberation. This is defined for Shankara as intuitive knowledge of the identity of *ātman* and *brahman*, not, it must be emphasized, as the reaching of unity with God. Within the great system created by Shankara, God or gods occupy an important place, but it is on the level of lower knowledge, not of higher. His Absolute Reality is not God, but must be understood as something quite different from any meaning usually given to conceptions of deity.

The selection given here is from Shankara's greatest work, his commentary on the *Vedānta Sūtra*. It illustrates his use of reason to prove that his position is a true exposition of the scriptures.

INTRODUCTION ON "SUPERIMPOSITION"

When it is well understood that "object" and "subject," comprehended as "you" and "I" and opposed in nature like darkness and light, cannot be of each other's nature, much less could the properties of the two be of each other's nature; therefore when one superimposes on the "subject" comprehended as "I" and consisting of intelligence, the "object" comprehended as "You" and its properties, and superimposes the "subject" which is the reverse thereof and its properties on the "object," this superimposition, it stands to reason to believe, is a thing to be denied.

Still, superimposing the nature and attributes of one thing on those of another and without discriminating from each other the two totally distinct things, namely, the "object" and the "subject," there is this natural usage in the world, "I am this" and "This is mine," which is due to a sublative notion and represents a confusion of the true and the false.

One may ask, what is this thing called "superimposition"? We say, it is the "appearance" in something of some other thing previously experienced and consists of a recollection. Some call it the superimposition of the attributes of one thing on another; some say that where a thing is superimposed on another, it is the illusion due to the nonperception of their difference; still others hold that where there is a superimposition, it is the fancying in a thing of a property contrary to its nature. In any case, it does not cease to have the character of one thing appearing to possess another's property. And so is our experience in the world: nacre shines like silver, and one moon, as if it had a second.

But how does the superimposition of "object" and its properties on the inner Self, which is not the "object," come about? On a thing before oneself one superimposes another thing, but you say, the inner Self, which falls outside the scope of what is comprehended as "you," is never an "object." The reply is: This inner Self is not a nonobject at all times, for it is the object of the notion "I" and there is the knowledge of the inner Self by immediate intuition. There is no such rule that a superimposition has to be made only in an object that exists in front of one; for even in an imperceivable thing like the ether, boys superimpose a surface, dirt, etc. Thus it is not contradictory to speak of superimposition on the inner Self of things which are non-Self.

The superimposition so characterized, the learned consider to be nescience, and the determination of the real nature of a thing by discriminating that which is super imposed on it, they say is knowledge. When this is so, that on which a thing is superimposed is not affected in the slightest degree by either the defect or the merit of the superimposed thing. And it is due to this superimposition over one thing of another in respect of the Self and the non-Self—which is termed nescience—that all worldly transactions, of the means of knowledge and the objects thereof, take place, and [under the same circumstance] again, do all the scriptures, with their injunctions, prohibitions, and means of liberation operate.

But how do you say that sources of valid knowledge like perception and the scriptures fall within the purview of that which is conditioned by nescience? I shall reply: One devoid of the sense of "I" and "Mine" in the body, senses, etc., cannot be a cognizer and cannot resort to a means of cognition; for without resorting to the senses, there can be no activity of perception, etc.; and without a basis [the body] the activity of the senses is not possible; and none ever acts without a body on which the sense of the Self has not been superimposed. Nor could the Self, the unattached, be a cognizer, when none of these [body, senses, etc.] exist; and without a cognizer, the means of cognition do not operate. Hence it is under what is conditioned by nescience that all means of knowledge, perception, etc., as also the scriptures, come. . . .

We said that superimposition is the seeing of a thing in something which is not that; thus, when son, wife, etc., are all right or not, one considers one's own Self as all right or not, one superimposes external attributes on the Self; even so does one superimpose on the Self the attributes of the *body* when one considers that "I am corpulent, I am lean, I am fair, I stand, I go, I jump"; similarly attributes of the *senses* when one says, "I am dumb, one-eyed, impotent, deaf, blind"; and in the same manner the properties of the *internal organs*, e.g., desire, volition, cogitation, and resolution. Even so, man superimposes the [conditioned] Self presented in the cognition of "I" on the inner Self which is the witness of all the activities of the internal organ; and that inner Self, the very opposite and the witness of all, on the inner organ. . . .

It is for casting away this superimposition which is the cause of [all] evil and for gaining the knowledge of the oneness of the Self that all the Upanishads are begun. And how this is the purport of all the Upanishads, we shall show in this system of thought called the investigation into the Self that presides over the body.

Of this system of thought [also] called the Vedānta Mīmāmsā [the enquiry into the purport of the Vedānta, i.e., the Upanishads], which it is my desire to explain, this is the first aphorism:

THEN THEREFORE THE DESIRE TO KNOW THE BRAHMAN

Therefore something must be set forth [as the preceding consideration] in close succession to which the inquiry into the Brahman is taught. I shall set it forth; the sense of discrimination as to things permanent and evanescent, nonattachment to objects of enjoyment here or in the hereafter, the accumulation of accessories like quietude and self-control, and a desire to be liberated. When these are present, whether before an inquiry into dharma or after it, it is possible for one to inquire into the Brahman and know it, not when they are absent. Therefore, by the word "then," it is taught that this desire to know the Brahman follows immediately after the full acquisition of the spiritual accessories set forth above. . . .

Now that Brahman may be well known or unknown; if it is well known, there is no need to desire to know it; if on the other hand, it is unknown, it could never be desired to be known. The answer to this objection is as follows: The Brahman exists, eternal, pure, enlightened, free by nature omniscient, and attended by all power. When the word "Brahman" is explained etymologically, it being eternal pure and so on, are all understood, for these are in conformity with the meaning of the root brh [from which Brahman is derived]. The Brahman's existence is well known, because it is the Self of all; everyone realizes the existence of the Self, for none says, "I am not"; if the existence of the Self is not well known, the whole world of beings would have the notion "I do not exist." And the Self is the Brahman.

It may be contended that if the Brahman is well known in the world as the Self, it has already been known, and again it becomes something which need not be inquired into. It is not like that, for [while its existence in general is accepted], there are differences of opinion about its particular nature. Ordinary people and the materialists are of the view that the Self is just the body qualified by intelligence; others think that it is the intelligent sense-organs themselves that are the Self; still others, that it is the mind; some hold it as just the fleeting consciousness of the moment; some others as the void; certain others say that there is some entity, which is different from the body, etc., and which transmigrates, does and enjoys; some consider him as the enjoyer and not as the doer; some that there is, as different from the above entity, the Lord who is omniscient and omnipotent. According to still others, it is the inner Self of the enjoyer. Thus, resorting to reasonings and texts and the semblances thereof, there are many who hold divergent views. Hence one who accepts some view without examining it might be prevented from attaining the ultimate good, and might also come to grief. Therefore, by way of setting forth the inquiry into the Brahman, here is begun the discussion of the meaning of the texts of the Upanishads, aided by such ratiocination as is in conformity to Scripture and having for its fruit the Supreme Beatitude.

It has been said that the Brahman is to be inquired into; on the question as to the characteristics of that Brahman, the blessed author of the aphorisms says:

WHENCE IS THE ORIGIN . . . OF THIS

. . Of this universe made distinct through names and forms, having many agents and enjoyers, serving as the

ground of the fruits of activities attended by specific
places, times, and causes, and whose nature and design
cannot be conceived even in one's mind—that omniscient
omnipotent cause wherefrom the origin, maintenance, and
destruction of such a universe proceeds is the Brahman
such is the full meaning to be understood. . . .

By showing the Brahman as the cause of the universe it
has been suggested that the Brahman is omniscient; now
to reinforce that omniscience the author of the aphorism
says:

AS IT IS THE SOURCE OF THE SCRIPTURE

Of the extensive scripture comprising the *Rig Veda*
etc., reinforced and elaborated by many branches of learn
ing, illumining everything even as a lamp, and like unto
one omniscient, the source is the Brahman. Of a scripture
of this type, of the nature of the *Rig Veda* and the like
endowed with the quality of omniscience, the origin can
not be from anything other than the omniscient one
Whatever teaching has, for purposes of elaborate exposi
tion, come forth from an eminent personage, as the sci
ence of grammar from Pānini, etc., though it is compre
hensive of that branch of knowledge, it is well understood
in the world that its exponent [e.g., Pānini] possesses
knowledge far more than what is in his work; it therefore
goes without saying that unsurpassed omniscience and
omnipotence is to be found in that Supreme Being from
whom, as the source, issued forth, as if in sport and with
out any effort, like the breathing of a person, this scripture
in diverse recensions, called *Rig Veda*, etc., which is the
repository of all knowledge and is responsible for the
distinctions into gods, animals, humans, classes, stages of
life, etc.; this is borne out by scriptural texts like: "This
that is called *Rig Veda* [and so on] is the breathings out
of this Great Being." . . . That Brahman, omniscient
omnipotent, and cause of the birth, existence, and dis
solution of the universe *is* known from the scripture as
represented by the Upanishads. How? "Because of textua

armony." In all the Upanishads the texts are in agreement in propounding, as their main purport, this idea. For example, "Dear one! this thing Existence alone was at the beginning"; "The one without a second"; "The Self, this one only, existed at first"; "This Brahman, devoid of anything before or after, inside or outside"; "This Self, the Brahman, the all-experiencing one"; "At first there was only this Brahman, the immortal one." When it is decisively known that the purport of the words in these texts is the nature of the Brahman, and when unity is seen, to imagine a different purport is improper, as thereby one will have to give up what is expressly stated and imagine something not stated. Nor could it be concluded that their purport is to set forth the nature of the agent, deity, etc.; for here are texts like "Then whom should It see and with what?," which refute action, agent, and fruit.

Because the Brahman is a thing already well established, it cannot be held to be the object of perception by senses, etc.; for the truth that the Brahman is the Self, as set forth in the text "That thou art," cannot be known without the scripture. As regards the objection that since there is nothing here to be avoided or desired, there is no use in teaching it, it is no drawback; it is from the realization that the self is the Brahman, devoid of things to be avoided or desired, that all miseries are ended and the aspiration of man is achieved.

from Shankara, *Brahmasūtra Bhasya*, I:1:1-4, in *Sources of Indian Tradition*, pp. 316-27)

Qualified Non-Dualism: The Vedānta of Rāmānuja

Although Shankara's interpretation of the *Upanishads* and of the scriptures in general has dominated Indian thought, other great theologians challenged his views. The most important of these was Rāmānuja, whose work dates from about 1100 A.D. Like Shankara he was a South Indian, a reminder that while the traditional home of Hinduism is in the north, many of the greatest exponents of its doctrines lived in the south.

According to Rāmānuja, the human soul and God, or Brah
man, were distinct identities, and salvation for him meant
communion of the individual soul with God, not a realizatio
of complete identity, as with Shankara. While he maintaine
that individual souls were ultimately dependent upon God fo
their existence, he insisted that they retained their separat
being even after the attainment of salvation. His system i
known as "qualified non-dualism," to distinguish it from Shar
kara's "unqualified monism," and also to indicate that it doe
not present a completely dualistic picture of the universe, sinc
he admitted that the individual souls were expressions of *brah
man*.

Rāmānuja's teaching played a very influential role in th
history of Indian religion by providing a metaphysical bas
for the devotional worship that had become common in h
time (see Part Four). Thus it might be argued that whi
Shankara's system has appealed to philosophers, Rāmānuja
has actually served a wider segment of the Indian people.

The selection given here is Rāmānuja's comment on one
the same passages from the *Vedānta Sūtra* that Shankara ha
commented upon. The famous formula from the *Upanishad*
"That art thou," had been used by Shankara to sum up h
monistic teachings, and Rāmānuja had to show that it coul
be interpreted in a non-monistic sense.

"Scripture does not teach that Release is due to the know
edge of a non-qualified Brahman.—The meaning of 'ta
tvam asi.'"

Nor can we admit the assertion that Scripture teache
the cessation of avidyâ to spring only from the cognition o
a Brahman devoid of all difference. Such a view is clear:
negatived by passages such as the following: 'I know tha
great person of sun-like lustre beyond darkness; knowir
him a man becomes immortal, there is no other path t
go;' 'All moments sprang from lightning, the Person—
none is lord over him, his name is great glory—they wh
know him become immortal.' For the reason tha
Brahman is characterised by difference all Vedic texts d
clare that final release results from the cognition of a qua

fied Brahman. And even those texts which describe Brahman by means of negations really aim at setting forth a Brahman possessing attributes.

In texts, again, such as 'Thou art that,' the co-ordination of the constituent parts is not meant to convey the idea of the absolute unity of a non-differenced substance: on the contrary, the words 'that' and 'thou' denote a Brahman distinguished by difference. The word 'that' refers to Brahman omniscient, &c., which had been introduced as the general topic of consideration in previous passages of the same section, such as 'It thought, may I be many'; the word 'thou,' which stands in co-ordination to 'that,' conveys the idea of Brahman in so far as having for its body the individual souls connected with non-intelligent matter. . . It, moreover, is not possible (while, however, it would result from the absolute oneness of 'tat' and 'tvam') that to Brahman, whose essential nature is knowledge, which is free from all imperfections, omniscient, comprising within itself all auspicious qualities, there should belong Nescience; and that it should be the substrate of all those defects and afflictions which spring from Nescience. . . If, on the other hand, the text is understood to refer to Brahman as having the individual souls for its body, both words ('that' and 'thou') keep their primary denotation; and, the text thus making a declaration about one substance distinguished by two aspects, the fundamental principle of 'co-ordination' is preserved. On this interpretation the text further intimates that Brahman— free from all imperfection and comprising within itself all auspicious qualities—is the internal ruler of the individual souls and possesses lordly power.

(from Rāmānuja, *Commentary on the Vedānta Sūtra*, I:1:1, in *Sacred Books of the East*, XLVIII, pp. 129-34, selections)

CHAPTER X

SACRED HISTORY

〰〰〰〰〰

The Hindu tradition, which is so rich in many varieties o
literature, has remarkably little historical literature of th
kind found in comparable periods either in Europe o
China, but it does possess a vast amount of writing tha
deals in a special way with the past. This is the literatur
known as the Purānas, a class of texts that is included i
the canon of scripture, although of a lesser degree of sanc
tity and authority than the Vedic writings. They are no
histories in the modern usage of the term, nor are the
even comparable to medieval chronicles, but they are sa
cred history, providing accounts of the origin of the un
verse, the deeds of the gods, and the genealogies of ancie
kings. Some of them, notably the Vishnu Purāna, contai
material that is undoubtedly factual, but their gener
scope and intention is so fundamentally unhistorical tha
it is virtually impossible to use them to reconstruct th
past. But their real function, the creation of a picture o
the universe in which the lives of men and gods interact,
admirably fulfilled, and their influence over the minds an
imaginations of the people of India has been enormous. :
is through them, rather than the great Vedic texts, th
the basic ideas of Hinduism have been communicated, an

eir mythological stories have been woven into the lives
the people in festivals and ceremonies of all kinds.

The Purānas are sectarian texts; they are identified with
particular god and his devotees, but the same stories,
ith variations, are repeated many times. Some of them
ay come from the early years of the Christian era, or
en earlier, but in their final form they date from after
o A.D., and many of them were added to as late as the
elfth century. According to the traditional count, there
e eighteen works that are genuine Purānas, but many
ore have received the title, and, at least in popular esti-
ation, not much distinction was made on the basis of
e. What apparently determined a work's influence was
e devotion it aroused for its particular deity. Most of the
irānas are concerned with the lives and deeds of Vishnu
id Shiva, or their incarnations, and this emphasis meant
at the older Vedic gods tended to become more and
ore subordinate. Often, for example, gods that originally
id no connection with either Vishnu or Shiva were pic-
red as their wives and children. Thus Ganesh, the
ephant-headed god, had probably been an extremely
icient deity of some primitive non-Aryan tribe, but he
is brought into the Shiva cult by making him the son of
hiva and his wife Pārvati, who herself was a mother god-
ss imported into the pantheon from some ancient
urce.

The Purānas thus looked two ways and performed two
nctions. From one side, they brought into the main
ream of Indian religious thought deities and concepts
om religious traditions that had not originally been related
the Brahmanical movement. On the other hand, they
ve to the local cults the prestige of the Vedic religion
id linked the various sects and groups with such domi-
int patterns of thought as respect for Brāhmans and ac-
ptance of the caste system. In these ways they were in-
spensable for the creation of a system that was able to
mprehend within itself the legacy of variegated cultures
id religious traditions.

A STORY OF ORIGINS:
THE CHURNING OF THE OCEAN

One of the most famous of the Puranic stories tells how th[e]
gods, when oppressed by a race of demons, called Daitya[s]
called on Vishnu (or Hari) to save them. After agreeing t[o]
help, Vishnu told them to make a brief truce with their en[e]-
mies and then to throw a variety of herbs into the ocean. I[n]
carnating himself as a tortoise, he then helped the gods chur[n]
the ocean to obtain *amrita*, the nectar of immortality, whic[h]
enabled them to defeat the demons. Among the many treasure[s]
thrown up at the same time were Lakshmī, the beautiful go[d]-
dess of prosperity who became Vishnu's consort.

Being thus instructed by the god of gods, the diviniti[es]
entered into alliance with the demons, and they jointl[y]
undertook the acquirement of the beverage of immorta[l]-
ity. They collected various kinds of medicinal herbs, an[d]
cast them into the sea of milk, the waters of which wer[e]
radiant as the thin and shining clouds of autumn. The[y]
then took the mountain Mandara for the staff; the serpen[t]
Vāsuki for the cord; and commenced to churn the ocea[n]
for the Amrita. The assembled gods were stationed b[y]
Krishna at the tail of the serpent; the Daityas and Dānava[s]
at its head and neck. Scorched by the flames emitted fro[m]
his inflated hood, the demons were shorn of their glor[y]
whilst the clouds driven towards his tail by the breath [of]
his mouth, refreshed the gods with revivifying showers. I[n]
the midst of the milky sea, Hari himself, in the form of [a]
tortoise, served as a pivot for the mountain, as it wa[s]
whirled around. The holder of the mace and discus wa[s]
present in other forms amongst the gods and demons, an[d]
assisted to drag the monarch of the serpent race: and i[n]
another vast body he sat upon the summit of the moun[-]
tain. With one portion of his energy, unseen by gods [or]

demons, he sustained the serpent king; and with another, infused vigour into the gods.

From the ocean, thus churned by the gods and Dānavas, first uprose the cow Surabhi, the fountain of milk and curds, worshipped by the divinities, and beheld by them and their associates with minds disturbed, and eyes glistening with delight. The troop of Apsarases, the nymphs of heaven, were then produced, of surprising loveliness, endowed with beauty and with taste. The cool-rayed moon next rose; and then poison was engendered from the sea, of which the snake gods (Nāgas) took possession. Dhanwantari, robed in white, and bearing in his hand the cup of Amrita, next came forth. . . . Then, seated on a full-blown lotus, and holding a water-lily in her hand, the goddess Lakshmī, radiant with beauty, rose from the waves. The great sages, enraptured, hymned her with the song dedicated to her praise. . . .

The sea of milk in person presented her with a wreath of never-fading flowers; and the artist of the gods decorated her person with heavenly ornaments. Thus bathed, attired, and adorned, the goddess, in the view of the celestials, cast herself upon the breast of Hari; and there reclining, turned her eyes upon the deities, who were inspired with rapture by her gaze. . . .

The powerful and indignant Daityas then forcibly seized the Amrita-cup, that was in the hand of Dhanwantari: but Vishnu, assuming a female form, fascinated and deluded them; and recovering the Amrita from them, delivered it to the gods. The deities quaffed the ambrosia. The incensed demons, grasping their weapons, fell upon them; but the gods, into whom the ambrosial draught had infused new vigour, defeated and put their host to flight, and they fled through the regions of space, and plunged into the subterraneous realms of hell. The gods thereat greatly rejoiced, did homage to the holder of the discus and mace, and resumed their reign in heaven. The sun shone with renovated splendour, and again discharged his appointed task; and the celestial luminaries again circled,

oh best of Munis, in their respective orbits. Fire once more
blazed aloft, beautiful in splendour; and the minds of all
beings were animated by devotion. The three worlds again
were rendered happy by prosperity; and Indra, the chief of
the gods, was restored to power.

(from *Vishnu Purāna*, I:9, trans. by H. H. Wilson, pp. 75-77)

THE PRICE OF DEVOTION:
THE TRIUMPH OF PRAHLĀDA

The *Purānas* have many stories of devotees who suffered for
their faith. One of the most famous of these is an account of
the tortures undergone by Prahlāda, a worshipper of Vishnu.
His father, the demon king Hiranyakashipu, enraged that his
son offered devotion to his great enemy, forbade him to con-
tinue his prayers. When the boy refused, the demon king
ordered that he be put to death, but despite all kinds of in-
genious tortures, he was always saved by Vishnu's intervention.
In the passage given here, Prahlāda's long sufferings end with
his father's death and repentance and his own assumption of
the throne.

This story has had a powerful appeal for the Indian imagination and allusions are frequent to it both in literature and
conversation.

Whilst with mind intent on Vishnu, Prahlāda thus pronounced his praises, the divinity, clad in yellow robes, suddenly appeared before him. Startled at the sight, with hesi-
tating speech Prahlāda pronounced repeated salutations
to Vishnu, and said, "Oh thou who removest all worldly
grief, Keshava, be propitious unto me; again sanctify me,
by thy sight." The deity replied, "I am pleased with the
faithful attachment thou hast shewn to me: demand from
me, Prahlāda, whatever thou desirest." Prahlāda replied,

"In all the thousand births through which I may be doomed to pass, may my faith in thee, never know decay; may passion, as fixed as that which the worldly-minded feel for sensual pleasures, ever animate my heart, always devoted unto thee." Vishnu answered, "Thou hast already devotion unto me, and ever shalt have it: now choose some boon, whatever is in thy wish." Prahlāda then said, "I have been hated, for that I assiduously proclaimed thy praise: do thou, oh lord, pardon in my father this sin that he hath committed. Weapons have been hurled against me; I have been thrown into the flames; I have been bitten by venomous snakes; and poison has been mixed with my food; I have been bound and cast into the sea; and heavy rocks have been heaped upon me: but all this, and whatever ill beside has been wrought against me; whatever wickedness has been done to me, because I put my faith in thee; all, through thy mercy, has been suffered by me unharmed: and do thou therefore free my father from this iniquity." To this application Vishnu replied, "All this shall be unto thee, through my favour: but I give thee another boon: demand it, son of the Asura." Prahlāda answered and said, "All my desires, oh lord, have been fulfilled by the boon that thou hast granted, that my faith in thee shall never know decay. Wealth, virtue, love, are as nothing; for even liberation is in his reach whose faith is firm in thee, root of the universal world." Vishnu said, "Since thy heart is filled immovably with trust in me, thou shalt, through my blessing, attain freedom from existence." Thus saying, Vishnu vanished from his sight; and Prahlāda repaired to his father, and bowed down before him. His father kissed him on the forehead, and embraced him, and shed tears, and said, "Dost thou live my son?" And the great Asura repented of his former cruelty, and treated him with kindness: and Prahlāda, fulfilling his duties like any other youth, continued diligent in the service of his preceptor and his father. After his father had been put to death by Vishnu in the form of the man-lion, Prahlāda became the sovereign of the Daityas; and possessing the splendours of royalty consequent upon his piety, exercised extensive sway, and was blessed with a numerous progeny. At the expiration of an authority which was the reward of his meritorious acts, he was freed from the consequences of moral merit or demerit, and obtained, through meditation on the deity, final exemption from existence.

Such was the Daitya Prahlāda, the wise and faithful worshipper of Vishnu, of whom you wished to hear; and such was his miraculous power. Whoever listens to the history of Prahlāda is immediately cleansed from his sins: the iniquities that he commits, by night or by day, shall be expiated by once hearing, or once reading, the history of Prahlāda.

(from *Vishnu Purāna*, I:20, trans. by H. H. Wilson, pp. 144-145)

THE LINEAGE OF KINGS

An important feature of the sacred history of the Puranic literature is the tracing of the genealogy of kings back to Manu, the first man, and, through him, back to primeval deities. These genealogies gave kings divine status, but the authors of the *Purānas* were probably not primarily motivated by political considerations. They were depicting their understanding of the universe, where the supernatural was commonplace, miraculous births were ordinary, and the dividing line between the divine and human was always being blurred. Indian kings generally traced their descent either to the sun or the moon, and royalty is usually designated as belonging to the "solar race" or the "lunar race." One of the most famous of the genealogies of kings is given in the *Vishnu Purāna*. The two lines of royalty are traced back to the great deity Brahmā through Manu, whose father was the sun, but whose daughter, Ila, had a child by the son of the deity of the moon. This is obviously not history in any conventional sense, but there is an interweaving of the stories of the gods with the records of actual kings, such as those of the Mauryan dynasty, that gives a new dimension to both gods and men. The selection given here tells of the origin of the lunar race of kings, and the descent of the divine nymph Urvashī to live with the earthly king Purūravas, illustrating the intricate blending of earthly and heavenly scenes. Such "history" is a vital element of the Hindu tradition; the complexities of the lineages may not be known, but the stories themselves, with their sometimes grotesque imagery, have fed the imaginations of countless generations.

Brahmā was the primeval, uncreated cause of all worlds. From the right thumb of Brahmā was born the patriarch Daksha; his daughter was Aditi, who was the mother of the sun. Manu . . . was the son of the celestial luminary. . . . Manu, being desirous of sons, offered a sacrifice for that purpose . . . but the rite being deranged through an irregularity of the ministering priest, a daughter, Ila, was produced. . . . Budha, the son of the deity of the moon, saw and espoused her, and by her a son named Purūravas.

Purūravas was a prince renowned for liberality, devotion, magnificence, and love of truth, and for personal beauty. Urvashī having incurred the imprecation of Mitra and Varuna, determined to take up her abode in the world of mortals; and descending accordingly, beheld Purūravas. As soon as she saw him she forgot all reserve, and disregarding the delights of heaven, became deeply enamoured of the prince. Beholding her infinitely superior to all other females in grace, elegance, symmetry, delicacy, and beauty, Purūravas was equally fascinated by Urvashī: both were inspired by similar sentiments, and mutually feeling that each was every thing to the other, thought no more of any other object. Confiding in his merits, Purūravas addressed the nymph, and said, "Fair creature, I love you; have compassion on me, and return my affection." Urvashī, half averting her face through modesty, replied, "I will do so, if you will observe the conditions I have to propose." "What are they?" inquired the prince; "declare them." "I have two rams," said the nymph, "which I love as children; they must be kept near my bedside, and never suffered to be carried away: you must also take care never to be seen by me undressed; and clarified butter alone must be my food." To these terms the king readily gave assent.

After this, Purūravas and Urvashī dwelt together, sporting amidst the groves and lotus-crowned lakes for sixty-one thousand years. The love of Purūravas for his bride increased every day of its duration; and the affection of Urvashī augmenting equally in fervour, she never called to recollection residence amongst the immortals. Not so with the attendant spirits at the court of Indra; and nymphs, genii, and quiristers, found heaven itself but dull whilst Urvashī was away.

Knowing the agreement that Urvashī had made with the king, Vishwavasu was appointed by the Gandharbas to effect its violation; and he, coming by night to the chamber where they slept, carried off one of the rams. Urvashī was awakened by its cries, and exclaimed, "Ah me! who has stolen one of my children? Had I a husband, this would not have happened! To whom shall I apply for aid?" The Rājā overheard her lamentation, but recollecting that he was undressed, and that Urvashī might see him in that state, did not move from the couch. Then the Gandharbas came and stole the other ram; and Urvashī, hearing it bleat, cried out that a woman had no protector who was the bride of a prince so dastardly as to submit to this outrage. This incensed Purūravas highly, and trusting that the nymph would not see his person, as it was dark, he rose, and took his sword, and pursued the robbers, calling upon them to stop, and receive their punishment. At that moment the Gandharbas caused a flash of brilliant lightning to play upon the chamber, and Urvashī beheld the king undressed: the compact was violated, and the nymph immediately disappeared. The Gandharbas, abandoning the rams, departed to the region of the gods.

Having recovered the animals, the king returned delighted to his couch, but there he beheld no Urvashī; and not finding her any where, he wandered naked over the world, like one insane. At length coming to Kurukshetra, he saw Urvashī sporting with four other nymphs of heaven in a lake beautified with lotuses, and he ran to her, and called her his wife, and wildly implored her to return. "Mighty monarch," said the nymph, "refrain from this extravagance. I am now pregnant: depart at present, and come hither again at the end of a year, when I will deliver to you a son, and remain with you for one night." Purūravas, thus comforted, returned to his capital. Urvashī said to her companions, "This prince is a most excellent mortal: I lived with him long and affectionately united." "It was well done of you," they replied; "he is indeed of comely appearance, and one with whom we could live happily for ever."

When the year had expired, Urvashī and the monarch met at Kurukshetra, and she consigned to him his first-born Āyus; and these annual interviews were repeated, until she had borne to him five sons. She then said to Purūravas, "Through regard for me, all the Gandharbas have expressed their joint purpose to bestow upon my lord their benediction: let him therefore demand a boon." The Rājā replied, "My enemies are all destroyed, my faculties are all entire; I have friends and kindred, armies and treasures: there is nothing which I may not obtain except living in the same region with my Urvashī. My only desire therefore is, to pass my life with her." When he had thus spoken, the Gandharbas brought to Purūravas a vessel with fire, and said to him, "Take this fire, and, according to the precepts of the Veda, divide it into three fires; then fixing your mind upon the idea of living with Urvashī, offer oblations, and you shall surely obtain your wishes." . . . In this way . . . Purūravas obtained a seat in the sphere of the Gandharbas and was no more separated from his beloved. (And his sons reigned in his kingdom, monarchs of the lunar line.)

(from the *Vishnu Purāna*, trans. by H. H. Wilson, pp. 348-50, 394-96)

SACRED GEOGRAPHY

One aspect of the Hindu tradition that helps to account for its great vitality through the centuries is the emphasis from very early times on India (*Bhāratavarsha*) as the holy motherland. There is hardly a river or other natural feature that has not some well-known incident of scripture connected with it. This means that there is always a sense of living in a land known intimately to the gods, of moving among scenes hallowed by deeds that were performed on earth but in which gods were the actors. The Himālayas and the Ganges (*Gangā*) are the most famous of holy places, and are part of the daily heritage of millions who have never seen them, but there are endless sites of scarcely less sanctity. In the passages given here, the holiness of India and the Ganges are especially praised, and it seems certain that this had the effect of giving the people a sense of the unity of India, even though it was divided politically. The numerous pilgrimages to sacred places must have also given the people a knowledge of the geography of the country. The great annual festivals at holy places like Prayāg (Allahabad) brought people from the far corners of India.

Bhārata is therefore the best of the divisions of the world, because it is the land of works: the others are places of enjoyment alone. It is only after many thousand births, and the aggregation of much merit, that living beings are sometimes born in Bhārata as men. The gods themselves exclaim, "Happy are those who are born, even from the condition of gods, as men in Bhārata-varsha, as that is the way to the pleasures of Paradise, or the greater blessing of final liberation. Happy are they who, consigning all the unheeded rewards of their acts to the supreme and eternal Vishnu, obtain existence in that land of works, as their path to him. We know not, when the acts that have obtained us heaven shall have been fully recompensed, where we shall renew corporeal confinement; but we know that those men are fortunate who are born with perfect faculties in Bhārata-varsha.

From the third region of the atmosphere, or seat of Vishnu, proceeds the stream that washes away all sin, the river Gangā, embrowned with the unguents of the nymphs of heaven, who have sported in her waters. Having her source in the nail of the great toe of Vishnu's left foot, Dhruva receives her, and sustains her day and night devoutly on his head; and thence the seven Rishis (Holy men) practise the exercises of austerity in her waters, wreathing their braided locks with her waves. The orb of the moon, encompassed by her accumulated current, derives augmented lustre from her contact. Falling from on high, as she issues from the moon, she alights on the summit of Meru, and thence flows to the four quarters of the earth, for its purification. . . . The offences of any man who bathes in this river are immediately expiated, and unprecedented virtue is engendered. Its waters, offered by sons to their ancestors in faith for three years, yield to the latter rarely attainable gratification. Men of the twice-born orders, who offer sacrifice in this river to the lord of sacrifice, Vishnu, obtain whatever they desire, either here or in heaven. Saints who are purified from all soil by bathing in its waters, and whose minds are intent on Vishnu, acquire thereby final liberation. This sacred stream, heard of, desired, seen, touched, bathed in, or hymned, day by day, sanctifies all beings; and those who, even at a distance of a hundred leagues, exclaim "Gangā, Gangā," atone for the sins committed during three previous lives. The place whence this river proceeds, for the purification of the three worlds, is the third division of the celestial regions, the seat of Vishnu.

(from *Vishnu Purāna*, II:3 and 8, trans. by H. H. Wilson, pp. 178, 228-29)

THE NATURE OF HISTORY

While it is impossible to speak of a "Hindu view of history," since this phrase implies a way of looking at the world that was foreign to Indian thought, there is, however, an understanding of the nature of the historical process that is of fundamental importance for the Hindu tradition. The principal feature of this understanding, which is given an elaborate analysis in the *Purānas*, is that human existence must be seen against a background of an almost unimaginable duration of time. In contrast to other civilizations which have been content to see man's history in terms of thousands of years, Indians—Buddhists and Jains as well as Hindus—spoke of billions of years. But even these figures, which are nearly meaningless in their magnitude, are dwarfed by the concept of cycles of aeons, endlessly renewing themselves, without beginning or end. Time and the historical process are parts of a vast cyclical movement, but not, as in some cyclical versions of history, a simple cycle of birth, growth, death and then rebirth with a repetition of the past. The Hindu model is of concentric circles, moving within each other in a complex series of retrogressive movements. The vastest cycle was "a year of Brahmā," which by some reckonings was 311,040,000 million years long, with Brahmā's life lasting for one hundred of these cycles. This was followed by dissolution of all the worlds—those of men and gods—and then creation once more took place.

Within these cycles there were other cycles which were of more imaginable dimensions, and it is these which are of primary significance for human history. A *kalpa*, or day of Brahmā, was 4,320 million years long, and within this were the smallest cycles, the four *yugas*. The *Krita Yuga*, the golden age, lasted for 1,728,000 years; the *Tretā*, for 1,296,000 years; the *Dvā-para* for 864,000 years; and the *Kali* for 432,000 years. The four ages are calculated as a descending arithmetical progression, marked by progressive physical and spiritual deterioration. Present history is taking place within the *Kali Yuga*, which explains the violence and evil of human history. When this age comes to an end, a new cycle will begin—one of the thousand cycles of *yugas* that make up a day of Brahmā.

Man cannot save the social process from the decay and dissolution that is an inherent part of its structure, but he can save himself from within the process. The point is made, indeed, that one mark of the wickedness of the *Kali Yuga* is that salvation has been made much easier than in the former ages, since men of this age could not be expected to fulfill the rigorous requirements of a better time.

The selection gives a graphic picture of the Kali Age as a time when the bonds of society are broken and virtue perishes from the earth. It is probably partly to be understood as a warning of things to come if men do not follow the teachings of religion, but it can also be read as a description of how the world seemed to a pious man living at a time when India was invaded by foreigners or *Mleccha*, "barbarians," as the Hindus referred to those outside the boundaries of India. Possibly this is a reference to an invasion by the Huns in fifth century or to the raids by the Turks in the tenth century. In any case, the times were so evil that, as the passage indicates, men looked for the coming of Vishnu in a new incarnation to restore the social order. With the coming of Vishnu as Kalki the Kali Age will end, and Krita, the golden age, will begin once more.

MAITREYA.—You have narrated to me, illustrious sage, the creation of the world, the genealogies of the patriarchs, the duration of the great cycles, and the dynasties of princes, in detail. I am now desirous to hear from you an account of the dissolution of the world, the season of total destruction, and that which occurs at the expiration of a Kalpa.

PARĀSHARA.—Hear from me, Maitreya, exactly the circumstances of the end of all things, and the dissolution that occurs either at the expiration of a Kalpa, or that which takes place at the close of the life of Brahmā. A month of mortals is a day and night of the progenitors: a year of mortals is a day and night of the gods. Twice a thousand aggregates of the four ages is a day and night of Brahmā. The four ages are the Krita, Treta, Dwāpara, and Kali; comprehending together twelve thousand years of the gods. There are infinite successions of these four ages, of a similar description, the first of which is always called the Krita, and the last the Kali. In the first, the Krita, is that age which is created by Brahmā; in the last, which is the Kali age, a dissolution of the world occurs. . . .

At that time there will be monarchs, reigning over the earth; kings of churlish spirit, violent temper, and ever addicted to falsehood and wickedness. They will inflict death on women, children, and cows; they will seize upon the property of their subjects; they will be of limited power, and will for the most part rapidly rise and fall; their lives will be short, their desires insatiable, and they will display but little piety. The people of the various countries intermingling with them will follow their example, and the barbarians being powerful in the patronage of the princes, whilst purer tribes are neglected, the people will perish. Wealth and piety will decrease day by day, until the world will be wholly depraved. Then property alone will confer rank; wealth will be the only source of devotion; passion will be the sole bond of union between the sexes; falsehood will be the only means of success in litigation; and women will be objects merely of sensual gratification. Earth will be venerated but for its mineral treasures; the Brahmanical thread will constitute a Brāhman; external types (as the staff and red garb) will be the only distinctions of the several orders of life; dishonesty will be the universal means of subsistence; weakness will be the cause of dependence; menace and presumption will be substituted for learning; liberality will be devotion; simple ablution will be purification; mutual assent will be marriage; fine clothes will be dignity; and water afar off will be esteemed a holy spring. Amidst all castes he who is the strongest will reign over a principality thus vitiated by many faults. The people, unable to bear the heavy burdens imposed upon them by their avaricious sovereigns, will take refuge amongst the valleys of the mountains, and will be glad to feed upon wild honey, herbs, roots, fruits, flowers, and leaves: their only covering will be the bark of trees, and they will be exposed to the cold, and wind, and sun, and rain. No man's life will exceed three and twenty years. Thus in the Kali age shall decay constantly proceed, until the human race approaches its annihilation.

When the practices taught by the Vedas and the institutes of law shall nearly have ceased, and the close of the Kali age shall be nigh, a portion of that divine being who exists of his own spiritual nature in the character of Brahmā, and who is the beginning and the end, and who comprehends all things, shall descend upon earth: he will be born as Kalki in the family of an eminent Brāhman of Sambhala village, endowed with the eight superhuman faculties. By his irresistible might he will destroy all the Mlechchhas and thieves, and all whose minds are devoted to iniquity. He will then reestablish righteousness upon earth; and the minds of those who live at the end of the Kali age shall be awakened, and shall be as pellucid as crystal. The men who are thus changed by virtue of that peculiar time shall be as the seeds of human beings, and shall give birth to a race who shall follow the laws of the Krita age, or age of purity. As it is said; "When the sun and moon, and the lunar asterism Tishya, and the planet Jupiter, are in one mansion, the Krita age shall return."

(from *Vishnu Purāna*, VI:1 and IV:24, selections, in H. H. Wilson, pp. 621 and 482-84)

PART FOUR

THE TRADITION AND
THE PEOPLE'S FAITH

INTRODUCTION

'or lack of a better term, the belief and practices of the
reat bulk of the people of India are often referred to as
Popular Hinduism," and very frequently the implication
1 this usage is that the religion of the masses is debased
nd corrupt, in contrast with the religion of the great
criptural texts. This suggestion is heightened by the use of
higher Hinduism" and "lower Hinduism" to distinguish
·hat seem to be obvious enough differences between the
aith of the ordinary people and that of the seers and
aints. But while it is true that in Hinduism, as in every
·adition, the realization of the ethical and spiritual ideals
· often at variance with the intention of the texts, never-
1eless, the divergence between the "high" culture and the
low" is not as great as it appears from the outside. The
arefied intellectual abstractions of the Vedānta philoso-
hy of Shankara, for example, may seem to have nothing
a common with the faith of the peasant as he worships
is crudely-formed idol beneath a tree, but, as has been
1ggested in the discussion of Vedānta, it is possible to
·ing both beliefs under one systematic statement.

It is a part of the genius of the Hindu tradition that the
·xternal dissimilarities between the levels of faith and
ractice have been transcended. One way in which this

was accomplished was through the recognition of inheren
differences in spiritual and moral capabilities—an accept
ance that found institutional form in the caste system a
well as in the ideal structures of the four classes, the fou
stages of life, and the four ends of man. Then the grea
assumptions of the tradition, a belief in *karma* and th
obligations of *dharma*, further enforced the acceptance o
differing standards of behavior and different levels of spir
itual attainment. But perhaps most important of all in
fluences working for a unity that bound together variou
levels of cultural and religious experience were the songs o
the poet-saints who expressed the values of the great trad
tion in the language of the common people. Thus it is tha
while the practice of the peasant may differ very radicall
from that of the learned man, and while he may not b
able to formulate his religious belief, nevertheless, th
hymns and songs that have been the source of nourishmen
for his spiritual life have brought him into contact wit
the fundamentals of the "high" religion.

The classical Sanskrit in which the literary and philo
sophical works of the Hindu tradition were written wa
the *lingua franca* of the learned and upper classes of Indi
but it was almost certainly never the language of th
people. In North India, the people spoke a variety of Indo
Aryan languages related to it, known as *Prākrits*, meanin
"natural" or "unrefined," and out of these developed th
great languages of modern India, such as Bengali, Marath
and Hindi. In South India, the people spoke Dravidia
languages, which were very different from the Indo-Arya
tongues of North India. The most important of these wer
Tamil and Telugu, and while Sanskrit became the lar
guage of religion in the South, these indigenous language
remained the medium of communication for all ordinar
purposes. To meet the needs of the people who did no
know Sanskrit, it was necessary that there be hymns an
songs written in the ordinary languages, and this need wa
amply fulfilled by a great number of religious poets in bot
North and South.

This new class of literature first made its appearance in South India, partly perhaps because the need was greater, since languages like Tamil were so alien to the Sanskrit, but also partly because there seems to have been a quite well-developed literary tradition among the Tamil-speaking people. The poetry that was written in the common languages gave particular expression to the devotional theism, *bhakti*, which had a long history of development. The ideas expressed in the *bhakti* hymns were not new, but they made more appeal to the hearts of the people than other forms of religion.

It was not only the devotion of *bhakti* religion, however, that found expression in the vernacular hymns. The great stories of the tradition, the mythological background, the exhortations to virtuous conduct, all these were given a place in the songs of the poets, who as agents of the high culture helped to create the pervasive unity of Hinduism.

The movement for expressing religious truth in the language of the people began in the South by at least the seventh century A.D. The time and place are both significant, for they make clear that the impetus towards devotional religion came from within the tradition itself, not, as has sometimes been suggested, from contact with Islam in the twelfth century. The devotional literature in Tamil, as in most of the Indian languages, was centered on either Shiva or Vishnu, with the hymns to Shiva being the earliest and most abundant. Along the western coast, a great succession of poets awakened love for Vishnu among the Marathi-speaking peoples from the thirteenth century on, and by the fifteenth century poets were praising him in the Hindi dialects of North India. In eastern India, both Shiva and Vishnu were the objects of a great literary movement by Bengali poets.

During the centuries when the poet-saints were winning the hearts of the people of India for Vishnu and Shiva, Hindu civilization was threatened by incursions by Islamic peoples from the north-west, the historic route taken by invaders of the country. The first invasions by Muslims date from the eighth century when Arab forces established themselves along the lower reaches of the Indus River, in what is now Pakistan, but this conquest had little effect on the rest of India, as the area was so remote from the main centers of life. The real threat to Hindu culture came from a Turkish people who had accepted Islam and had settled in Afghanistan. Beginning at the end of the tenth century they raided North India, plundering the great temples and carrying away people as slaves, but not attempting to set up kingdoms. At the end of the twelfth century, however, one of the ablest of the Turkish rulers defeated Prithvi Rāj, the last important northern Hindu king, at a great battle in 1192 at Tarain, north of Delhi.

Muhammad Ghori's victory did not mean that India, or even all of North India, came under Muslim rule, for many Hindu rulers survived. Their effective leadership, however, had disappeared. In succeeding centuries various Muslim dynasties ruled from Delhi, which had become the chief city of North India after the defeat of Prithvi Rāj, and eventually they expanded their power throughout the country. In the extreme South, Hindu kingdoms survived up to the sixteenth century, when the last one, Vijayanagar, was finally destroyed. Meanwhile, elsewhere in India, a large number of Muslim generals and military adventurers had carved out kingdoms for themselves whenever the ruler at Delhi had been unable to exert his authority.

In the sixteenth century new Muslim invaders, the people from Central Asia known as the Mughals, captured Delhi, and under four great rulers, Akbar (1556-1605), Jahāngīr (1605-1627), Shāh Jahān (1627-1658), and Aurangzīb (1658-1707), created an imposing empire. At the death of Aurangzīb most of India was under the control of the dynasty, but in fact the Muslim hegemony was nearing its end. Within fifty years western powers were struggling for supremacy, and by the end of the eighteenth century the British had firmly entrenched themselves in Bengal. Thus political power was to pass, not to the followers of the ancient tradition, but to another group, like the Muslims, alien in religion, race, and language.

The effects of Islamic conquest on India were great—the most striking evidence of this is the existence of at least one hundred and thirty million Muslims in the area at the present time—but the long centuries of alien domination had not destroyed either Hindu religion or culture. In all of history, no other civilization has ever been subjected to such a strain and managed to endure so unchanged in fundamentals as did the Hindu. There are many reasons for this, such as the vast Hindu population in comparison with the small number of invaders, the strength of the Hindu class system, and the attitudes of the Muslim rulers themselves, but much credit must be given to the poet-saints who made the immemorial tradition a living reality for the people of India. The songs of Hinduism were the products of a passionate faith that enabled men to live by old standards and old values by giving them relevance in a world that must have seemed hostile and menacing.

CHAPTER XI

IN PRAISE OF SHIVA

~~~~~~~~

Although Shiva was known throughout India in ancien[t]
times—what appears to be his image was found in th[e]
ruins of the Indus Valley civilization—his worship wa[s]
most widespread in the South. While little is known wit[h]
certainty of religious developments there, the Brahmanica[l]
religion from North India, with its great literature an[d]
ritual, had gained a strong position by the early centurie[s]
of the Christian era. In addition, both Buddhism and Jain[-]
ism had many adherents, especially, as the many artisti[c]
remains suggest, among kings and wealthy merchants[.]
Around the seventh century A.D., however, there appear[s]
to have been a great revival of emphasis on the worship o[f]
Shiva and an assertion of the claims of Hinduism agains[t]
Buddhism and Jainism. As a result, the two unorthodo[x]
faiths lost their standing in the South, as they did else[-]
where.

The instruments of this awakening or renewal of Shiv[a]
worship were a series of poet-saints who between the se[v-]
enth and eleventh centuries produced a literature that i[s]
remarkable for both literary beauty and devotional pas[-]
sion. According to tradition there were sixty-three of thes[e]
nāyanārs, or singers of the praises of Shiva, but four o[f]

em have left most of the legacy of poetry and song to
e Tamil-speaking people of India. Of these, Appar
lso known as Tirunāvukkarashu) and Sambandar (or
ānasambandha) lived in the seventh century, Mānik-
vāchakar, who lived in the eighth century, and Sundara-
ūrthi, who lived in the ninth century. Their poems
ntain many references to the legends of Shiva, suggest-
g that the stories themselves were well-known, and
eded only an allusion on the part of the poet to bring
em to the mind of the people.

Paralleling the worship of Shiva, and frequently coalesc-
g with it, was the worship of shakti, which literally
eans "power," the personification of the dynamic, active
rces of the universe. Sometimes Shiva himself was
ought of as these powers—as, for example, when he is
ctured as Lord of the Dance,—but more often shakti is
entified with the consort of Shiva, under the name of
āli or Durgā. The worship of shakti as a goddess under
ese or some other names is widespread not only in the
uth but also in Bengal, and probably can be traced back
very ancient fertility cults. This form of worship, which
a very vital element in Hinduism, was expounded in eso-
ric works known as Tantras. One of the many methods
r gaining salvation advocated by the Tantras is the ritual
e of forbidden, or normally unlawful, acts, such as the
ting of meat, the drinking of liquor, or promiscuous sex-
l intercourse, as a religious rite. One explanation of the
troduction of these elements into worship of Shiva and
s consort is that through them the worshipper asserts the
eness of all life, even those aspects usually considered
clean. Another possible explanation is that poison is
ed to drive out poison. By deliberately engaging in repul-
ve acts the devotee makes clear that he is not depending
on external goodness for his salvation. He does demon-
rates his willingness to break with all conventional life. It
ints out, in any case, the recognition by Hinduism of the
ssibility of every facet of life being used for the great

end of salvation, and it speaks "to many fears and passio
that are deep in the human soul and seem to be part of th
secret of the universe." [1]

A DESCRIPTION OF SHIVA

Descriptions of Shiva's physical appearance, and references
his special attributes, occupy an important place in the dev
tional literature. Associated with him, on the one hand, a
all the dark and terrifying products of the human imaginatie
—skulls, graveyards, demons, blood sacrifices; on the oth
hand, there are many songs in praise of his matchless beaut
Furthermore, he is the deity who has claimed the minds ar
hearts of many of India's greatest intellectual figures, notab
Shankara (see Chapter IX). The explanation, as the followir
passage from the *Mahābhārata* suggests, is that Shiva comp
hends in his purpose all forms of being. For the philosophe
Shiva stands as a symbol for the Absolute; for the simple d
votee, he is present in the form of an image. Shiva's most co
mon symbolic form, the *lingam*, or phallus, can be understoo
as the passage shows, as an indication that all living beings a
marked with a sign that proclaims Shiva's omnipresence. Th
speaker here is a great saint, Upamanyu, whose mother ha
told him of having had the glory of Shiva revealed to her. Th
passage provides a useful background for the poet-saints wh
wrote in praise of Shiva.

My mother said,—Mahādeva is exceedingly difficult to l
known by persons of uncleansed souls. These men are i
capable of bearing him in their hearts or comprehendir
him at all. They cannot retain him in their minds. The
cannot seize him, nor can they obtain a sight of him. Me
of wisdom aver that his forms are many. Many, again, a

[1] Nicol Macnicol, *Indian Theism* (London: 1915), p. 185.

the places in which he resides. Many are the forms of his Grace. . . .

Shiva assumes the forms of Brahmā and Vishnu and the chief of the celestials; of the Rudras, the Ādityas, and the Ashwins; and of those deities that are called Vishwedevas. He assumes the forms also of men and women, of ghosts and spirits and of all aquatic animals. . . . He assumes the forms of tortoises and fishes and conchs. He it is that assumes the forms of those coral sprouts that are used as ornaments by men. Indeed, the illustrious god assumes the forms of all creatures too that live in holes. He assumes the forms of tigers and lions and deer, of wolves and bears and birds, of owls and of jackals as well. He it is that assumes the forms of swans and crows and peacocks, of chameleons and lizards and storks. . . . He it is that assumes the form of Shesha (the snake), who sustains the world on his head. He has snakes for his belt, and his ears are adorned with ear-rings made of snakes. Snakes form also the sacred thread he wears. An elephant skin forms his upper garment. He sometimes laughs and sometimes sings and sometimes dances most beautifully. Surrounded by innumerable spirits and ghosts, he sometimes plays on musical instruments. Diverse again are the instruments upon which he plays, and sweet the sounds they yield. He sometimes wanders (over crematoria), sometimes yawns, sometimes cries, and sometimes causes others to cry. He sometimes assumes the guise of one that is mad, and sometimes of one that is intoxicated, and he sometimes utters words that are exceedingly sweet. He sometimes performs penances and sometimes becomes the deity for whose adoration those penances are undergone. He sometimes makes gifts and sometimes receives those gifts; sometimes disposes himself in Yoga and sometimes becomes the object of the Yoga contemplation of others. He may be seen on the sacrificial platform or in the sacrificial stake; in the midst of the cowpen or in the fire. He may not again be seen there. He may be seen as a boy or as an old man.

He sports with the daughters and the spouses of the Rishis. His hair is long and stands erect. He is perfectly naked, for he has the horizon for his garments. He is endued with terrible eyes. He is fair, he is darkish, he is dark, he is pale, he is of the color of smoke, and he is red. He is possessed of eyes that are large and terrible. He has empty space for his covering and he it is that covers all things.

He is the cause of the continuance and the creation (of the universe). He is the cause of the universe and the cause also of its destruction. He is the Past, the Present, and the Future. He is the parent of all things. Verily, he is the cause of every thing. He is that which is mutable, he is the unmanifest, he is Knowledge; he is Ignorance; he is every act; he is every omission; he is righteousness; and he is unrighteousness. Him, Behold, O Indra, in the image of Mahādeva the indications of both the sexes. That god of gods, Shiva, that cause of both creation and destruction, displays in his form the indications of both the sexes as the one cause of the creation of the universe.

If Maheshwara be not accepted, tell me, if thou hast ever heard of it, who else is there whose sign has been worshipped or is being worshipped by all the deities? He whose sign is always worshipped by Brahman, by Vishnu by thee, O Indra, with all the other deities, is verily the foremost of all adorable deities. Brahman has for his sign the lotus. Vishnu has for his the discus. Indra has for his the thunder-bolt. But the creatures of the world do not bear any of the signs that distinguish these deities. On the other hand, all creatures bear the signs that mark Mahādeva and his spouse, Umā. Hence, all creatures must be regarded as belonging to Maheshwara. All creatures of the feminine sex, have sprung from Umā's nature as their cause, and hence it is they bear the mark of femeninity that distinguishes Umā; while all creatures that are masculine, having sprung from Shiva, bear the masculine mark that distinguishes Shiva. That person who says that there is, in the three worlds with their mobile and immobile creatures, any other cause than the Supreme Lord, and

that which is not marked with the mark of either Mahādeva or his spouse, should be regarded as very wretched.

(from *Mahābhārata*, Anushāsana Parva in P. C. Roy, XII, pp.
62-65, 72-73)

APPAR

According to tradition, Appar (seventh century) was born into
a Hindu family but became a Jain monk. He was reconverted
to Hinduism, however, when having contracted an incurable
disease, he was saved through the prayers of his sister to Shiva.
Because of this, he devoted the rest of his life to singing songs
in praise of Shiva and to preaching about him to the people.
His most illustrious convert is said to have been the king of the
Pallava country, the territory on the south-east coast of India.
This tradition probably indicates the return of the people, notably the kings, from allegiance to Buddhism and Jainism, to
the orthodox tradition.

In the first poem, the worshipper dedicates himself to Shiva,
naming over the parts of the body. The fourth verse is often
recited by the dying or to them. The second poem speaks of
the true freedom that comes to one who serves Shiva as a
servant. The reference in the first poem to Shiva drinking "the
dark sea's bane" recalls the churning of the ocean by Vishnu
(see Chapter X), when among the things churned up was a
poison. To save mankind from being harmed by it, Shiva drank
it. This is understood by his devotees to be a measure of his
love for mankind.

Consecration to Shiva

Head of mine, bow to Him,
　　True Head, skull garlanded,
A skull was His strange begging-bowl,
　　Bow low to Him, my head.

Eyes of mine, gaze on Him
  Who drank the dark sea's bane.
Eight arms He brandishes in dance,
  At Him agaze remain.

Ears of mine, hear His praise,
  Shiva, our flaming king.
Flaming as coral red His form:
  Ears, hear men praises sing.

What kinsmen in that hour
  When life departs, have we?
Who but Kuttālam's dancing lord
  Can then our kinsman be?

How proud shall I be there,
  One of His heavenly host,
At His fair feet who holds the deer,
  How proud will be my boast!

I sought Him and I found.
  Brahmā sought in vain on high.
Vishnu delved vainly underground.
  Him in my soul found I.

Triumph Through Shiva

We are not subject to any; we are not afraid of death;
  We will not suffer in hell; we live in no illusion;
We feel elated; we know no ills; we bend to none;
  It is all one happiness for us; there is no sorrow,
For we have become servants, once for all,
        Of the independent Lord,
And have become one at the beautiful flower-strewn feet
        Of that Lord.

(from Appar, in F. Kingsbury and G. E. Phillips, *Hymns of
the Tamil Saivite Saints*, pp. 53-55, and *Sources of Indian
Tradition*, p. 353)

SAMBANDAR

Sambandar (seventh century) is reputed to have composed ten thousand hymns before he died at the age of sixteen. His marvellous songs are credited with having helped in the reconversion of many Jains and Buddhists to Hinduism. The first hymn given here was supposed to have been written when he was three years old. The second one makes the claim that Shiva is so all-encompassing in his power that he is the source of both good and evil.

Shiva's Glory

The serpent is his ear-stud, he rides the bull, he is
    crowned with the pure white crescent;
He is smeared with the ashes of destroyed forests;
He is decked with a garland of full-blossoming flowers;
When of old his devotees called him, he came to glittering
    Piramapuram,
He bestowed his grace upon all;
He is indeed the thief who has stolen my soul away.

The Lord Is Everything

Thou art error, thou art merit, O Lord of Kūdal Ālavāi!
    Thou art kith and kin, Thou art master!
Thou art the light which shines without a break.
Thou art the inner meaning of all the sacred texts.
Material gain, the joys of love, all that man seeks, Thou
    art.
What can I utter in praise before Thee?

(from Sambandar, in R. C. Majumdar, *The Classical Age*, p. 330, and *Sources of Indian Tradition*, p. 354)

MĀNIKKAVĀCHAKAR

Mānikkavāchakar is said to have been the Prime Minister of
the King of the Pāndya Kingdom (the southern tip of India)
in the eighth century. Becoming a devotee of Shiva, he renounced the world and spent his life seeking to win followers
for him.

In many temples the images of the gods are put to bed at
night, and then awakened in the morning. This poem is a
song sung to awaken Shiva, and admirably expresses the attitude of the pious worshipper towards the image itself. Modern
interpreters frequently argue that the idol is only an aid to
worship, but this is almost certainly a rationalization of what
the devotee genuinely feels as he bows in reverence: for him
the idol is in a very real sense the dwelling place of God. G. U
Pope, whose translation is used here, suggested that for the
poet there was an identity between the god imagined in his
mind and the visible image to which he offered his devotion,
and this seems to be the mood of the poem. "If it is remembered," Pope wrote, "that some of these images have been actually worshipped . . . for a thousand years . . . that each
generation has done them service and lavished gifts upon
them; that they are connected by association with the long line
of saints and sages, and that it is earnestly believed that
(Shiva's) method of gracious manifestation is by, through, and
in, these,—or what we should call sacraments of his perpetual
presence—we shall understand with what profound awe and
enthusiastic affection even images . . . can be beheld by
multitudes of good and excellent people."

A Song to Awaken Shiva

Hail! Being, Source to me of all life's joys! 'Tis dawn;
    upon Thy flower-like feet twin wreaths of blooms we lay
And worship, 'neath the beauteous smile of grace benign
    that from Thy sacred face beams on us. Shiva-Lord,
Who dwell'st in Perun-turrai girt with cool rice-fields,

where 'mid the fertile soil th' expanding lotus blooms!
Thou on Whose lifted banner is the Bull! Master!
  Our mighty Lord! FROM OFF THY COUCH IN GRACE ARISE!

The sun has neared the eastern bound; darkness departs;
  dawn broadens out; and, like that sun, the tenderness
Of Thy blest face's flower uprising shines; and so,
  while bourgeons forth the fragrant flower of Thine eyes'
  beam,
Round the King's dwelling fair hum myriad swarms of bees.
  See, Shiva-Lord, in Perun-turrai's hallowed shrine Who
  dwell'st!
Mountains of bliss, treasures of grace Who com'st to yield!
  O surging Sea! FROM OFF THY COUCH IN GRACE ARISE!

The tender Koel's note is heard; the cocks have crowed;
  the little birds sing out; sound loud the tuneful shells;
Starlights have paled; day's lights upon the eastern hill
  are mustering. In favouring love O show to us
Thy twin feet, anklet-decked, divinely bright;—
  Shiva-Lord, in Perun-turrai's hallowed shrine Who
  dwell'st!
Thee all find hard to know; easy to us Thine own!
  Our mighty Lord! FROM OFF THY COUCH IN GRACE ARISE!

There stand the players on the sweet-voiced lute and lyre;
  there those that utter praises with the Vēdic chaunt;
There those whose hands bear wreaths of flowers entwined;
  there those that bend, that weep, in ecstasy that faint;
There those that clasp above their heads adoring hands;—
  Shiva-Lord, in Perun-turrai's hallowed shrine Who
  dwell'st!
Me too make Thou Thine own, on me sweet grace bestow!
  Our mighty Lord! FROM OFF THY COUCH IN GRACE ARISE!

(from Mānikkavāchakar, in G. U. Pope, *The Tiruvācagam*, pp.
207-09)

SUNDARAMŪRTHI

Known as the "Friend of God," Sundaramūrthi (ninth century) is credited with the performance of many miracles. The great significance attached to particular places associated with Shiva is brought out in these verses from some of his best-known hymns. Another noteworthy feature is the striking metaphor that compares Shiva to a madman; this indicates the ecstatic passion that fills the songs of many of the mystic poets.

Shiva's Dwelling Places

Ah sinful, I have left the path of love and service
    pure!
    Now know I well the meaning of my sickness
      and my pain.
    I will go worship. Fool! how long can I so far
      remain
From Him, my pearl, my diamond rare, the king
    of great Ārūr.

O madman with the moon-crowned hair,
    Thou lord of men, thou fount of grace,
How to forget Thee could I bear?
    My soul hath aye for Thee a place.
Venney-nallūr, in "Grace's shrine"
    South of the stream of Pennai, there
My father, I became all thine;
    How could I now myself forswear?

I roamed, a cur, for many days
    Without a single thought of Thee,
Roamed and grew weary, then such grace
    As none could win Thou gavest me.
Venney-nallūr, in "Grace's shrine"
    Where bamboos fringe the Pennai, there

My Shepherd, I became all thine;
  How could I now myself forswear?

Henceforth for me no birth, no death,
  No creeping age, bull-rider mine.
Sinful and full of lying breath
  Am I, but do Thou mark me Thine.
Venney-nallūr, in "Grace's shrine"
  South of the wooded Pennai, there
My Master, I became all thine;
  How could I now myself forswear?

. . . .

Linked to naught else in life, my mind thinks only
    of Thy holy feet.
  I'm born anew, from this time forth I pass the
    way of birth no more.
In Kodumudi, lord austere, where wise men Thee
    with praises greet,
  Should I forget Thee, my own tongue 'Hail,
    Siva'! crying, would adore.

When will the end draw nigh, sense fade, life
    close, and I the bier ascend?
  This, naught but this, is all my thought. But,
    lord of speech, Thou light on high,
Where the bright streams of Kāviri to Kodumudi
    coolness lend,
  Should I forget Thee, my own tongue to Thee
    would loud 'Hail, Siva' cry.

from Sundaramūrthi, in F. Kingsbury and G. E. Phillips, pp.
5-9)

RĀMAPRASĀD

Rāmaprasād's dates—1718 to 1775—are a reminder that the
great tradition of *bhakti* literature in praise of Shiva had an

unbroken tradition of over a thousand years. One of the great
est of the many poets of Bengal, Rāmaprasād sang hymns in
honor of a number of gods, but those he wrote for Kālī, the
mother goddess, consort of Shiva and embodiment of *shakti*
or power, have a special importance. That Kālī is usually por
trayed as dark and fearsome did not deter the poet from speak
ing of her in tones of great affection.

Shiva's Consort, Kālī

When you lie down,
Think you are doing obeisance to Her;
When you sleep, meditate on the Mother.
When you eat,
Think you are offering oblations to the Mother;
Whatever you hear with the ear is Her sacred incantation
Each one the fifty letters of the alphabet represents Her
    alone.
Rāmaprasād declares in joy:
The Mother pervades everything;
When you move about in the city, you are walking around
    the Mother.

(from Rāmaprasād, in *Sources of Indian Tradition*, pp. 364–
365)

LALLĀ

Kashmir was a center of Shiva worship, and, according to some
traditions, it was from there that devotional Shaivism passed
to the rest of India. Of the many mystics and poets of Kashmir
who sang Shiva's praises, the most famous was a woman, Lallā
who lived in the fourteenth century. One of her poems is given
here. Like many of the *bhakti* poets, she emphasized the need
of inward experience, and the uselessness of formal worship
that did not express true devotion. At the same time, Lallā

makes use of the same metaphysical and theological structure
of thought that one finds in the great intellectual statements,
such as that of Shankara. Her hymns, which are still very popular in Kashmir, illustrate the way in which the teachings of the
high tradition were passed on to the ordinary people.

The Indwelling Lord

I, Lallā, went far in search of Shiva,
  The Omnipresent Lord;
After wandering, I found Him within my own self,
  Abiding in His own Home.

The temples and images that you have fashioned
  Are no better than stone;
The Lord is immeasurable and consists of intelligence;
What is needed to realize him is unified concentration
  Of breath and mind.

Let them blame me or praise me or adore me with flowers;
  I will become neither joyous nor sad,
For I rest in myself and am drunk with the nectar
  Of the Pure Lord.

With the help of the gardeners called Mind and Love,
Plucking the flower called Steady Contemplation,
Offering the water of the flood of the Self's own Bliss,
Worship the Lord with the sacred formula of silence!

(from Lallā, in *Sources of Indian Tradition*, p. 360, revised)

CHAPTER XII

IN PRAISE OF VISHNU
AS KRISHNA AND RĀMA

◈◈◈◈◈◈◈

Although the worship of Vishnu as supreme deity was ver
ancient, the great flowering of the cult dedicated to hir
took place after the eleventh century. Like the worship o
Shiva, the cult found its first wide acceptance in th
South. The poets who sang Vishnu's praise are known o
the Ālvārs, and, along with the Shaivite nāyanārs, the
have provided a rich religious literature. The intellectu
framework for the Vishnu cult was provided by the gre
theologian Rāmānuja, whose philosophical position h
already been noted (Chapter IX). Building on his inte
pretation of the Bhagavad Gītā as a work that exal
Vishnu as God, he argued that the weight of the Ved
tradition supported the worship of a personal deity, n
the abstract Absolute of the followers of Shankara.

Unlike Shiva, Vishnu was usually worshipped under th
form of one of his incarnations, not in his own perso
The best known of these incarnations were Krishna an
Rāma, with Krishna undoubtedly representing an old
strain of religion, since he is the central figure of the Bha
avad Gītā which predates the first Christian centur
When Krishna appears in the Purānas his character, or o
least the legends associated with him, has undergone
considerable change from its portrayal in the Gītā, wit

*the emphasis on his activities as a lover of the milkmaids
and as the performer of mighty deeds. The stories of his
many loves, but especially his love for Radha, are among
the most familiar themes of Indian art, and when his
praises were sung by the poets in the languages of the
people the image frequently used is that of a passionate
woman longing for the embrace of her lover. Thus the
union of man and woman becomes the great symbol for
the devotees of Krishna for the union of the soul with
God.*

*The first of the Ālvārs lived some time between the sixth
century and the ninth, but beyond that their dates cannot
be ascertained with any certainty. There were twelve of
them in all, and they have left four thousand hymns that
are still the basis of devotion for the followers of Vishnu in
the Tamil-speaking areas. In the fifteenth century a spiritual descendant of the Ālvārs, Vallabāchārya (c. 1479-
1531), went to North India and gave new life to the Krishna
cult in Mathura, the ancient homeland of Lord Krishna.
His influence was seen in Sūrdās (sixteenth century), in
Mīrābāi, a Rajput Princess, and above all in Chaitanya
(c. 1485-1533), who was said to have been his son-in-law.
Chaitanya's teaching that the passionate longing that
filled Radha's soul for union with Krishna should be redu-
plicated in the soul of each devotee as he sought for God
placed a great emphasis on emotional experience. Like
many of the mystics, he repudiated caste restrictions, and
welcomed outcastes and Muslims into his movement. This
attitude never became, however, a full-fledged social protest, and as his followers were absorbed into the complex
web of Hindu society their particular religious emphasis
proved attractive to many but they did not in any way
threaten the main structure of religious beliefs and practices.*

*Even before the Krishna movement had spread to the
Hindi and Bengali areas, it had firmly established itself
along the western coast and among the hills in the
Marāthi-speaking areas. The pioneer in the use of the*

Marāthi language for learned purposes was Jnānadeva (c
1275-1296), but the most famous of the Marātha saint
was Tukārām (1598-1649). The particular deity which he
and the Marāthas worshipped was called Vitobhā, and
whether or not he was originally identified with Krishna
by Tukārām's time the Krishna legends and stories had
been transferred to him.

Many of the devotees of Vishnu as Supreme God at
times would praise Krishna and at times his other great
incarnation, Rāma, but most of the poets tended to focus
their worship rather exclusively on one or the other. Rāma,
the Prince and King of Ayodhya, had, like all great kings in
the Indian epics, a semi-divine quality, but in Valmiki's
poem (see Chapter VII) he was not the deity he had become by the eleventh or twelfth century. Probably his dei-
fication was a long process and owed much to the faith of
ordinary people in North India, but it was a South Indian
Rāmānanda, who, early in the fifteenth century, settled at
Benares, the holiest of Hindu cities, and formed the nu-
cleus of a cult devoted to the spreading of his worship
From this center radiated influences that have profoundly
affected the religious life of India ever since.

Two different streams of devotional piety can be traced
to Rāmānanda's circle. One of these drew for inspiration
from Muslim sources as well as Hindu, and, indeed, there
is good reason for supposing that the greatest figure of this
blended movement, Kabīr (c. 1440-1518), came from a
Muslim home. His poetry and that of some of his followers will be noted in the following chapter. The other
stream of bhakti religion coming from Rāmānanda is
purely Hindu in its inspiration. The greatest ornament of
this movement is Tulasīdās (c. 1532-1623), and it would
be difficult to overestimate his significance for the religious and moral life of North India.

The claim made by Sir George Grierson, a great nineteenth century student of Indian literary history, that no
figure except Buddha so profoundly influenced as many
Indians as did Tulasīdās, seems well-founded. Through

his poem, Rāmācharitamanas, "The Lake of the Deeds of
Rāma," the story of Rāma and Sītā has become as famil-
ar to the people of North India as the daily events of their
own lives. Through his poem, rather than through the
great Sanskrit scriptures, the ideas and concepts of Hindu-
sm have permeated the lives of the people. Westerners
used to say that Tulasīdās' work was the Bible of India,
but that comparison is inadequate now, for Tulasīdās' book
s probably better known today in North India than the
Bible is in any country in the West. A selection from this
work is given to suggest something of its nature, but even
more than the other works, its attraction is not translata-
ble. As is the case with all devotional poetry, the believing
hearer or reader brings to it an attitude of reverence, and a
desire to be brought nearer to the deity it exalts, that nei-
her sympathy nor interest alone can really duplicate.

PURANDARADĀSA

Purandaradāsa (1480-1564) was the leading figure in a sect of
Krishna devotees in Karnataka (the modern Mysore). Like
most of the followers of Vishnu, he emphasized that what was
needed for salvation was inward devotion of the heart, not outward ritual observances, nor, as the following poem argues,
mortification of the body and fasting. The translation of the
original title, "Stomach Austerity," indicates the poet's contempt for those whose piety was ostentatious but devoid of
true devotion.

Stomach Austerity

This austerity is really for the sake of the stomach:
This austerity devoid of devotion to the Lord—
This rising at early dawn, this telling, with shivering frame,
Of having bathed in the river,

While all the time the mind is filled with jealousy and
    anger;
This display of large numbers of images, like a bronze shop
    in the bazaar,

This conducting of worship with bright lights, to impress
    others. . . .
All these acts done without the abandonment of the sense
    of "I,"
Without communion with holy souls,
Without belief that everything depends only upon the
    Lord,
Without the vision in silence of the Lord,
All these are austerities practiced merely for livelihood.

(from Purandaradāsa, in *Sources of Indian Tradition*, p. 358)

JNĀNADEVA

Jnānadeva (1275-1296) is said to have written his great work
Jnāneśvari, a commentary on the *Bhagavad Gītā* in Marāthī
at the age of nineteen. There are a number of legends illustrating his saintliness, such as the famous story of how he
caused a water-buffalo to recite the *Vedas* to show a Brāhman
that the rote memorization of the scriptures was a sign neither
of intelligence nor piety.

A Prayer for Grace

Let the Lord of the Universe be pleased with this sacred
literary activity of mine, and being pleased, let him bestow
on me this grace:
May the wicked leave their crookedness,
May they cultivate increasing love for the good;
Let universal friendship reign among all beings,

Let the darkness of evil disappear.
Let the sun of true religion rise in the world,
Let all beings obtain their desires.
May all beings be endowed with happiness,
May they offer ceaseless devotion to the Primeval Being. . . .

(from *Jnāneśvari*, in *Sources of Indian Tradition*, p. 358)

TUKĀRĀM

The songs of Tukārām (1598-1649) are the common property of the Marāthi speaking people of western India, and his influence on their lives has been very great. In most Indian devotional literature it is difficult to see much awareness of social conditions, or to trace any connection of religious movements with political events. The Marāthi saints are an exception to this general rule, for in their poetry one senses a strong note of dissatisfaction with the prevailing social arrangements, and in the seventeenth and eighteenth century their poetry helped bind the Marāthas together in their great struggle against the Mughals. Like many of the leaders of the *bhakti* movement, Tukārām came from a low caste, and this perhaps explains his strong egalitarian emphasis and his insistence that righteous living is the only criterion of worth. His writings are characterized by a passionate plea for moral living and a sense that life imposes almost intolerable burdens on man. Perhaps in no other author of the Indian tradition is there such an overwhelming feeling of the horror of the human condition because of man's accumulation of sin through endless rebirths. Escape from this is found through faith in the grace of Nārāyana, or Vishnu, who bears men's burden without consideration of their merit.

The Burden of the Past

I have been harassed by the world.
I have dwelt in my mother's womb and I must enter the
    gate of the womb eight million times.
I was born a needy beggar and my life is passed under a
    stranger's power.
I am bound fast in the meshes of my past and its fated
    influence continues with me,
It puts forth its power and whirls me along.
My stomach is empty and I am never at rest.
I have no fixed course or home or village.
I have no power, O God, to end my wanderings;
My soul dances about like rice in a frying pan.
Ages have passed in this way and I do not know how many
    more await me.
I cannot end my course, for it begins again;
Only the ending of the world can set me free.
Who will finish this suffering of mine?
Who will take my burden on himself?
Thy name will carry me over the sea of this world,
Thou dost run to help the distressed.
Now run to me, Nārāyana, to me, poor and wretched as I
    am.
Consider neither my merits nor my faults.
Tukārām implores thy mercy.

(from Tukārām in J. N. Fraser and K. B. Marathe, *The Poems
of Tukārām*, pp. 114-15, revised)

MĪRĀBĀĪ

Many stories are told of how the devotion of Mīrābāī (c. 1500-
1550) for Krishna led her to abandon her husband, who was
the ruler of the ancient Rajput state of Mewār, and to pass her

ife in complete dedication to the praise of her God. Once, for
example, her husband, hearing her talking in a closed room to
a man, rushed in with drawn sword to kill her for her unfaith-
fulness. But it was Krishna with her, and he transformed her
into a multitude of forms so that the king could not tell which
one was really his wife. In response to her continual pleading
for a demonstration of his love for her, Krishna finally revealed
himself in his glory and absorbed her soul into his. Her haunt-
ingly lovely songs are still popular in western India and Rajas-
than. In this poem, Giridhar Gopāl is a name of Krishna.

Krishna's Bride

My only Lord is Giridhar Gopāl,
None else, none else, in this false world;
  have forsaken my family and friends,
  sit among saintly souls,
  have lost regard for wordly fame and honor.
My heart swells at the sight of the godly,
t shrinks at the sight of the worldly.
  have watered the creeper of God's love with my own
    tears.
Churning the curds of life, I have taken out the butter,
  and thrown away the rest.
The King, my husband, sent me a cup of poison:
  drank it with pleasure.
The news is now public, everyone knows now
That Mīrābāī has fallen in love with God!
t does not matter now: what was fated to happen, has
  happened.

from Mīrābāī, in *Sources of Indian Tradition*, p. 359, revised)

SŪRDĀS

Sūrdās (c. 1485-1563) was a follower of Vallabācharya, the theologian who provided a systematic basis for the Krishna cult. Sūrdās himself, however, cared little for systematic statements of theology, and his poetry is an intense outpouring of his love for Krishna. All that mattered was to lose oneself in an emotion that in some way duplicated the experience of Krishna. As he put it in a remarkable verse, "Whether through passion, anger, love or friendship, if a man thinks of God constantly, he becomes God." In the following poem, which uses the metaphor of the abandoned dancing of the professional dancing girl, the poet conveys his sense of the futility of life apart from God. Gopāl is a name that recalls Krishna's life as cowherd. Nanda is the name of his foster father.

I have danced my full now, O Gopāl!
With passion and fury for my petticoat,
With lust for physical pleasure as my necklace,
With delusion jingling as my anklets,
With words of abuse as poetry,
With my mind full of false ideas as the big drum,
With my movement in the company of the sinful as the
    steps,
With avarice as the earthen pitcher making sound inside
Beating time in various ways,
I have danced enough.
I have worn illusion as my girdle,
I have put on material craving as the mark on my fore-
    head;
I have endlessly demonstrated my wants, without regard to
    time or place;
O Son of Nanda, put an end to all this nonsense!

(from Sūrdās, as in *Sources of Indian Tradition*, p. 362-63, revised)

CHAITANYA

Chaitanya (c. 1485-1533) was one of the vital forces in the shaping of Bengali religion and literature. Unlike the other mystic poets and preachers, however, he did not leave a large legacy of songs, but only the memory of his extraordinary sense of the presence of the deity with him. He is credited with a number of important statements on the teaching of his sect, and one of them is given here. As a catechism of the Vaishnavite faith, it sums up the teachings of many of the groups. It is cast in the form of a dialogue between Chaitanya and a high official of the Kingdom of Orissa.

Question	Which knowledge is the highest of all?
Answer	There is no knowledge but devotion to Krishna.
Ques.	What is the highest glory in all types of glory?
Ans.	Being reputed to be Krishna's devotee.
Ques.	What is counted wealth among human possessions?
Ans.	He is immensely wealthy who has love for Rādhā-Krishna.
Ques.	What is the heaviest of all sorrows?
Ans.	There is no sorrow except separation from Krishna.
Ques.	Who is considered liberated among those who are liberated?
Ans.	He is the foremost of the liberated who practices devotion to Krishna.
Ques.	Among songs what song is natural to creatures?
Ans.	It is the song whose heart is the love-sports of Rādhā-Krishna.
Ques.	What is the highest good of all creatures?
Ans.	There is none except the society of those who are devoted to Krishna.
Ques.	Whom do creatures incessantly remember?

Ans.   The chief things to be remembered are Krishna'
            name, qualities and sports.
Ques.   Among objects of meditation which should crea
            tures meditate on?
Ans.   The supreme meditation is on the lotus-feet o
            Rādhā-Krishna.
Ques.   Where should creatures live leaving all behind
Ans.   It is the glorious land of Brindāban, where th
            rās-līlā is eternal.
Ques.   What is the best of things to be heard by crea
            tures?
Ans.   The Rādhā-Krishna love sports are a delight t
            the ear.
Ques.   What is chief among the objects of worship?
Ans.   The name of the most adorable couple, Rādhā
            Krishna.

(from *Chaitanya Charitamrita*, II:8, in M. T. Kennedy, *Th
Chaitanya Movement*, pp. 115-16)

TULASĪDĀS

Tulasīdās retold the familiar story of Rāma's exile in the fore
with his wife Sītā and his brother Lakshman and of Sītā's ca
ture by Rāvan, the demon king of Ceylon, but the epic ta
was transformed to exalt Rāma as Supreme Lord. The auth
fulfilled his intention of awakening devotion to Rāma as cr
ator of the Universe and Lord of all life by writing a work tha
combined to a perhaps unique degree the most lofty religio
themes with a story calculated to appeal to the imagination
an unsophisticated audience. This does not mean that Tul
sīdās' work appeals only to the uneducated, since it is in fa
beloved by all classes, but only that it can speak directly to me
and women on all levels of cultural and spiritual attainment.
   As an example of the blending of ethical and religious teac
ing with narrative excitement the famous passage describin
the attempt of the Vulture King, Jatāvu, to prevent the abdu

ion of Sītā by Rāvan, the demon king of Ceylon, is given
ere. In the original story, Rāma had been lured away from
he hermitage by a trick, but in Tulasīdās' version, as Supreme
God he knows perfectly well that the deer he is hunting is a
mirage called up by the demon Rāvan. But the poet's concern
is to inspire his hearers with faith in Rāma's grace, not to tell
a convincing story.

Rāvan angrily seized Sītā and seated her in his chariot. As
he took his way through the air, he was so agitated with
fear that he could scarcely drive. . . . Manifold were the
lamentations that Sītā uttered. "My affectionate and loving lord is far away; who will tell him of my calamity; that
an ass is devouring the oblation intended for the gods!"
At the sound of Sītā's woeful lament every created being,
whether animate or inanimate, was made sad. The vulture-
king, too, heard her piteous cry and recognized the wife of
the glory of Raghu's line, whom the vile demon was carrying away, as it were the famous dun cow that had fallen
into the hands of some savage. "Fear not, Sītā my daughter, I will annihilate this monster." The bird darted forth
in its fury, like a thunderbolt launched against a mountain.
"Stop, you villain, how dare you go on thus and take no
heed of me." . . . The vulture rushed on in a fury, crying: "Hearken Rāvan, to my advice; surrender Sītā and
go home in peace; if not, despite your many arms, it will
turn out thus; Rāma's wrath is like a fierce flame, and your
whole house will be consumed in it like a moth." The warrior demon gave no answer. Then the vulture rushed wildly
on and clutched him by the hair and dragged him from
his chariot so that he fell to the ground. Again, having
sheltered Sītā, the vulture turned and with his beak tore
and rent his body. For nearly half an hour the demon was
in a swoon, then gnashed his teeth with rage and drew his
monstrous sword and cut off Jatāyu's wings. The bird fell
to the ground, calling upon Rāma, and doing marvellous
feats of courage. Then Rāvan again seated Sītā in the
chariot and drove off in haste. Sītā was borne through the

air lamenting, like a frightened fawn in the power of a
huntsman.

Though he tried every kind of threat and blandishment
the monster could not make her yield to him, and at last
after exhausting all his devices he left her under the Asoka
tree. With Rāma's beauteous form impressed upon her
heart, as he appeared when pursuing the mimic deer, Sītā
was incessantly invoking his name, 'O Hari, Hari!' . . .
When Rāma found the hermitage bereft of Sītā, he was
as agitated as any common man. "Alas! Jānaki, my pre-
cious Sītā, so beautiful and amiable, so divinely pious
and devoted! . . . How can I endure this cruelty at your
hands; why do you not at once disclose yourself, my beloved?" In this manner the Lord searched and lamented
like a fond lover distressed by separation. Rāma, who has
no wish unsatisfied, the perfection of bliss, the uncreated
and the everlasting, acted the part of a man. Further on he
saw the vulture-king lying, with his thoughts fixed on the
prints of Rāma's feet.

The compassionate Raghubīr laid his lotus hands upon
his head. At the sight of Rāma's lovely face all his pain was
forgotten, and the vulture recovered himself and spoke as
follows: "Hearken Rāma, remover of life's troubles. My
lord, this is Rāvan's doing; he is the wretch, who has carried off Janak's daughter. He took her away, sire, to the
south, crying as piteously as an osprey. I have kept alive,
my lord, only to see you; now, O most merciful, I would
depart." Said Rāma: "Remain alive, father." He smiled
and answered: "He, by the repetition of whose name at the
hour of death the vilest sinner, as the scriptures declare, attains salvation, has come in bodily form before my eyes:
what need is there, sire, for me to live any longer?" Raghu-
rāi's eyes filled with tears as he replied: "Father, it is your
own good deeds that have saved you. There is nothing in
the world beyond the reach of those who devote their soul
to the good of others. When you pass out of the body, father, ascend to my sphere in heaven. What more can I give
you? your every wish is gratified." Dropping the form of a

vulture, he appeared in all the beauty of Hari, bedecked with jewels and in gorgeous yellow attire, with dark-hued body and four mighty arms, and with his eyes full of tears he chanted this hymn of praise:

"Glory to Rāma of incomparable beauty; the bodiless, the embodied; the veritable source of every bodily element; who with his mighty arrows has broken the might of the arm of the ten-headed demon; the ornament of the earth. With his body dark as a rain-cloud, with his lotus face and his eyes large as the lotus flower, I unceasingly worship Rāma the merciful, the mighty-armed, the dispeller of all life's terrors; of immeasurable strength; without beginning and unborn; the indivisible; the one; beyond the reach of all the senses; the incarnate Govinda; the annihilator of duality; the profound in wisdom; the supporter of the earth; an everlasting delight to the soul of the saints, who practise the spell of Rāma's name. I unceasingly worship Rāma, the friend of the unsensual, the destroyer of lust and every other wickedness. He, whom the scriptures hymn under the name of the passionless Brahm, the all-pervading, the supreme spirit, the unbegotten; to whom the saints attain after infinite study and contemplation, penance and abstraction; he the all-merciful, the all-radiant, the unapproachable, has now become manifest for the delight of the world. He who is at once inaccessible and accessible, like and unlike, the essentially pure, the unfailing comforter, whom ascetics behold only when they have laboriously subdued their mind and senses; even Rāma, the spouse of Lakshmi, who is ever at the command of his servants, though the lord of the three spheres, may he abide in my heart, the terminator of transmigration, whose praises make pure."

After asking the boon of perfect faith, the vulture departed for Hari's sphere. Rāma with his own hands performed his funeral rites with all due ceremony.

The tender-hearted and compassionate Raghunāth, who shows mercy even on the undeserving, bestowed upon a vulture, an unclean flesh-eating bird, such a place in heaven as the greatest ascetics desire. Hearken, then: the most miserable of men are they who abandon Hari and become attached to objects of sense.

(from Tulasīdās, *Rāmacaritamānasa*, III, selections in F. S. Growse, *The Rāmāyana of Tulsīdās*, pp. 345-56)

CHAPTER XIII

THE MEETING OF HINDU
AND MUSLIM DEVOTION

∞∞∞∞∞

As noted in the last chapter, of the two main groups of
poets and religious singers affected by the influence of
Rāmānanda, one, represented by Tulasīdās, remained
wholly within the framework of traditional Hindu orthodoxy; the other, represented by Kabīr, was influenced by
Islam and had a tendency to either move outside orthodoxy or at least to be related to it very loosely.

Although in general the spirit and temper of Islam was
not congenial to any kind of meeting with Hinduism,
there was one aspect of the invaders' faith that provided a
common meeting ground. This was the religious experience of the Sūfīs, the Islamic mystics, who like the followers of Hindu bhakti religion sought salvation through an
ardent and passionate love for God. Often suspect within
Islamic orthodoxy because they spoke of a union with the
Divine that seemed at variance with the insistence on the
majesty and oneness of God, the Sūfīs found India a congenial home for their teachings. Many of the converts
made to Islam in India were attracted by the message of
these mystics and were not, as is sometimes thought, impelled by force or fear. And even when conversion did not
take place, the Sūfī emphasis on experience as over against

doctrine made it possible for them to influence, and be influenced by, the poet-saints of Hinduism.

Three great figures stand out in the religious history of India for their attempt to blend into a living faith concepts and values drawn from both Islam and Hinduism. Kabīr (1440-1518) was the earliest of the three and his influence was probably the most widespread. Nānak (1469-1538), the founder of the Sikh religion, owed much to Kabīr but he had also read the works of the Sūfīs. The third, Dādū (1544-1603), was also influenced by Kabīr, but his teachings had a stamp of originality. All of them would have denied that they were innovators, claiming that they were restoring the true religion which had become corrupted and superstitious, but in fact they introduced very real changes into the religious life of the peoples of North India, where they all had their homes. The surest evidence for this is that they were attacked by the guardians of the orthodox traditions, both Hindu and Muslim, as perverters of the true faith. But while they were innovators, it is also true that they contributed to the strengthening of Hinduism in North India—even Nānak, whose sect was markedly different from Hinduism. If one sought an analogy for their lives in Western religion one would find it not in the Protestant reformers of the fifteenth and sixteenth centuries of Europe, but rather in saints and mystics of the Middle Ages, who brought about internal change in the Church without altering its structure. Like all the great leaders of the bhakti movement, they were "mad after God," and although they might denounce caste and class and all the external things of Hinduism, such as fasts and pilgrimages, their real concern was with singing the praises of God, and getting men to experience his grace and love.

These poets—Kabīr, Nānak and Dādū—differed from the other bhakti singers in one important way: they tended to define God in somewhat abstract terms, and did not call upon him under the form of any of the incarnations of Shiva or Vishnu. This emphasis is probably an indication of Muslim influence, although there is precedent for it within Hinduism itself.

KABĪR

Kabīr (c. 1440-1518) was the first great spokesman for a faith that drew upon both Islamic and Hindu sources, and it is indictative of the esteem in which he was held by the common people, if not by the orthodox, that both religions claimed him as their own. As a child, he was apparently brought up as a Muslim, but he came under the influence of Rāmānanda, the mystic and theologian, and most of his ideas can be accounted for from within the Hindu tradition. His strict monotheism, however, as well as his rejection of caste and his contempt for idol worship, show Muslim influence. It is true that he addresses God as "Rāma" but this is not an incarnation, as is the Rāma of ordinary Hindu thought; it is, rather, a word for God, used, very likely, for lack of a better one, and also because at this time Rāma was assuming many characteristics of a Supreme God.

He wrote many poems in a dialect of Hindi and these have helped to give the language a literary form. Many of his sayings were expressed in brief form, and have the appearance of proverbs or folk wisdom, rather than deliberate compositions —many of them have actually passed into the common language. The first translations given here are by Rabīndranāth Tagore, the most famous of modern Indian poets. They express the warm humanity and deep sense of God's presence that have made Kabīr one of the most beloved of India's many singers of religious songs. Since Tagore's translations are rather more elegant than the originals, a few familiar verses are given in a more literal translation.

Open your eyes of love, and see Him who pervades this world! consider it well, and know that this is your own country.

When you meet the true Guru, He will awaken your
 heart;
He will tell you the secret of love and detachment, and
 then you will know indeed that He transcends this universe.

This world is the City of Truth, its maze of paths enchants
 the heart:
We can reach the goal without crossing the road, such is
 the sport unending.
Where the ring of manifold joys ever dances about Him,
 there is the sport of Eternal Bliss.
When we know this, then all our receiving and renouncing is over;
Thenceforth the heat of having shall never scorch us more.

He is the Ultimate Rest unbounded:
He has spread His form of love throughout all the world.
From that Ray which is Truth, streams of new forms are
 perpetually springing: and He pervades those forms.
All the gardens and groves and bowers are abounding
 with blossom; and the air breaks forth into ripples of
 joy. . . .
There the Eternal Fountain is playing its endless life-
 streams of birth and death.
They call Him Emptiness who is the Truth of Truths, in
 Whom all truths are stored!
There is an endless world, O my Brother! and there is the
 Nameless Being, of whom naught can be said.
Only he knows it who has reached that region: it is other
 than all that is heard and said.
No form, no body, no length, no breadth is seen there:
 how can I tell you that which it is?
He comes to the Path of the Infinite on whom the grace of
 the Lord descends: he is freed from births and deaths
 who attains to Him.
Kabīr says: "It cannot be told by the words of the mouth,
 it cannot be written on paper:

It is like a dumb person who tastes a sweet thing—how
shall it be explained?"

(from Kabīr, in Rabīndranāth Tagore, *Songs of Kabīr*, pp.
118-21)

O Saints, the world has gone mad; if I tell the truth it
comes down upon me to kill me, but believes a lie. I have
seen the devout and the pious who regularly bathe in the
mornings. They forsake God and worship stones; in them
there is no wisdom. . . . They have commenced to worship brass and stones and are proud of their pilgrimages.
They wear garlands, caps and frontal marks and signs on
their arms, and engage in singing the praises of their gods;
they have forsaken God.

The beads are of wood, the gods of stone, the Ganges
and the Jumna are water. Rāma and Krishna are dead.
The four Vedās are fictitious stories.

If by worshipping stones one can find God, I shall worship a mountain: better than these stones (idols) are the
stones of the flour mill with which men grind their corn.

Although I entreat much, even falling at their feet, with
tears in my eyes, the Hindus do not forsake idol-worship
and the Muhammadans are too stiff-necked to hear any
thing.

Kabīr says, I am completely at a loss; Is the holy place
great or the servant of God?

(from Kabīr, in G. H. Westcott, *Kabīr and the Kabīr Panth*,
pp. 58-59)

NĀNAK

Nānak (1469-1538) has an important place in the history of
India as the founder of Sikhism, one of the most remarkable
religious movements of modern times. However, his actual

teachings do not have a direct causal connection with the later growth of this militant sect, which should be understood largely in terms of the historical events of the seventeenth and eighteenth centuries, when the chances of history made the Sikhs bitter enemies of the Muslim rulers. At that time the distinguishing marks of the faith were adopted—the un-cut hair, the turban, the iron bracelet and dagger—and the followers of Nānak were welded into a fighting community.

The transformation of the Sikhs into a group hostile to Islam is one of the ironies of history, for Nānak's message aimed at the reconciliation of Hindus and Muslims through a common faith. This message was not by any means an artificial syncretism of what he considered the best features of both religions, but the influences that came to him from both can be discerned. His emphasis on monotheism, on the oneness and uniqueness of the Creator God, on the necessity of worshipping One who is the source of one's own existence, is Islamic in its inspiration. Also Islamic is his insistence on obedience to God. But his underlying metaphysical structure is Hindu: the belief in *karma* and rebirth, a feeling that ultimately Reality is undifferentiated, that there is no barrier between the human soul and the Absolute. These concepts keep Nānak and Sikhism firmly within the Hindu tradition.

The passage given here is from the *japjī*, the morning prayer, which is said by Sikhs every morning. In the convention of Indian poetry, Nānak included his name in each of the main verses.

Morning Prayer

There is but one God whose name is true, the Creator, devoid of fear and enmity, immortal, unborn, self-existent. The True one was in the beginning; the True One was in the primal age.
The True One is now also, O Nanak; the True One also shall be.

By thinking I cannot obtain a conception *of Him*, even though I think hundreds of thousands of times.

Even though I be silent and keep my attention firmly fixed on Him, I cannot preserve silence.

The hunger of the hungry *for God* subsideth not though they obtain the load of the worlds.

If man should have thousands and hundreds of thousands of devices, even one would not assist him in obtaining God.

How shall *man* become true before God? How shall the veil of falsehood be rent?

By walking, O Nanak, according to the will of the Commander as preordained.

True is the Lord, true is His name; it is uttered with endless love.

People pray and beg, 'Give us, give us'; the Giver giveth His gifts;

Then what can we offer Him whereby His court may be seen?

What words shall we utter with our lips, on hearing which He may love us?

At the ambrosial hour of *morning* meditate on the true Name and God's greatness.

The Kind One will give us a robe of honour, and by His favour we shall reach the gate of salvation.

Nanak, we shall thus know that God is altogether true.

If I knew Him, should I not describe Him? He cannot be described by words.

My Guru hath explained one thing to me—

That there is *but* one Bestower on all living beings; may I not forget Him!

(from Nānak, in M. A. Macauliffe, *The Sikh Religion*, I, pp. 195-96)

DĀDŪ

Dādū (1544-1603) was the third of the important teachers in whose verses and songs can be seen the influence of Islamic doctrines on traditional Hindu thought. Born to a family whose members were probably recent converts to Islam from Hinduism, Dādū broke with Islam as the result of a religious experience. While the inspiration of this experience may have been Hindu, Dādū did not find his spiritual home within Hindu orthodoxy but in the *bhakti* movements that were reinvigorating the religious life of North India at that time. Nor did he make any conscious attempt, as did Nānak, to bridge the gap between the two faiths; rather, he appears to have been repelled by what he saw in both. Turning from both, he urged men to find truth through devotion to the Living God who is known only in the heart. But despite his attacks on Islam and Hinduism, Dādū had been influenced, as was Nānak, by the ethical monotheism of Islam, and, even more than Nānak, his general religious outlook was thoroughly Hindu.

His teachings are contained in a collection of poems known as *Bāni*, or inspired speech. This is revered as scripture by many sects of modern India; one of the most curious of these was a group of warrior ascetics who, in the nineteenth century, served as border guards for Jaipur State.

In many bonds is this wretched soul bound.
Of its own strength it cannot escape. The Beloved is the
    Deliverer.
Dadu is the prisoner, Thou the Master who sets him free.
Keep me no longer in bondage, O gracious Lord.
The heart is soiled within: it is full of clamant desires.
Reveal and take them wholly away: this is Dadu's cry.
All things possess me, O Rama: nothing departs.
What should I hide from Thee? Behold all that is within.

When a mighty thorn is lodged in the mind, how can one
forget Rama?

How am I to endure this pain? Help me, O Lord.

Keep Thou, O Keeper, keep this heart of mine.

There is no other but Thou: the saints bear witness.

Let my mind flee from illusion and the distractions of
sense;

Make it such, O Lord, that it may delight in Thee.

Give me those eyes by which the self beholds the Self.

Grant me, O my Master, this boon, that Dadu may behold
Thee.

Give me each day new devotion, each day a new Name by
which to call Thee;

Give me each day new love. I offer myself in sacrifice.

Lord, give me true contentment, love, devotion, trust;

Give me uprightness, patience, truth: this does Thy servant Dadu beg.

Lord, take away my misgivings, destroy my doubts,

Dispel the error, the suspense, the awful pain. Make me
truly one with Thee. . . .

Dadu stands at the Master's door and cries night and day:

Be gracious, O my Lord: O Master, grant me the vision.

Dadu is athrist for love: O Lord Rama, give me to drink;

Fill the cup before mine eyes, and give life to the dead.

O Allah, Lord of Light, ever fill the cup and give me to
drink;

Make me to drink of Thy love: intoxicate me with it.

Many hast Thou such as I; I have no other such as Thou.

Cast not Dadu away: remain Thou before mine eyes. . . .

What was pleasing to myself have I done, not what Thou
didst please.

Dadu is a sinner: I have beheld my mind within.

Do with me as Thou wilt: I surrender myself to Thee.

If it please Thee, pardon Thy servant; if it please Thee, lay
hold of him and slay him.

Says Dadu: If the Lord should call me to account, then
would he behead and impale me.

If, of His goodness and compassion, He forgives, then do I
live indeed.

(from Dādū, *Bāni*, in W. G. Orr, *A Sixteenth Century Indian
Mystic*, pp. 89-91)

PART FIVE

THE TRADITION AND THE MODERN WORLD

INTRODUCTION

After reaching its maturity, Hindu civilization had to withstand the shock of two alien intrusions. The first of these, already briefly noted in the last section, was the series of invasions by Islamic peoples from Central Asia that ended in the establishment of political control over almost all of India. The second shock was the coming of the European peoples as a part of the great wave of expansion that had begun late in the fifteenth century and, as far as India was concerned, reached its height in the nineteenth century. Of the two, the Islamic period of domination was longer than the European, and left a legacy of a large Islamic population, but the ultimate effects of the Western intrusion have probably been greater. Not only have the political and economic structures of Indian society been far more profoundly modified by the Western impact than they were by the Islamic, but the cultural and religious life of the people has been challenged by the pervasive forces of Western modernity. In this final section, the selections are focused on the nature of these modifications that have taken place in the great tradition and on the ways in which the challenges to the ancient faith were met by its defenders.

The age of European expansion into India began with

the arrival of the Portuguese expedition under Vasco da
Gama in 1498. The ultimate result of this first voyage was
that the Portuguese gained control of the trade between
Asia and Europe, which for centuries had been in the
hands of Muslim traders. The fundamental feature of the
Portuguese maritime empire was the possession of strate-
gically located bases around the rim of the Indian Ocean:
she did not have the resources to expand her power into
the interior. From the great city of Goa, which she built
on the western Indian coast, Portugal ruled her mercantile
empire for over a century until she was challenged by the
arrival in the Eastern seas of other European powers, notably the Dutch and English.

Throughout the seventeenth century the European
trading companies competed with each other for the trade
between the East and Europe, and for concessions from
the Mughal Emperor, but none of them made important
territorial gains in India. The traders were not representatives of national states, even though their companies had
trading monopolies from their different governments, and
their impact on the life of India was minimal until the end
of the first half of the eighteenth century. Then, with the
breakdown of the Mughal Empire after the death of Aurangzīb in 1707, change took place. A many-sided con-
test for power ensued, with the Europeans, particularly the
French and English, fighting each other and also fighting
the rulers of Indian states which had been created from
the wreckage of the Mughal Empire. The English
emerged victorious among the European powers, while the
Marāthas, whose great religious revival was noted in Chapter XII, were the chief Indian contenders for control of
the subcontinent. It was not until 1818 that the English
administered a final defeat to the Marāthas, and even then
they remained one of the groups most hostile to British
rule. This was evidenced to some extent by the support
given to the rebels in the Mutiny of 1857 by a few Marātha princes, but even more at the end of the century by

the vigorous opposition to British rule that arose in the Marāthi-speaking regions of western India.

Up until the beginning of the nineteenth century there is very little indication of the reaction of Indians to the ideas and values of the West, even though there was opportunity at least from the beginning of the fifteenth century for cultural interchange. It was widely believed in the nineteenth century that the *bhakti* movement, with its many very striking resemblances to Christianity, had been influenced through contact with the ancient Christian Church of South India, but few scholars would now feel that this interpretation of the evidence was justified. It seems reasonably clear that the great movements that took place within Hinduism in earlier ages arose from forces long latent within the tradition itself. This is not the case, however, with the changes that took place in the nineteenth century; here the results of Western influence are plain. But while emphasizing this, it is important to avoid the impression that the cultural and religious movements of nineteenth and twentieth century India lack roots in the Hindu tradition. All the essential ideas and values of Hinduism remained, and, while challenged, were not destroyed. Instead, the educated, urban middle-classes—in a sense, a product of westernization, but, in most cases, drawn from the Brāhman class—drew freely upon the West for social and political concepts to meet the problems of the new day. Almost always, however, in their personal style of living and in the intimacy of family life they maintained the traditional values and customs.

The variety of responses made by Indians to the impact of the West can be roughly classified under four headings. One reaction was indifference, and this was not purely negative in its results, for it meant that religious and social movements that had their roots in the Hindu tradition continued to flourish, and the nineteenth century saw a remarkable proliferation of cults and sects of all kinds with Hinduism. But even though these movements seem com-

pletely indigenous in their inspiration, it is quite possible
that they were reflecting a general malaise and unrest
caused by the intrusion of the West. Of the numerous
saints and mystics that had local fame, one achieved a
wider reputation. This was Srī Rāmakrishna, who stands
in direct spiritual succession to the great mystics of an earlier period. Another, and very different response, was the
rejection of the old tradition and the acceptance of everything Western, including Christianity. This attitude was
not very common, but it contributed something to the
general process of growth and change that characterized
the time. More common, and of much greater significance,
was the reaction to the West that was both critical and
selective. Aware of weaknesses within traditional Hindu
society, many sought to reform it by using features of
Western culture, particularly its political arrangements or
its science and technology. This classification covers a very
wide spectrum of opinion, including individuals of the
most antithetical views, such as Rāmmohan Roy, K. C.
Sen, the Tagore family, Vivekānanda, Aurobindo Ghose,
Gokhale, Rānade, and Gāndhi.

The fourth reaction was outright and hostile rejection of
the values and ideas of the Western world. This response
must have been fairly widespread, and even though it did
not receive literary form until late in the nineteenth century, it was an important element in the Mutiny of 1857.
Dayānanda Saraswatī and B. G. Tilak are the most famous names among those who adopted this general attitude, but here again the range of opinion, and degree of
rejection, varied greatly.

Out of the mingling of these reactions came the intellectual ferment of the nineteenth and twentieth centuries
in India. Perhaps nowhere else in the history of the world
can one see a meeting of cultures and traditions comparable to that which took place in India as Western civilization, confident of its own greatness and proud of its
achievements, met the Hindu tradition. Although for a
time uncertain and confused, Hinduism rallied to assert an

equal pride and confidence in its greatness. Something of the fruitfulness—and the losses—of the confrontation of the two cultures is seen in the following selections. More important, they indicate the enduring richness and variety of the Hindu tradition.

As will be seen from the readings, one of the most important features of the period was the reinterpretation that took place of the meaning of many of the values and ideals of the tradition. This was a characteristic both of those who, like Rāmmohan Roy, enthusiastically welcomed the ideas of the West, and of those like Dayānanda who rejected them. The general aim of those who were involved in this process was to show that the ancient scriptures were relevant to the needs of the time, and that they need not be rejected because of the new forces of the West that were at work in Indian life. Like most religious reformers, they were anxious to show they were calling for a return to the pure springs of doctrine and not advocating anything new, but there can be little doubt that in many ways they departed from the original meanings of the texts. Another important aspect of this work of reinterpretation was the claim that the ancient scriptures of India contained all the ideas that were being held up as new and Western. This was partly a necessary defence against the charges of the orthodox that the new forces were utterly alien and should be rejected, but probably more often it sprang from the desire to prove that Indian culture was not inferior to that of the West. But whatever the motivation, this task of reinterpretation was necessary for the renaissance of Hinduism to meet the conditions of the modern world.

CHAPTER XIV

ACCEPTANCE
AND REFORM

〰〰〰〰

One of the most fruitful responses to the impact of the West came from a small group of Hindus who throughout the nineteenth and on into the twentieth century sought, through a blending of the most valuable elements of the Western with the Hindu tradition, to create a purified Hinduism and a reformed social order. As interpreters of the West, they endeavored to convince their fellow countrymen that change did not mean destruction of the old order but rather that it pointed to its renewal. Deeply rooted in their own tradition, they were convinced that the future of Hinduism—and of India—lay in an acceptance of the modern world.

The first figure in this movement is Rāmmohan Roy (1772-1833), one of the most interesting minds produced in modern India. The son of orthodox Hindu parents, he had a brief but successful career as a revenue official in the services of the East India Company, into whose hands the control of Bengal had passed in the last half of the eighteenth century.

From his youth he had been convinced that Hinduism was infected by evils which must be removed, and after his retirement from the Company's service in 1815 he devoted his energy to religious and social reform. The sources of his reforming zeal are not altogether clear, but they appear to have been partly Indian in origin—an acquaintance with the Muslim as well as the Hindu tradition—and partly a knowledge of the main currents of European thought, especially the criticism of orthodox religion associated with Deism. Both these influences are reflected in his criticism of the idol-worship and polytheism that seemed to him to disfigure and corrupt Hinduism. Another of his main concerns, the removal of social disabilities from Indian women, appears to have had its origin in his sensitive reaction to the custom, then common in Bengal, of women burning themselves on their husband's funeral pyres. The method of reform that he adopted was generally adopted by later reformers. Hinduism had been corrupted, he argued, because the people had forgotten the ancient scriptures: if these were appealed to, it would be discovered that the customs and beliefs that disfigured society had no sanctions in the sacred texts. In pursuit of this goal, he translated the Upanishads into English and Bengali, and in his commentaries on them he argued that they spoke of belief in one God, showing no signs of such later developments as idol-worship and caste.

At the same time that he was urging reform on his fellow Hindus, Rāmmohan felt it necessary to defend Hinduism against the attacks that were made on it by a number of Europeans, especially the missionaries who had begun to come to Bengal in increasing numbers. Believing that their denunciations of Hinduism were unfair in that they identified it completely with its worst features, he countered by charging that Christianity in its current forms was as much marred by superstition as was Hinduism. He was fighting, then, on two fronts: against the orthodox Hindus who accused him of injecting Christian ideas into the Upanishads, and against orthodox Christians who thought his interpretation of the Bible had been colored by Hinduism.

Rāmmohan's ideas found institutional expression in the Brāhmo Samāj, an organization he founded in 1828. Like many other religious reformers, he claimed that he was not starting a new sect, but only purifying the old religion. There were elements in Rāmmohan's thought, however, that made it virtually certain that the Brāhmo Samāj would separate itself from the main stream of Hinduism. His rejection of the use of idols in worship, his attachment to eighteenth century rationalism, his disbelief in transmigration, all ran counter to traditional Hinduism. But although the Brāhmo Samāj moved away from Hinduism, it rendered the parent religion great services. Negatively, the Samāj's criticism of existing customs and beliefs forced orthodoxy to examine its own position. More positively, through the leadership taken by 15 members in social reform movements, it helped Hindu society adjust itself to the challenges of the modern world. It also provided its members, many of whom were men of great ability, with an opportunity to discuss the important issues of the time. The Samāj's strength was confined to Bengal, but it was from there that the new currents of thought were radiating in the first half of the nineteenth century.

The leadership of the Brāhmo Samāj passed to Debendranāth Tagore (1817-1905), the son of one of Rāmmohan's closest associates. A man of deep religious feeling, he emphasized, as Rāmmohan had not, the mystical elements of faith. He turned to the Upanishads for his inspiration, finding the ancient texts a record of mystical experience that echoed the teachings of the great European mystics

The third great leader of the Brāhmo Samāj was Keshub Chunder Sen (1838-1884). A far more ardent advocate of social reform than were his predecessors, he vehemently denounced caste distinctions and child marriage. He was also more influenced by evangelical Christianity than they had been, and he made much use of Christian terminology. Yet, despite frequent avowals of his acceptance of the divinity of Christ, he remained a Hindu. He was, indeed, within the great tradition of bhakti religion, and his use of Christian terms is as much an indication of the similarities of bhakti to Christianity as it is of actual influence.

The three figures mentioned above were all from Bengal, but western India also felt the stirring of new patterns of thought and action at this time. Among the Marāthi-speaking peoples particularly, the stimulus provided by the growth of Bombay as a great commercial center led to an attempt to bring the old religion into the modern world. A number of Marātha Brāhmans of great energy and intellectual brilliance argued for the acceptance of the challenge posed by the impact of the West through an abandonment of customs that hindered social progress. The whole complex of social customs that buttressed the Hindu family system—the seclusion of women, the institution of child marriage, the prohibition of widow remarriage—was attacked. In addition they argued that Indians, as a preliminary step towards national reform, should seek more active participation in the new structure of government created by the British.

The representative of this western Indian group chosen for inclusion here is Mahadev Govind Rānade (1842-901). He was one of the many gifted Indians who found a career in the courts of law established by the British in the nineteenth century. A member of the Prārthana Samāj, or Prayer Society, a religious organization closely modeled on the Brāhmo Samāj, Rānade was the most forceful spokesman for social reform in western India. Rānade argued that reform meant the revitalization of Hinduism, not its abandonment, and he and his friends remained more definitely a part of Hindu society than was the case with some of their counterparts in Bengal. Conceivably this was because a tradition of social and religious protest was indigenous to the Marāthi-speaking peoples, and therefore the reformers did not feel constrained to move outside the bounds of the old society. But, all of the men, whether from Bombay or Bengal, who accepted the experience of the West as valuable for India and sought in its light to reform Hindu society, helped to create the temper and mood of modern India.

RĀMMOHAN ROY:
RATIONALIST PROPHET

One of the ways in which Rāmmohan sought to convince hi
fellow Hindus of the corruption of contemporary religion wa
by translating the *Upanishads* into Bengali and English, s
that all might understand the grandeur of the ancient faith
The first selection is from the preface to the translation of th
Isha Upanishad, published in 1816. In it he emphasizes hi
conviction that original Hinduism did not worship idols bu
acknowledged one supreme God. The second selection show
another important aspect of his teaching—a defence of Hir
duism against the attacks of Christian polemicists. Rāmmo
han wanted to make clear that although Hinduism was co
rupted, its basis was a pure rationalism. In this article Rām
mohan wrote under a pseudonym, speaking of himself in th
third person, a device which he frequently adopted.

Original Hinduism

Sorrow and remorse can scarcely fail sooner or later to b
the portion of him, who is conscious of having neglecte
opportunities of rendering benefit to his fellow creature
From considerations like these, it has been that I, (a
though born a *Brahmin*, and instructed in my youth in a
the principles of that sect,) being thoroughly convinced o
the lamentable errors of my countrymen, have been stim
lated to employ every means in my power to improve the
minds, and lead them to the knowledge of a purer syste
of morality. Living constantly amongst *Hindoos* of diffe
ent sects and professions, I have had ample opportunity o
observing the superstitious puerilities into which they hav
been thrown by their self-interested guides; who, in de
ance of the law as well as of common sense, have su
ceeded but too well in conducting them to the temple o
Idolatry; and while they hid from their view the true su

tance of morality, have infused into their simple hearts a
weak attachment for its mere shadow.

For the chief part of the theory and practice of *Hindoo-
ism*, I am sorry to say, is made to consist in the adoption of
a peculiar mode of diet; the least aberration from which,
even though the conduct of the offender may in other
respects be pure and blameless) is not only visited with
the severest censure, but actually punished by exclusion
from the society of his family and friends. In a word, he is
doomed to undergo what is commonly called loss of cast.

On the contrary the rigid observance of this grand article of *Hindoo* faith is considered in so high a light, as to
compensate for every moral defect. Even the most atro-
cious crimes weigh little or nothing in the balance against
the supposed guilt of its violation.

Murder, theft, or perjury, though brought home to the
party by a judicial sentence, so far from inducing loss of
cast, is visited in their society with no peculiar mark of
infamy or disgrace.

A trifling present to the *Brahmin*, commonly called
'rāyaschit, with the performance of a few idle ceremonies,
are held as a sufficient atonement for all those crimes; and
the delinquent is at once freed from all temporal incon-
venience, as well as all dread of future retribution.

My reflections upon these solemn truths have been most
painful for many years. I have never ceased to contemplate
with the strongest feelings of regret, the obstinate adherence of my countrymen to their fatal system of idolatry,
inducing, for the sake of propitiating their supposed Deities, the violation of every humane and social feeling. And
this in various instances; but more especially in the dreadful acts of self-destruction and the immolation of the nearest relations, under the delusion of conforming to sacred
religious rites. I have never ceased, I repeat, to contemplate
these practices with the strongest feelings of regret, and to
view in them the moral debasement of a race who, I cannot help thinking, are capable of better things;—whose
susceptibility, patience and mildness of character render

them worthy of a better destiny. Under these impressions
therefore, I have been impelled to lay before them genuine
translations of parts of their scripture, which inculcate
not only the enlightened worship of one God, but the pur
est principles of morality, accompanied with such notice
as I deemed requisite to oppose the arguments employed
by the *Brahmins,* in defiance of their beloved system. Most
earnestly do I pray, that the whole may sooner or later
prove efficient in producing on the minds of *Hindoos* in
general, a conviction of the rationality of believing in and
adoring the Supreme Being only; together with a complete
perception and practice of that grand and comprehensive
moral principle—*Do unto others as ye would be done by*

(from Rāmmohan Roy, *Translations of the Isa Upanishad,* pp.
ii-v)

A Defence of Hinduism

A few queries written in the Bengali language, having
again issued from the Mission Press, Sreerampore, directed
against the Vedanta system of religion, and a missionary
gentleman having brought these queries to the notice of
our friend, Rammohun Roy, I naturally expected that the
latter would publish a reply.

Disappointed in my expectation, and much hurt at the
stigma thrown upon the religion which I profess, following
the divine guidance of the Vedas and the dictates of pure
reason, I deem it incumbent upon me to defend what I
believe to be true, against so unprovoked an aggression.

In his prefatory lines, the author says, that from reading
the translation of the Vedanta by Rammohun Roy, he un
derstands that the Vedas declare a knowledge of God to
be unattainable by man, and therefore he begs that Ram
mohun Roy will cease to impart their doctrines until he
shall acquire a knowledge of the Deity from some other
religious source.

This author, in common with a great number of his fe

low-believers, not resting contented with the perversion and misrepresentation of the purport of his own Bible, has been zealously endeavouring to misquote the writings, revered by others as sacred authority, for the purpose of exposing them to ridicule. To prove this assertion I quote here the very first passage of the translation of the abridgement of the Vedanta by Rammohun Roy, to which the querist refers in his prefatory lines.—viz.

"The illustrious Vyasa, in his celebrated work, the Ve-"danta, insinuates in the first text, that it is absolutely "necessary for mankind to acquire knowledge respecting "the Supreme Being; but he found from the following pas-"sages of the Vedas that this inquiry is *limited to very* "*narrow bounds.*—Vyasa also, from the result of various "arguments coinciding with the Veda, found that an "*accurate* and *positive* knowledge of the Supreme Being, "is not within the boundary of comprehension, *i.e., what* "and *how* the Supreme Being is, cannot be *definitely* ascer-"tained. He has, therefore, in the second text, *explained* "the Supreme Being by his *effects* and *works*, without "attempting to *define* his *essence*."

Now my readers will plainly perceive in the above quotation, that a perfect knowledge respecting the nature and essence of the Deity is, declared in the Vedanta "to be unattainable:" while a knowledge of his existence through "his effects and works" is duly revealed by the Veda and consequently is zealously studied and imparted by us. We find in the Christian Scriptures declarations to the same purport. Psalm CXLV. "Great is the Lord and greatly to be praised; and his greatness is *unsearchable.*" Job XXVI. 26. God is great and we *know him not: neither* can the number of his years *be searched out.*" Will the author of these queries justify any one in following his example, by suggesting to the missionary gentlemen not to inculcate Christian doctrines; on the ground that the Scriptures declare a knowledge of God and the number of the years of his existence *unsearchable?* I think he will not listen to such a suggestion, and will perhaps say in defence of the

missionaries, that since the real nature of God is said in
Scripture to be unsearchable, they have never attempted
to preach the divine nature and essence. If such be their
defence, how could prejudice completely shut the eyes of
this interrogator against the plain declaration found in the
translation of the Vedanta both in Bengalee and English
which he says he has read: *viz.*, "He (Vyasa) has, there-
"fore, in the second text, explained the Supreme Being by
"his *effects* and *works* without attempting to define his es-
"sence."

In answer to his first query, *i.e.*, "Did one God creat
"the world or not?" I refer him to the next passage and to
a subsequent passage of the same translation of the Vedanta, *viz.*, "He, by whom the birth, existence, and anni-
"hilation of the world is regulated, is the Supreme Being."
"All the Vedas prove nothing but the *unity* of the Supreme Being." "God is indeed one and has *no second*."
These passages will, I hope, be sufficient to convince the
querist, that the doctrine of the *unity* of God is an essential principle of the Vedanta system, however unwelcome
it may be to him, as opposing his favorite notion of three
Gods, or three Persons equally powerful under an *abstract
idea of Godhead*.

Now, unbiassed readers will judge, which of these two
opinions is the more consistent with reason and divine revelation, to wit, the denying of properties to God according
to the human notion of qualities in objects, as done by the
Vedanta; or the equalising of the number of Gods, or persons under a Godhead, with the number of the supposed
principal qualities belonging to the Deity (namely Creation, Redemption, and Sanctification) as practised by the
querist and his fellow-believers, who have provided themselves with a God the Father, for the work of creation,
God the Son, for redemption and a God the Holy Ghost
for sanctification.

I do not wonder, that our religious principles are compared with those of atheists, by one, whose ideas of the
divine nature are so gross, that he can consider God, a

having been born and circumcised, as having grown and been subject to parental authority, as eating and drinking, and even as dying and as having been totally annihilated (though for three days only, the period intervening from the crucifixion of Christ to his resurrection); nor can it give me any concern, if a person, labouring under such extravagant fancies, should, at the same time, insinuate atheism against us, since he must thereby only expose himself to the derision of the discerning public.

As to his sixth and seventh queries, viz. "Do not wicked "actions proceed in this world from the depravity of man- "kind?" 7th. "By what penance can that guilt be expiated, "which men contract by the practice of wickedness?" I beg to observe, that a desire of indulging the appetites and of gratifying the passions is, by nature, common to man with the other animals. But the Vedas, coinciding with the nat- ural desire of social intercourse implanted in the human constitution, as the original cause of sympathy with others, require of men to moderate those appetites and regulate those passions, in a manner calculated to preserve the peace and comfort of society, and secure their future hap- piness; so that mankind may maintain their superiority over the rest of the animal creation, and benefit by one another. For each person to indulge without restraint all the appetites and passions, would be destructive of the harmony of society, which mankind is naturally desirous to preserve. These sentiments are contained in the following passages of the same translation of the Vedanta, viz., "A "command over our passions and over the external senses "of the body, and good acts, are declared by the Veda to "be indispensable in the mind's approximation to God. "They should, therefore, be strictly taken care of, and at- "tended to both previously and subsequently to such ap- "proximation to the Supreme Being."

In the constant internal struggles between this desire of indulgence, always working powerfully upon the mind, and the social inclination, displayed in various modes, ac- cording to the difference of circumstances, of habits, and

of education, some yield often to the passions. In that case
the only means of attaining an ultimate victory over them
is sincere repentance and solemn meditation, which occasion mental disquiet and anxiety forming the punishment
of sin; and which are calculated to prevent future surren-
ders to the passions on similar occasions. The sin which
mankind contracts against God, by the practice of wickedness, is believed by us to be expiated by these penances
and not, as supposed by the querist, by the blood of a son
of man or son of God, who never participated in our
transgressions.

(from Rāmmohan Roy, *The English Works of Raja Rammohan Roy,* pp. 181-87)

DEBENDRANĀTH TAGORE:
MYSTICISM AND REFORM

Although Debendranāth Tagore's personal religious experience
reflected the language and thought of the *Upanishads,* he was
critical of all existing texts as a possible basis of the purified
religion that he sought to establish in the Brāhmo Samāj. In
a remarkable passage in his autobiography, he tells how he
selected those parts of the *Upanishads* which were congenial
to his thought and rejected those that he found distasteful. He
tells how, to his surprise, he discovered that there were not
eleven *Upanishads,* but one hundred and forty seven.

These Upanishads could not meet all our needs; could not
fill our hearts. Then what was to be done now? What
hope was there for us? Where should we seek a refuge for
Brahmaism? It could not be founded on the Vedas, it
could not be founded on the Upanishads. Where was its
foundation to be laid?
    I came to see that the pure heart, filled with the light of
intuitive knowledge,—this was its basis. Brahma reigned in

ıe pure heart alone. The pure, unsophisticated heart was
ıe seat of Brahmaism. We could accept those texts only
f the Upanishads which accorded with that heart. Those
ıyings which disagreed with the heart we could not ac-
ept. These were the relations which were now established
etween ourselves and the Upanishads, the highest of all
ıastras. In the Upanishad itself we read that God is re-
ealed through worship to the heart illumined by an intel-
ect free from all doubt. To the soul of the righteous is
evealed the wisdom of God. The Rishi of old who by
ıeans of contemplation and the grace of wisdom had
een the Perfect Brahma in his own pure heart, records his
xperience in these words: "The pure in spirit, enlight-
ıed by wisdom, sees the holy God by means of worship
ıd meditation."

These words accorded with experience of my own heart,
ence I accepted them.

Again I read in the Upanishads that those who remain
ı their own villages and perform sacrifices and other pre-
cribed rites, after death attain the region of smoke. From
noke they pass into night, from night to the dark fort-
ight, from the dark fortnight to the months of the sum-
ıer solstice, from those months to the region of the
ıthers, from that region to the sky, from the sky to the re-
on of the moon; and having enjoyed the fruit of their
ood actions in that region, they, in order to be born again
ıto this world, fall from the region of the moon into the
cy, from the sky they pass on to the air, from air they
ecome smoke, from smoke they turn into vapour, from
ıpour to cloud, from the clouds they are rained down and
ıring up here as wheat, barley, food-plants, trees, sesame,
ıd pulse. Of those men and women who eat that wheat,
arley, and other food-stuffs they are born here as living
reatures. These appeared to me to be unworthy vain im-
ginings. I could not respond to them. They were not the
anscription of the prompting of my heart.

But my heart assented fully to the following noble say-
ıg of the Upanishad:

After having studied the Vedas in your preceptor's home
and having duly served your spiritual guide, return to you
home; and after marriage read the Vedas in some holy spo
instruct your pupils and pious sons in the way of wisdom
and after having brought the senses under perfect contro
support your life by wealth justly earned without givin
pain to any living creature. He who lives thus for the whol
term of his life upon this earth enters Brahma-loka afte
death, and never returns to this world again; no, never agaiï

He who purifies his soul in this world by the doing o
virtuous deeds in obedience to God's commandments, a
tains to sacred regions upon leaving this earth; and castin
off his animal nature receives a body divine. In that sacre
sphere he obtains a brighter vision of the glory of Go
and having reached higher stages of wisdom, love, and vi
tue he is translated to higher regions. Thus rising high
and higher he progresses from holy to holier spheres, fro
innumerable heavens to other heavens, and returns not t
earth again. In heaven there is no animality, no hunger, n
thirst; there is no desire of women or wealth, neither lus
nor anger, nor greed. There is eternal life, eternal youtl
Thus from one heaven to another, the tides of wisdon
love, virtue, and goodness carry that divine soul onwar
towards everlasting progress, and from his heart the four
of joy perennially springs. . . . By the grace of God th
soul is infinitely progressive. Overcoming sin and sorro
this progressive soul must and will progress onwards an
upwards; it will not decline again upon earth. Sin nev
reigns triumphant in God's holy kingdom. The soul is fir
born in the human body. After death it will assume appr
priate forms, and pass from sphere to sphere in order t
work out the fruits of its merit and demerit, and will n
again return here.

Again, when I saw in the Upanishads that the worshi
of Brahma leads to Nirvâna, my soul was dismayed at th
idea:

Deeds, together with the sentient soul, all become one
Brahma.

f this means that the sentient soul loses its separate con-
:iousness, then this is not the sign of salvation but of ter-
ble extinction. What a vast difference between the eter-
al progress of the soul according to the Brahma Dharma
n the one hand, and this salvation by annihilation on the
ther! This Nirvâna-salvation of the Upanishads did not
nd a place in my heart. This soul instinct with conscious-
ess—whether it dwells in high heaven or upon this lowly
arth—when all its worldly desires become extinct, and
hen the only desire that burns night and day within it is
iat of attaining the Supreme indwelling Soul; when it is
ee from desire and desirous of the Spirit, and when in
iat state it performs all the good works commanded by
{im, serving Him with all humility and patience; then it is
ee from its mortal coil, and crossing to this world's far-
ier shore finds refuge in the bosom of the Eternal
rahma, which is beyond the pale of darkness, radiant
ith wisdom, and anointed with love! There, filled with
ew life, and purified by His grace, it remains eternally
nited in wisdom, love, and joy with that Infinite Wis-
om, Love, and Joy, even as shadow unto light. That mo-
ient lasts for ever. "This Kingdom of Brahma eternally
ines."

This is its final goal, this is its uttermost gain, this is its
highest heaven, this is its supreme bliss.

At these sublime words of the Vedas, the mind is satis-
ed, the soul finds peace, and the heart, filled to the brim
ith joy, says perpetually: "O how great is the freedom
om fear which is attained by the realisation of Brahma!"

Perfect Wisdom,
Vhen will thy truth, ever new and full of light,
hine in the sky of my heart?
hrough the long night I wait
nd watch the eastern horizon,
Vith face upturned and folded hands,

In hope of new happiness, new life, and a new dawn ¢
  day.
What shall I see, what shall I know?
I know not what that joy shall be.
New light within my inmost heart;
By that light, full of great joy I will go singing towards m
  home—
Who would desire to linger in dreary exile?

Now this blessing of His has descended upon my hear
"May your way to Brahma-loka be safe and clear on th
farther side of this world of darkness!" Having receive
this blessing I can feel the eternal Brahma-loka from th
world.

(from D. Tagore, *Autobiography*, pp. 160-66)

KESHUB CHUNDER SEN:
CHRIST AND INDIA

K. C. Sen's emphasis on Christ as the center of his worsh
antagonized many members of the Brāhmo Samāj. But whi
it seemed as if he had moved very close to an acceptance of
Christian position, actually he remained within the Hin
tradition, even in his most extravagant praise of "the Asiat
Christ." He declared that Christ was the unique Son of Go
but his interpretation of the phrase was not that of orthod
Christianity, for he was equally insistent that all religions a
one, although using different symbols to speak of the san
truth. Here he was moving on a level of understanding th
was congenial to many strands of the Hindu tradition, ar
although there are not many Hindus today who would acce
K. C. Sen's position fully, his general emphasis would probab
be approved by a wide range of opinion.

You will find on reflection that the doctrine of divine h
manity is essentially a Hindu doctrine, and the picture

Christ's life and character I have drawn is altogether a picture of ideal Hindu life. Surely, the idea of absorption and
immersion in the Deity is one of those ideas of Vedantic
Hinduism which prevail extensively in India. From the
highest sage to the humblest peasant, millions of men in
his land believe in the pantheistic doctrine of man's identity with the Godhead. The most illiterate man is heard to
say he and the Lord are one! The doctrine of absorption in
the Deity is India's creed, and through this idea, I believe,
India will reach Christ. Will he not fulfil the Indian scripture? I am reminded of the passage in the Gospel in which
he says,—"I am not come to destroy but to fulfil." The
Mosaic dispensation only? Perhaps the Hindu dispensation also. In India he will fulfil the Hindu dispensation.
The earliest scriptures of our nation are full of pantheism,
and though there are errors therein, the truths of pantheism will be fulfilled and perfected in Christ. The religion
of our ancestors was pantheism from the beginning to the
end. But what is Hindu pantheism? Essentially, it is nothing but the identification of all things with God. I do not
mean that you should adopt pantheism as it exists in
Hindu books. Far from it. Oh! there are mischievous errors
and absurd ideas mixed up with it, which you must es-
chew. Christ's pantheism is a pantheism of a loftier and
more perfect type. It is the conscious union of the human
with the Divine Spirit in truth, love and joy. The Hindu
sage realizes this union only during meditation, and he
seeks unconscious absorption in his God, with all his faults
and short-comings about him. His will is not at one with
the will of God. But Christ's communion is active and
righteous; it combines purity of character with devotion.
Hindu pantheism in its worst form is proud, being based
upon the belief that man is God; it is quietism and trance.
Christ's pantheism is the active self-surrender of the will.
It is the union of the obedient, humble and loving son
with the Father. In the midst of activity, Christ was absorbed in God. . . . In Christ you see true pantheism.
And as the basis of early Hinduism is pantheism, you, my

countrymen, cannot help accepting Christ in the spirit [
your national scriptures. You have already seen how in h
outward form and appearance, with his flowing garmen
he is acceptable to you. Now, you find that even the spir
of Christ draws you through your national instincts. Yc
have a national affinity to the invisible as well as to th
visible Christ. Can you deny it?

Behold Christ cometh to us as an Asiatic in race, as
Hindu in faith, as a kinsman and a brother, and he d
mands your heart's affection. Will you not give him yo
affection? He comes to fulfil and perfect that religion [
communion for which India has been panting, as the ha
panteth after the waterbrooks. Yes, after long centuri
shall this communion be perfected through Christ. F
Christ is a true Yogi, and he will surely help us to reali:
our national ideal of a Yogi. India must, therefore, hon
him. You have learnt to give the homage of your hearts
dear Chaitanya, the prophet of Nuddea, and you have al
learnt to give honor unto Guru Nanuk, the prophet of th
Punjab. These are your national prophets, and you do we
to love and revere them. And if you look upon Asia as yo
home, you cannot but regard Christ, too, as one of yo
Eastern prophets, entitled to your loyalty and attachmer
He comes to you after all as a Yogi, full of Hindu devotic
and communion. . . . He gave his Father not only h
soul but also his will. In accepting him, therefore, you a
cept the spirit of a devout Yogi, and a loving Bhakta,—th
fulfilment of your national scriptures and prophets. . .
Young men of India, who are so jealous in the cause
reformation and enlightenment, turn your attention
this point. Believe and remember what Christ has sai
and be ready to receive him. He is coming, and in th
fulness of time he will come to you. He will come to you
self-surrender, as asceticism, as Yoga, as the life of God
man, as obedient and humble sonship. For Christ is not
ing else. The bridegroom cometh. Do not, like the fooli:
virgins, fall asleep. But trim your lamps, put on your be
apparel, and go forth with the enthusiasm and joy whic

all oriental nations display upon such occasions, to receive the bridegroom. Oh! the bridegroom is coming; there is no knowing when he cometh. Let India, beloved India, be decked in all her jewellery,—those "sparkling orient gems," for which this land is famous, so that at the time of the wedding we may find her a really happy and glorious bride. The bridegroom is coming. Let India be ready in due season.

(Keshub Chunder Sen, *Lectures in India*, pp. 257-61)

M. G. RĀNADE: THE NEED
FOR SOCIAL REFORM

Few Hindus have written so critically, yet with such insight, about their tradition as has Rānade. He watched the rise of the revivalist movements, described in the next chapter, with great disquietude. He was convinced that the appeal to the past was based on a false understanding both of the nature of India's tradition and of the modern world. A patriot and a religious man, he believed that if India was to gain its freedom from British domination it would first have to see a radical transformation in the cultural values that determined social life.

It is not the outward form but the inward form, the thought and the idea which determines the outward form, that has to be changed, if real reformation is desired. Now what have been the inward forms or ideas which have been hastening our decline during the past three thousand years? These ideas may be briefly set forth as isolation, submission to outward force or power more than to the voice of the inward conscience, perception of factitious difference between men and men, due to heredity and birth, a passive acquiescence in evil or wrong-doing, and a general indifference to secular well-being, almost bordering upon fatalism. These have been the root ideas of our social system. They have, as their natural result, led to the existing family arrangements, where the woman is entirely subordinated to the man, and the lower castes to the higher castes, to the length of depriving men of their natural respect for humanity. All the evils we seek to combat flow from the prevalence of these ideas. They are mere corollaries to these axiomatic assumptions. They prevent our people from realising that they really are in all conscience neither better nor worse than their fellows, and that the average man, whatever garb he may put on, is the worse for his assuming dignities and powers which do not, in fact, belong to him. As long as these ideas remain operative on our mind we may change our outward forms and institutions, and be none the better for the change. These ideas have produced their results, and we must judge of their good or bad qualities, as St. Paul says, by their fruits. Now that these results have been disastrous nobody disputes or doubts, and the lesson to be drawn for our guidance in the future from this fact is that the current of these ideas must be changed, and in the place of the old worship, we must accustom ourselves and others to worship and reverence new ideals. In place of isolation we must have fraternity, or rather elastic expansiveness. At present it is everybody's ambition to pride himself upon being a member of the smallest community that can be conceived, and the smaller the number of those with whom you can dine or marry or associate, the higher your purity and perfection. The purest person is he who cooks his own food, and does not allow the shadow of his nearest friend to fall upon his cooked food. Every caste and every sect has thus a tendency to split itself into smaller castes and smaller sects in practical life. Even in philosophy, it is a received maxim that knowledge and salvation are only possible for the esoteric few, with whom only is true wisdom and power, and for the rest of mankind, they must be left to grovel in superstition and vice, with only a colouring of so-called religion to make them respectable. Now all this must be changed. The new mould of thought must be cast, as stated above, in fraternity, or all-attracting expansiveness, and cohesion in society. Increase your circle of friends and associates, slowly and cautiously if you will, but the tendency must be to turn our face towards a general recognition of the essential equality between man and man. That will beget sympathy and power. It will strengthen your own hands by the sense that you have numbers with you, and not against you, or, as you foolishly imagine, below you. The next idea which lies at the root of our helplessness is that we were always intended to remain children, to be subject to outside control, and never to rise to the dignity of self-control by making our conscience and our reason the sole guides to our conduct. All our past history has been a terrible witness to the havoc committed by this misconception. We are children, no doubt, but the children of God, and not of man, and the voice of God in us is the only voice to which we are bound to listen. Of course, all of us cannot listen to that voice when we desire it, because from long neglect we have benumbed the faculty of conscience in us. With too many of us, a thing is true or false, righteous or sinful, simply because somebody else has said that it is so. Duties and obligations are duties and obligations, not because we feel them to be so, but because somebody, reputed to be wise, has laid it down to be so. Of course, in small matters of manners and courtesies, this outward dictation is not without its use. But when we abandon ourselves entirely to this helplessness, and depend on others' wills, it is no wonder that we become as helpless as children. Now, the new idea which should take its place is not the idea of rebellious independence and overthrow of all authority, but that of freedom responsible to God alone. Great and wise men in the past or in the present, have a claim on our regards. But they must not come between us and our God—the Divine principle seated within everyone of us, high or low. It is this sense of self-respect, or rather of respect to the God in us, which has to be cultivated, and it is a tender plant which takes years and years to cultivate. But we have the capacity, and we owe it as a duty to ourselves to undertake the task. Reverence all human authority, pay your respects to all prophets and revelations, but subordinate that reverence to the Divine command in us.

(M. G. Rānade, *Religious and Social Reform*, pp. 170-75)

CHAPTER XV

REJECTION

AND REVIVAL

In the last half of the nineteenth century the intellectual movement associated with Rāmmohan Roy and his successors, which was characterized by a general tendency to adapt the Hindu tradition to Western values, met strong opposition. The criticism of Hindu institutions and beliefs which had been engendered by the first contacts with modern Western thought was replaced by a mood of resurgent self-confidence. Instead of an attempt to show that pure Hinduism was basically similar to the highest reaches of Western thought, there was a proud assertion that the Hindu tradition needed no support from the finding of identities, real or fancied, with Christianity. The leaders of this new movement, to which the title "Hindu Renaissance" is sometimes given, did not speak with one voice since they differed widely on the correct interpretation of the traditional values, but the cumulative effect of their teaching was to give Hinduism a self-awareness and a pride in its greatness that had long been lacking.

Three quite distinct groups can be identified within this general movement of rejection of Western values and revival of the Hindu tradition. There were, first of all, those who agreed that Hinduism needed reform, but who believed that this could be achieved through the revival of

*virtues of Hinduism itself, not through those of the West.
Dayānanda Saraswatī (1824-1883), one of the most influential figures in modern Indian history, was one of these.
He found no satisfaction in the religious orthodoxy of his
family, and, following the classic Indian model, set out as a
young man to wander through India seeking truth. After
years of travel to the sacred places he became convinced
that the contemporary leaders of Hinduism were corrupt
and ignorant. The root cause of this condition, he believed, was that the great original scriptures, particularly
the Rig Veda, had been abandoned, and that their place
had been taken by later religious texts, such as the Purānas. For Dayānanda, the Vedas were not only true,
but they contained all truth, including the ideas of modern
science. Above all, they taught a rigorous monotheism,
giving no sanction to either the polytheism or idol-worship
of later Hinduism. From these two basic principles—the
inerrancy of the Vedas and monotheism—he mounted a
wide-ranging criticism of all aspects of contemporary Hinduism. Along with this went a fierce polemic against other
religious groups, particularly Islam and Christianity, as
false alien religions that sought to destroy the Hindu faith.
This was an unfortunate emphasis in the eyes of those who
regarded religious toleration as a primary virtue, but it was
undoubtedly of great importance in giving Hindus a sense
of their own value and significance.*

*Unlike most Indian religious leaders, Dayānanda was
not content with inspiring a personal loyalty in a group of
followers, but sought to create institutions that would embody his ideas. This led to the formation of the Ārya
Samāj, or the society of true Aryan believers. Motivated by
a missionary enthusiasm that paralleled, and was no doubt
to a degree copied from, that of Christian missionaries, the
Ārya Samāj moved into the villages and created a network
of schools and colleges. The movement enjoyed its greatest
success in the Panjāb, where the revival of a strong Hindu
self-consciousness was to later play an important role in
the nationalist struggle.*

Similar to Dayānanda in general temperament and outlook, but differing in that he was primarily a political leader, was Bāl Gangādhar Tilak (1856-1920). At a time when the other leaders of the Indian National Congress, which had been founded in 1885, were committed to a program of social reform on Western lines, Tilak made a bold demand for a nationalism rooted in Indian religious and social values. More than any other individual, he changed the mood of Indian political life from one of co-operation with the British rulers, coupled with an appeal to British good intentions, to one of outright defiance. Central to this achievement was his interpretation of Hinduism as a dynamic social religion, concerned with action in this world. He rejected as a perversion of the truth the widely held view that the scriptures enjoined a life of meditation and world-negation, arguing that in the days of its glory Hinduism had inspired men to deeds of heroic valor in war. The text to which he turned for support for his interpretation was the Bhagavad Gītā, which he read as a rallying call to a life of action. Krishna's advice to the hesitant Arjuna to fight in battle was taken to be a message to the young men of India to fight the British, by violence if necessary, in order to regain political supremacy.

The second religious group that gave Hindus a renewed confidence in their own tradition was associated with Srī Rāmakrishna (1834-1886), the most famous of nineteenth century Indian saints. Rāmakrishna was of a totally different temperament from either Dayānanda or Tilak; he had no concern with either social or political reform, living a life wholly dedicated to religious experience. His influence, nevertheless, was felt throughout the social life of Bengal where he passed his life in continuation of the bhakti tradition so deeply-rooted in that region. He stands, not as a defender of the Hindu way, but as one who accepted the tradition in all its richness and contradictions, and his great achievement was to show to his generation that sainthood, as understood within the Hindu tradition, had a unique value for India's life in the modern world.

*Rāmakrishna was, as he himself once said, "mad fc
God." The central object of his devotion was the goddes
Kālī, but his passionate longing to experience God i
every conceivable way led him to seek communion with a
the deities of Hinduism as well as with Buddha, Chris
and Allah. Through enormous spiritual struggles he a
tained his goals, and thousands flocked to see him, draw
by the tales of his sanctity.*

*The heart of his message, insofar as it can be separate
from the appeal of his personality, was the claim that i
his own personal religious experience he had discovere
that all the deities, Kālī, Christ, or Allah, were identical i
the communion of the mystic. All experience, religious c
otherwise, was seen by him as part of a total unity. Th
led Rāmakrishna to perform acts which must, to moder
Western man, seem bizarre and aberrant, as when he wer
about dressed as a woman to enter more fully into the po
sion enjoyed by Rādha in her communion with Krishn
Coupled with this emphasis on the need for complete al
sorption in life of the deity being worshipped, went a
acceptance of all aspects of the tradition, even those th
to reformers seemed most in need of alteration, includin
the worship of Kālī herself.*

Among the crowds that went to see Rāmakrishna wer
Keshub Chunder Sen (see Chapter XIV), then at th
height of his fame as an orator and preacher, and a youn
college student, Narendra Nāth Datta (1863-1902). Se
found in the saint's presence evidence of the universalit
of religious experience, but young Datta found a maste
He became Rāmakrishna's favorite disciple, and took th
name of Vivekānanda. Although he had been brought u
in the atmosphere of the Brāhmo Samāj, he abandone
the westernized Calcutta life he had known, and became
sannyāsī, or hermit. In 1892 he aroused interest in Ind
by his remarkable personal presence and his oratory, an
the following year he went to Chicago to attend the Pa
liament of Religions. He made an enormous impressio
and for the next three years toured the United States an

England. On his return to India he organized the Rāma-krishna Mission, whose members are devoted to social service and the spread of Rāmakrishna's message.

The ideas that Vivekānanda enunciated are simple enough, but he expressed them in such a way that they caught the imagination of both Indians and Westerners. To the familiar argument that all religions were true, being but different pathways to the same goal, Vivekānanda tended to add the suggestion that Hinduism was the only one of the great religions profound enough to recognize this fact. The insight of Hinduism meant that India had a spiritual secret that sharpened the contrast between her and the materialistic nations of the West. It was true that India could learn from the technology of the West, but, he argued, the West must learn to drink from the fountain of Indian spirituality. This idea became one of the most common clichés on India in relation to the West, and whatever its validity, it played an important part in giving Indians a sense of the worth and value of their Hindu tradition.

A third group that must be distinguished in the general category of those that helped restore Hindu self-confidence were not Indian in origin, but found their home there. The Theosophical Society was founded in New York in 1875, but its significance both as a world and Indian movement came when Mrs. Annie Besant went to India as its leader. With her appearance, Indians for the first time heard Hinduism exalted by a Westerner as superior to Christianity in its ethics and institutional life, including the caste system, so long denounced by both Indians and Westerners as the most malevolent feature of Indian life. This emphasis provided a link with the revivalism of Tilak and Dayānanda as well as with the emotional fervor of Vivekānanda, while the rationalistic formulations of the Theosophical creed made an appeal to a number of intellectuals.

The influences of these three groups flowed together to strengthen the Hindu tradition at the very moment

when it seemed most likely to have been overwhelmed b
the assault of the West. In addition to giving Hindus
new awareness of the greatness of their faith, they empha
sized the spoken languages of the people rather than th
foreign medium, English, which was used by the reform
ers. Another result was a growth of interest in the India
past, and great rulers, notably Ashoka and Sivaji, wer
made to serve as symbols of a unity that India had onc
enjoyed and might know again. There was a revival of in
terest, too, in the study of Sanskrit and of the ancient rel
gious texts. After ages of neglect the great art forms of th
past were studied with enthusiasm, and the wealth o
sculpture, music and dance forms became known to th
common people as well as to scholars.

In every area of life the defence of the Hindu traditio
led to a revitalization of a way of life that a hundred year
before had seemed moribund and marked for destructio
The result is that Hinduism is almost certainly stronge
and more vigorous today than it was at the beginning o
the nineteenth century. In the process of revival man
changes took place, and in many instances what was re
vived was not the same as the ancient forms that wer
imitated—this is true both in art and religion—but th
line of continuity is clear between the great ages of Hindu
ism and the present.

DAYĀNANDA SARASWATĪ:
AGGRESSIVE REFORMER

The selections chosen from Dayānanda's writings illustrat
two important aspects of his influence. The first passage
a summary of his teaching that the Vedas teach a pu
monotheism. The others are examples of his polemical wri
ings directed against the great missionary faiths, Islam an

Christianity, which had won many converts from Hinduism. However illiberal this phase of the Hindu revival may appear, it was a vital element in the emergence of modern India. Christians and Muslims have often charged Hindus with being superstitious; in these passages Dayānanda returns the indictment with interest. One of the unforeseen consequences of this new polemic was to harden the lines of division between Hindus and Muslims, thus making possible the demand in the twentieth century by Muslims for a separate homeland.

God and the Veda

They are atheists and of weak intellect, and continually remain sunk in the depths of misery and pain who do not believe in, know, and commune with Him who is Resplendent, All-glorious, All-Holy, All-knowledge, sustainer of the sun, the earth and other planets, Who pervades all like ether, is the Lord of all and is above all *devatās*. It is by the knowledge and contemplation of God alone that all men attain true happiness.

Q.—There are more gods than one mentioned in the *Vedas*. Do you believe this or not?

A.—No, we do not; as nowhere in all the four *Vedas* there is written anything that could go to show that there are more gods than one. On the other hand, it is clearly said in many places that there is only one God.

Q.—What is meant by the mention of various *devatās* in the *Vedas* then?

A.—Whatsoever or whosoever possesses useful and brilliant qualities is called a *devatā*, as the earth for instance; but it is nowhere said that it is God or is the object of our adoration. Even in the above *mantra* it is said that He, who is the sustainer of all *devatās*, is the adorable God, and is worthy of being sought after. They are greatly mistaken who take the word *devatā* to mean God. He is called *devatā* of *devatās*—greatest of all *devatās*,—because He alone is the author of Creation, Sustenance and Dissolution of the Universe, the Great Judge and Lord of all. . .

Q.—Does God incarnate or not?

A.—No; because it is said in the *Yajur Veda.* "He is un
born" again "He overspreads all. He is pure, is never born
never takes on a human form." It is clear from these quo
tations that God is never born.

Q.—But *Krishna* says in the *Gita.* "Whenever there i
decay of virtue I take on a human form." What is you
answer to this?

A.—Being opposed to the *Veda* it can not be held to b
an authority. Though it is possible that *Krishna,* being ver
virtuous and being extremely anxious to further the caus
of righteousness, might have wished that he would like t
be born again and again at different times to protect th
good and punish the wicked. If such was the case, there i
no harm in it; because 'whatever the good and the grea
possess—their wealth, their bodies, aye even their hearts—
is at the service of humanity.' In spite of all this *Krishn*
could never be God.

Q.—If this be the case, why do people then believe i
the twenty-four incarnations of God?

A.—From want of knowledge of the *Vedas,* from bein
led astray by the sectarians and being themselves unedu
cated, people are involved in ignorance and, therefore, n
wonder, believe in and say such false things. . . . Whoso
ever ponders over the great things that God has done i
this universe, can not but come to the conclusion tha
"There is no one like Him, nor shall ever be." Nor can th
incarnation of God be demonstrated by reason, just as th
saying of a man, that space entered a womb or was put in
closed hand, can never be true, for space being Infinit
and omnipresent can neither go in, nor come out; similarly
God, being Infinite and All-pervading, it can never b
predicated of him that He can go in or come out.

Q.—Does God forgive the sins of His devotees or not

A.—No; for, were He to forgive their sins, His Law o
Justice would be destroyed, and all men would becom
most sinful. Knowing that their sins will be forgiven, the

will become fearless and will be greatly encouraged to commit sins. . . . Therefore it is God's duty to give souls the just fruits of their deeds and not to forgive their sins.

(Dayānanda Saraswatī, *Satyārtha Prakāsh*, pp. 230-231, 249-251)

Against Christianity

The Christians go about preaching "Come, embrace our religion, get your sins forgiven and he saved." All this is untrue, since had Christ possessed the power of having sins remitted, instil faith in others and purifying them, why would he have not freed his disciples from sin, made them faithful and pure. When he could not make those who went about with him pure, faithful and sinless, how could he now that no one knows where he is purify any one? Now disciples of Christ were destitute of as much faith as a grain of mustard seed and it is they that wrote the Bible, how could then such a book be held as an authority. Those who seek happiness should not believe in the works of the faithless, the impure (at heart) and the unrighteous. . . . All such things as one's being possessed of devils, or casting them out, curing of disease without proper medicine and diet are impossible as they are opposed to the dictum of knowledge and contrary to the laws of nature. Only the ignorant people can believe in them. . . .

Are these things any better than the tricks of a wonder-worker or of a juggler of to-day? Where did all these loaves come from (to feed the multitude)? Had Christ possessed such miraculous powers, why would he have hankered after the fruit of a fig tree when he was hungry? Why did he not turn stones, earth and water into loaves and delicious sweets? These things look more like children's play. Many a *Vairagee* and other mendicants defraud guileless, ignorant men of their money by such tricks (as these). . . .

—If the conversion of a man by the offering of his will be the cause of his entering into heaven and his not doing so the cause of his going to hell, it is clear then that no one can take upon himself the sins or virtues of another. And the use of the expression "except ye . . . become as little children," etc., shows that most of the teaching of Christ were opposed to the dictum of knowledge and contrary to the laws of nature, and he also wished that the people should accept them like children without questioning their validity, in other words, accept them with their eyes closed. Plenty of Christians have blind faith like children, otherwise why should they believe in such things as are opposed to reason and science. It is also clear that had not Christ himself been as destitute of knowledge and understanding as a child, he would not have taught others to become as children, since a man always wants to make others like himself.

(Dayānanda Saraswatī, *Satyārtha Prakāsh*, pp. 708-711)

Against Islam

(In the following attack on Islam, Dayānanda used the method of selecting verses from the Koran that seemed to be contrary to common sense and morality.)

"The true religion with God is Islam." Quran, III:17.

—Is God the Lord of the Muslims alone? Did no Divine religion exist at all thirteen hundred years back? It shows that the Quran is not the word of God, but of some bigot. . . .

"And fight for the cause of God against those who fight against you. And kill them wherever ye shall find them, and eject them from whatever place they have ejected you, for civil discord is worse than courage. Fight therefor against them until there be no more civil discord."
(Quran, II:186, 187, 189.)

—Had not such teachings existed in the Quran, the Muslims would not have been so cruel to the non-Muslims. They have greatly sinned by slaughtering the innocent. They hold that one who does not believe in the Muslim religion is an infidel, and that it is better to put the infidels to sword. They have always lived up to their professions in this respect. They have lost their political supremacy while "fighting" for the cause of their God. This religion does indeed teach cruelty toward the non-Muslims. . . . Such things can never be taught by God nor by one of His enlightened votaries, nor could they be found in His Word. They can only be the utterances of an ignorant and selfish man.

Is it not sheer prejudice to call those, who do not profess Islam, infidels? That Being can not be God who teaches that the Muslims should not associate even with good people of other faiths, while they may take even the wicked Muslims for their friends. One is therefore fully justified in inferring that this Quran, its God and the Muslims are embodiments of bigotry and ignorance. Now reader mark! How clever Mohammad is! He makes his God say in this verse that God will love those who follow Mohammad and even their sins will be forgiven. This shows that the heart of Mohammad was not pure. It appears that Mohammad (made or) had the Quran made in order to serve his selfish interests.

(Dayānanda Saraswatī, *Satyārtha Prākāsh*, pp. 754, 758, 759)

B. G. TILAK:

THE CALL TO ACTION

The leaders of the Hindu Renaissance attached great importance to the interpretation of the great scriptural texts. The application of the methods of modern scholarship to the texts was first made by European and American scholars, and while Indians were quick to adopt the techniques, many objected to the interpretations given by the Western scholars. B. G. Tilak found particularly objectionable the assumption made by Western scholars that the scriptures provided no basis for social action. If this were so, then inspiration would have to come from the West, and, more specifically, from Christianity. In the *Bhagavad Gītā* Tilak found a gospel of life-affirmation and a call to action that was admirably suited to the needs of that time. That this interpretation is, in fact, true to the *Gītā* would be denied by many scholars, including many Indians, but Tilak's vigorous argument was welcomed by those who wanted to engage in social action without having to acknowledge a debt to Western idealism.

Let me begin by telling you what induced me to take up the study of *Bhagavad Gita*. When I was quite a boy, I was often told by my elders that strictly religious and really philosophic life was incompatible with the hum-drum life of every day. If one was ambitious enough to try to attain Moksha, the highest goal a person could attain, then he must divest himself of all earthly desires and renounce this world. One could not serve two masters, the world and God. I understood this to mean that if one would lead a life which was the life worth living, according to the religion in which I was born, then the sooner the world was given up the better. This set me thinking. The question that I formulated for myself to be solved was: Does my religion want me to give up this world and renounce it before I attempt to, or in order to be able to, attain the perfection of manhood? In my boy-hood I was also told that *Bhagavad Gita* was universally acknowledged to be a book containing all the principles and philosophy of the Hindu religion, and I thought if this be so I should find an answer in this book to my query; and thus began my study of the *Bhagavad Gita*. I approached the book with a mind prepossessed by no previous ideas about any philosophy, and had no theory of my own for which I sought any support in the *Gita*. A person whose mind is prepossessed by certain ideas reads the book with a prejudiced mind, for instance, when a Christian reads it he does not want to know what the *Gita* says but wants to find out if there are any principles in the *Gita* which he has already met within Bible, and if so the conclusion he rushes to is that the *Gita* was copied from the Bible. It have dealt with this topic in my book *Gita Rahasya* and I need hardly say much about it here, but what I want to emphasise is this, that when you want to read and understand a book, especially a great work like the *Gita*—you must approach it with an unprejudiced and unprepossessed mind. To do this, I know is one of the most difficult things. Those who profess to do it may have a lurking thought or prejudice in their minds which vitiates the reading of the book to some extent. However I am describing to you the frame of mind one must get into if one wants to get at the truth and however difficult it be, it has to be done. The next thing one has to do is to take into consideration the time and the circumstances in which the book was written and the purpose for which the book was written. In short the book must not be read devoid of its context. This is especially true about a book like *Bhagavad Gita*. Various commentators have put as many interpretations on the book, and surely the writer or composer could not have written or composed the book for so many interpretations being put on it. He must have but one meaning and one purpose running through the book, and that I have tried to find out. I believe I have succeeded in it, because having no theory of mine for which I sought any support from the book so universally respected, I had no reason to twist the text to suit my theory. There has not been a commentator of the *Gita* who did not advocate a pet theory of his own and has not tried to support the same by showing that the *Bhagavad Gita* lent him support. The conclusion I have come to is that the *Gita* advocates the performance of action in this world even after the actor has achieved the highest union with the supreme Deity by Gnana (knowledge) or Bhakti

(Devotion). This action must be done to keep the world going by the right path of evolution which the Creator has destined the world to follow. In order that the action may not bind the actor it must be done with the aim of helping his purpose, and without any attachment to the coming result. This I hold is the lesson of the *Gita*. Gnanayoga there is, yes. Bhaktiyoga there is, yes. Who says not? But they are both subservient to the Karmayoga preached in the *Gita*. If the *Gita* was preached to desponding Arjuna to make him ready for the fight—for the action—how can it be said that the ultimate lesson of the great book is Bhakti or Gnana alone? In fact there is blending of all these Yogas in the *Gita* and as the air is not Oxygen or Hydrogen or any other gas alone but a composition of all these in a certain proportion so in the *Gita* all these Yogas blended into one.

I differ from almost all commentators when I say that the *Gita* enjoins action even after the perfection in Gnana and Bhakti is attained and the Deity is reached through these mediums. Now there is a fundamental unity underlying the Logos (Ishvara), man, and world. The world is in existence because the Logos has willed it so. It is His Will that holds it together. Man strives to gain union with God; and when this union is achieved the individual Will merges in the mighty Universal Will. When this is achieved will the individual say; "I shall do no action, and I shall not help the world"—the world which is because the Will with which he has sought union has willed it to be so? It does not stand to reason. It is not I who say so; the *Gita* says so. Shri Krishna himself says that there is nothing in all the three worlds that He need acquire, and *still* he acts. He acts because if He did not, the world will be ruined. If man seeks unity with the Deity, he must necessarily seek unity with the interests of the world also, and work for it. If he does not, then the unity is not perfect, because there is union between two elements out of the 3 (man and Deity) and the third (the world) is left out. I have thus solved the question for myself and I hold that serving the world, and thus serving His Will, is the surest way of Salvation, and this way can be followed by remaining *in* the world and not going away from it.

(B. G. Tilak, *His Writings and Speeches*, pp. 258-63)

SRĪ RĀMAKRISHNA: SAINTHOOD AND THE MODERN WORLD

Rāmakrishna's teachings, such as the presence of God in all human experience, are deeply rooted in the Hindu tradition. His great achievement, which was not the product of conscious intention but of his own personality, was to make the life of an Indian saint relevant to the people of nineteenth and twentieth century India. His sayings, in the form of dialogues with his disciples and visitors, were preserved by his followers, and this selection is taken from the collection made by one of them. The brief descriptive passage indicates the effect the saint had on many of his visitors.

(i)

The disciple asked: "Bhagavân, one may believe that God is with form, but surely He is not in the earthen images that are worshipped?" Srî Râmakrishna replied: "My dear sir, why do you say earthen images? The image of the Divine Being is made of the spirit." The disciple could not understand the meaning of this, but answered: "Yet should it not be one's duty to make clear to those who worship images that God is not the same as the images and that at the time of worship they should think of God Himself and not of the image made of clay?" The Bhagavân said: "The Lord of the universe teaches mankind. He who has made the sun and moon, men and brutes; He who has created things for them to live upon, parents to tend and rear them; He who has done so many things will surely do something to bring them to the light. The Lord dwells in the temple of the human body. He knows our innermost thoughts. If there is anything wrong in image worship, does He not know that all worship is meant for Him? He will be pleased to accept it knowing that it is for Him. Why should you worry yourself about things which are beyond your reach? Try to realize God and love Him. This is your first duty.

"You speak of images made of clay. Well, there often comes a necessity for worshipping such images and symbols. In Vedânta it is said, the absolute Existence-Intelligence-Bliss pervades the universe and manifests itself through all forms. What harm is done by worshipping the Absolute through images and symbols? We see little girls with their dolls. How long do they play with them? So long as they are not married. After marriage they put away those dolls. Similarly, one needs images and symbols so long as God is not realized in His true form. It is God Himself who has provided these various forms of worship. The Master of the universe has done all this to suit different men in different stages of spiritual growth and knowledge. The mother so arranges the food for her children that each one gets what is best for him. Suppose a mother has five children with one fish to cook for all. She will make different dishes of it that she may give to each just what suits him,—the rich *pilau* for one, soup for another, fried fish for a third, fish with sour tamarind for a fourth, and so on, exactly according to the power of digestion of each. Do you now understand?"

The disciple replied: "Yes, Bhagavân, now I do. But, Revered Sir, how can one fix one's mind on God?"

Srî Râmakrishna: To that end one must always sing forth the Holy Name of God and talk without ceasing of His glory and attributes. Then one must seek the company of holy men. One must from time to time visit the Lord's devotees or those who have given up attachment to the things of the world for the sake of the Lord. It is, however, difficult to fix one's mind upon God in the midst of worldly cares and anxieties; hence the necessity of going into solitude now and again with a view to meditating on Him.

The disciple asked: "Bhagavân, is it possible to see God?"

Srî Râmakrishna: Certainly. The following are some of the means of seeing God: Going from time to time into solitude; singing forth His name and His attributes; discrimination.

The disciple: Bhagavân, what state of mind leads to God-vision?

Srî Râmakrishna: Cry to God with a yearning heart and then you will see Him. People will shed a jugful of tears for the sake of their wife or children; they will be carried away by a stream of their own tears for the sake of money; but who sheds a tear for God? Cry for Him, not for show, but with a longing and yearning heart. The rosy light of the dawn comes before the rising sun; likewise a longing and yearning heart is the sign of God-vision that comes after.

Extreme longing is the surest way to God-vision. Through extreme longing the mind remains fixed on the Supreme Being. One should have faith like that of an innocent child and such longing as a child has when it wants to see its mother.

(ii)
SOME INCIDENTS IN THE LIFE OF SRÎ RÂMA-KRISHNA (AS TOLD BY HIMSELF)

I practised austerities for a long time. I cared very little for the body. My longing for the Divine Mother was so great that I would not eat or sleep. I would lie on the bare ground, placing my head on a lump of earth, and cry out loudly: "Mother, Mother, why dost Thou not come to me?" I did not know how the days and nights passed away. I used to have ecstasy all the time. I saw my disciples as my own people, like children and relations, long before they came to me. I used to cry before my Mother, saying: "O Mother! I am dying for my beloved ones (Bhaktas); do Thou bring them to me as quickly as possible."

When I reached the state of continuous ecstasy, I gave up all external forms of worship; I could no longer perform them. Then I prayed to my Divine Mother: "Mother, who will now take care of me? I have no power to take care of myself. I like to hear Thy name and feed Thy Bhaktas and help the poor. Who will make it possible for me to do these things? Send me someone who will be able to do these for me." As the answer to this prayer came Mathura Bâbu, who served me so long and with such intense devotion and faith! . . .

(iii)

In referring to the time of joyous illumination which immediately followed His enlightenment, He exclaimed:

What a state it was! The slightest cause aroused in me the thought of the Divine Ideal. One day I went to the Zoological Garden in Calcutta. I desired especially to see the lion, but when I beheld him, I lost all sense-consciousness and went into Samâdhi. Those who were with me wished to show me the other animals, but I replied: "I saw everything when I saw the king of beasts. Take me home." The strength of the lion had aroused in me the consciousness of the omnipotence of God and had lifted me above the world of phenomena. . . .

(iv)

Bhagavân Srî Râmakrishna, again losing all sense-consciousness, entered into God-consciousness and remained motionless like a carven image. Seeing this wonderful sight, some of the devotees shed tears of joy and happiness while others kneeled and began to pray to the Bhagavân. Each one fixed his eyes upon Srî Râmakrishna and, according to the innermost feeling of his heart, realized his Ideal in Him. Some saw in Him the Ideal Devotee, while others recognized the Divine Incarnation in a human form. Mahima, with tears of joy in his eyes chanted: "Behold, behold, the embodiment of Divine Love!" And after a few minutes, as if catching a glimpse of the Absolute Brahman in Râmakrishna, he exclaimed: "Infinite Existence, Intelligence and Love, beyond Unity and Diversity!"

After remaining in this state for a long time, Bhagavân Râmakrishna came down once more on the human plane and said: God incarnates Himself in a human form. It is true that He dwells everywhere, in all living creatures, but the desires of the human soul cannot be fulfilled except by an *Avatâra* or Divine Incarnation. The human being longs to see Him, touch Him, be with Him and enjoy His Divine company. In order to fulfill such desires, the Incarnation of God is necessary.

(*The Gospel of Râmakrishna*, pp. 62-65, 70-71, 206-09, 408-409)

VIVEKÂNANDA: HINDU PROPHET
TO THE WESTERN WORLD

The following selection differs from others in this book in that it is addressed to those who stand outside the Hindu tradition, not to those who accept in some form its presuppositions. This in itself indicates the magnitude of the change that was at work in India at the end of the nineteenth century. Hinduism had reached a stage of self-awareness that made it possible for Vivekânanda to declare to America and Europe that India had spiritual resources to cure the maladies of the West. As the editor of Vivekânanda's papers remarked, when this speech was given at the Parliament of Religions in 1893, "Hinduism had been created." The image of Hinduism that Vivekânanda presented to the world—a religion tolerant of all faiths, profoundly spiritual, yet utterly simple in its creed—was widely accepted. It became, in effect, the stereotype that vied with the earlier image of Hinduism as corrupt and superstitious.

. . . . The Hindu believes that he is a spirit. Him the sword cannot pierce—him the fire cannot burn—him the water cannot melt—him the air cannot dry. The Hindu believes that every soul is a circle whose circumference is nowhere, but whose centre is located in the body, and that death means the change of this centre from body to body. Nor is the soul bound by the conditions of matter. In its very essence, it is free, unbounded, holy, pure and perfect. But somehow or other it finds itself tied down to matter, and thinks of itself as matter.

Why should the free, perfect and pure being be thus under the thraldom of matter, is the next question. How can the perfect soul be deluded into the belief that it is imperfect? . . . . The Hindu is sincere. He does not want to take shelter under sophistry. He is brave enough to face the question in a manly fashion; and his answer is, "I do not know. I do not know how the perfect being, the soul, came to think of itself as imperfect, as joined to and conditioned by matter." . . .

The human soul is eternal and immortal, perfect and infinite, and death means only a change of centre from one body to another. The present is determined by our past actions, and the future by the present. The soul will go on evolving up or reverting back from birth to birth and death to death. But here is another question: is man a tiny boat in a tempest, raised one moment on the foamy crest of a billow and dashed down into a yawning chasm the next, rolling to and fro at the mercy of good and bad actions—a powerless, helpless wreck in an ever-raging, ever-rushing, uncompromising current of cause and effect; a little moth placed under the wheel of causation, which rolls on crushing everything in its way, and waits not for the widow's tears or the orphan's cry? The heart sinks at the idea, yet this is the law of Nature. Is there no hope? Is there no escape?—was the cry that went up from the bottom of the heart of despair. It reached the throne of mercy, and words of hope and consolation came down and inspired a Vedic sage, and he stood up before the world and in trumpet voice proclaimed the glad tidings: "Hear, ye children of immortal bliss! even ye that reside in higher spheres! I have found the Ancient One, who is beyond all darkness, all delusion: knowing Him alone you shall be saved from death over again." . . .

Thus it is that the Vedas proclaim not a dreadful combination of unforgiving laws, not an endless prison of cause and effect, but that at the head of all these laws, in and through every particle of matter and force, stands One, "By whose command the wind blows, the fire burns, the clouds rain, and death stalks upon the earth." . . .

The Vedas teach that the soul is divine, only held in the bondage of matter; perfection will be reached when this bond will burst, and the word they use for it is therefore *mukti*—freedom, freedom from the bonds of imperfection, freedom from death and misery. So the best proof a Hindu sage gives about the soul, about God, is "I have seen the soul; I have seen God." And that is the only condition of perfection. The Hindu religion does not consist in struggles and attempts to believe a certain doctrine or dogma, but in realizing—not in believing, but in being and becoming.

Thus the whole object of their system is by constant struggle to become perfect, to become divine, to reach God and see God, and this reaching God, seeing God, becoming perfect even as the Father in Heaven is perfect, constitutes the religion of the Hindus.

And what becomes of a man when he attains perfection? He lives a life of bliss infinite. He enjoys infinite and perfect bliss, having obtained the only thing in which man ought to have pleasure, namely God, and enjoys the bliss with God.

So far all the Hindus are agreed. This is the common religion of all the sects of India; but then perfection is absolute, and the absolute cannot be two or three. It cannot have any qualities. It cannot be an individual. . . .

Therefore, to gain this infinite universal individuality, this miserable little prison-individuality must go. Then alone can death cease when I am one with life, then alone can misery cease when I am one with happiness itself; then alone can all errors cease when I am one with knowledge itself; and this is the necessary scientific conclusion. Science has proved to me that physical individuality is a delusion, that really my body is one little continuously changing body in an unbroken ocean of matter and *Advaitam* (unity) is the necessary conclusion with my other counterpart. Soul. . . .

Descend we now from the aspirations of philosophy to the religion of the ignorant. At the very outset, I may tell you that there is no *polytheism* in India. In every temple, if one stands by and listens, one will find the worshippers applying all the attributes of God, including omnipresence, to the images. . . .

As we find that somehow or other, by the laws of our mental constitution, we have to associate our ideas of infinity with the image of the blue sky, or of the sea, so we naturally connect our idea of holiness with the image of a church, a mosque or a cross. The Hindus have associated the ideas of holiness, purity, truth, omnipresence, and such other ideas with different images and forms. But with this difference that while some people devote their whole lives to their idol of a church and never rise higher, because with them religion means an intellectual assent to certain doctrines and doing good to their fellows, the whole religion of the Hindu is centred in realization. Man is to become divine by realizing the divine; idols or temples or churches or books are only the supports, the helps, of his spiritual childhood: but on and on he must progress. . .

If a man can realize his divine nature with the help of

an image, would it be right to call that a sin? Nor even when he has passed that stage, should he call it an error. To the Hindu, man is not travelling from error to truth, but from truth to truth, from lower to higher truth. To him all the religions, from the lowest fetichism to the highest absolutism, mean so many attempts of the human soul to grasp and realize the Infinite, each determined by the conditions of its birth and association, and each of these marks a stage of progress; and every soul is a young eagle soaring higher and higher, gathering more and more strength till it reaches the Glorious Sun. . . .

To the Hindu, then, the whole world of religions is only a travelling, a coming up, of different men and women, through various conditions and circumstances, to the same goal. Every religion is only an evolving a God out of the material man, and the same God is the inspirer of all of them. Why, then, are there so many contradictions? They are only apparent, says the Hindu. The contradictions come from the same truth adapting itself to the varying circumstances of different natures. . . .

This, brethren, is a short sketch of the religious ideas of the Hindus. The Hindu may have failed to carry out all his plans, but if there is ever to be a universal religion, it must be one which will have no location in place or time; which will be infinite, like the God it will preach, and whose sun will shine upon the followers of Krishna and of Christ, on saints and sinners alike; which will not be Brahmanic or Buddhistic, Christian or Mahommedan, but the sum-total of all these, and still have infinite space for development; which in its catholicity will embrace in its infinite arms, and find a place for, every human being, from the lowest grovelling savage not far removed from the brute, to the highest man towering by the virtues of his head and heart almost above humanity, making society stand in awe of him and doubt his human nature. It will be a religion which will have no place for persecution or intolerance in its polity, which will recognize divinity in every man and

woman, and whose whole scope, whose whole force, will
be centred in aiding humanity to realize its own true, divine nature.

(Vivekānanda, *Complete Works*, I, pp. 4-17)

MRS. ANNIE BESANT:
THEOSOPHY'S INTERPRETATION
OF HINDUISM

Mrs. Annie Besant is remembered in India for two contributions: her services to the cause of Indian independence as a
member of the Indian National Congress Party, and her defence of the values and institutions of Hinduism. An example
of her method of handling the tradition is shown in her
interpretation of the famous story of Lord Krishna's theft of
the clothes of the milkmaids while they were bathing. For
critics of Hinduism, such stories had long been used to illustrate the licentious character of the religion and of its devotees. Many Hindus had come to share this embarrassment,
and reformers like Dayānanda had denounced the Krishna
legends as perversions of the true faith. Mrs. Besant argued
that such stories were really instructive morality dramas, and
she transformed them through an allegorical treatment.

Let me take one instance which ignorant lips have used
most in order to insult, to try to defame the majesty that
they do not understand. But let me say this: that I believe
that in most cases where these bitter insults are uttered
they are uttered by people who have never really read the
story, and who have heard only bits of it and have supplied
the rest out of their own imaginations. I therefore take a
particular incident which I have heard most spoken of
with bitterness as a proof of the frightful immorality of
Shrī Krishna.

While the child of six was one day wandering along, as He would, a number of the Gopîs were bathing nude in the river, having cast aside their cloths—as they should not have done, that being against the law and showing carelessness of woman modesty. Leaving their garments on the bank they had plunged into the river. The child of six saw this with the eye of insight, and He gathered up their cloths and climbed up a tree near by, carrying them with Him, and threw them round His own shoulders and waited to see what would chance. The water was bitterly cold and the Gopîs were shivering; but they did not like to come out of it before the clear steady eyes of the child. And He called them to come and get the garments they had thrown off; and as they hesitated, the baby lips told them that they had sinned against God by immodestly casting aside the garments that should have been worn, and must therefore expiate their sin by coming and taking from His hands that which they had cast aside. They came and worshipped, and He gave them back their robes. An immoral story, with a child of six as the central figure! It is spoken of as though he were a full grown man, insulting the modesty of women. The Gopîs were Rishis, and the Lord, the Supreme, as a babe is teaching them a lesson. But there is more than that; there is a profound occult lesson below the story—a story repeated over and over again in different forms—and it is this: that when the soul is approaching the supreme Lord at one great stage of initiation, it has to pass through a great ordeal; stripped of everything on which it has hitherto relied, stripped of everything that is not of its inner Self, deprived of all external aid, of all external protection, of all external covering, the soul itself, in its own inherent life, must stand naked and alone with nothing to rely on, save the life of the Self within it. If it flinches before the ordeal, if it clings to anything to which hitherto it has looked for help, if in that supreme hour it cries out for friend or helper, nay even for the Guru himself, the soul fails in that ordeal. Naked and alone it must go forth, with absolutely none to aid it save

the divinity within itself. And it is that nakedness of th
soul as it approaches the supreme goal, that is told of i
that story of Shrî Krishna, the child, and the Gopîs, th
nakedness of life before the One who gave it. You fin
many another similar allegory. When the Lord comes i
the Kalki, the tenth, Avatâra, He fights on the battlefiel
and is overcome. He uses all His weapons; every weapo
fails Him; and it is not till He casts every weapon aside an
fights with His naked hands, that He conquers. Exactl
the same idea. Intellect, everything, fails the naked sou
before God.

If I have taken up this story specially, out of hundred
of stories, to dwell upon, it is because it is one of th
points of attack, and because you who are Hindus by birt
ought to know enough of the inner truths of your ow
religion not to stand silent and ashamed when attacks ar
made, but should speak with knowledge and thus prever
such blasphemies.

(Annie Besant, *Avatāras*, pp. 100-04)

CHAPTER XVI

FOUR TWENTIETH CENTURY STATEMENTS

〰〰〰〰

It is curious that while the Hindu tradition in the nineteenth and twentieth centuries produced saints and social reformers it has produced few theologians or philosophers whose works have won acclaim from their peers in the West, or, indeed, in India itself. The reason for this may be bound up with the cultural and political conditions of the last hundred years: intellectual energy has gone into the reforming of the old society and the building up of a new political structure. Or it may be that fundamentally the Hindu tradition is interested in the verification of religious and philosophical truth through personal experience, and current intellectual movements in the West are perhaps not congenial to the Hindu pragmatism that examines statements in terms of their usefulness to man's search for salvation. There have, however, been many attempts made in India on the part of Hindu thinkers to express the values of the tradition in statements that will be relevant to the needs of those who have accepted the methods and presuppositions of Western science and humanistic learning. Four of the most famous of these have been chosen to suggest the problems that have presented themselves to their minds, and the ways that they dealt with them. All of them had first-hand experience of the

West but were deeply committed to Hinduism, and all of them, with the exception of Rabīndranāth Tagore, were involved in political life. Two of them, Tagore and Sarvepalli Rādhakrishnan, conform to familiar patterns of Western intellectual achievement, while the other two, Mohandās Gāndhi and Aurobindo Ghose, lived lives that at points contradicted normal patterns of both Indian and Western experience.

Rabīndranāth Tagore (1861-1941) was the son of Debendranāth Tagore, who had revitalized the Brāhmo Samāj in the middle of the nineteenth century, and, although not very closely identified with the Samāj as an organization, his relationship to its particular intellectual milieu is clear. In many ways he is the spiritual legatee of the movement that attempted to bring new life into India by simultaneously returning to the sources of the Hindu tradition and turning to the West. From a very early age he was familiar with the poetry of the humble people of Bengal, especially of the Bāuls, a sect noted for their devotional songs and the unconventionality of their lives. The contrast between the scion of one of the wealthiest and most intellectual families of Bengal and the wandering, illiterate Bāuls is great, but they shared a passion for spiritual freedom and a desire to express in poetry the pain and glory of man's search after God.

But Tagore was more than a poet; he was also one of the most famous Indians of his generation. The award of the Nobel Prize in 1913 for his poetry made him a world figure and gave him enormous prestige in India. This meant that, whatever his own inclinations might be, he had to relate himself to the nationalist movement then gaining momentum. Profoundly patriotic, he desired India's political freedom; at the same time he was repelled by many features of the nationalist movement. It seemed to him that Indian nationalism threatened India with the same evils that were destroying the West, and he refused to give his wholehearted support to the Indian National Congress. This led him into conflict with some of the nationalist leaders, but *the greatest of them, including Gāndhi, recognized that his opposition arose from the splendor of his vision of India's role in the world, not from any attachment to British rule. He did not stress, as had Vivekānanda, the materialism of the West over against the spirituality of India, but he saw India's destiny as the creator of a new order of civilization and culture. A narrow and parochial nationalism, he believed, would make this impossible; therefore, India should strive to keep open the channels of spiritual communication with all the world. Although his vision fades with the passing years, he remains as one of the most attractive exponents of a vital element of the Hindu tradition.*

The career of Aurobindo Ghose (1872-1950) was very different from that of Tagore, although they came from somewhat similar backgrounds. His father wanted him to receive a thoroughly Western education to fit him for public service under the British government, so he was sent as a small boy to England to be educated, and a deliberate attempt was made to cut him off from all Indian contacts. After his return to India in 1893, however, he threw himself whole-heartedly into the nationalist movement, and became the great exponent of a nationalism that would be wholly Indian in its origin. The result was a fusing of the demand for political freedom with a mystical interpretation of India's past that made an irresistible appeal to many Hindu students at the end of the century. Accused by the Government of advocating terrorism and violence, Aurobindo withdrew from all political activity and dramatically retired to Pondicherry, the small French territory in South India, to devote himself to religious exercises and writing.

Aurobindo's intention in his years of retirement was to create a new synthesis of truth by drawing upon both Hindu and Western thought in such a way that an original theological and philosophical construct would emerge. In engaging in this task he was attempting to do for the modern world what Shankarāchārya had done for Hinduism in the ninth century and St. Thomas Aquinas for Christianity in the thirteenth, but it is impossible to say how successful he has been. His writings are frequently obscured by a use of the familiar language of Western philosophy to apply to states and conditions of existence that are related to his private religious experience; furthermore, he gives terms meanings peculiar to his own system. Yet at all times his writings are marked by brilliant insights that illumine Hindu thought.

The heart of Aurobindo's system is a complex doctrine of spiritual evolution, of the movement of the human soul from lower to higher forms of spiritual consciousness. This evolution can be aided by man's own efforts. This view is elaborated at great length in works of a half poetical, half philosophical nature, and while it has not won wide acceptance in India, it is conceivable that it may play an important part in Hindu religious thought. In any case, his life as an ardent nationalist and then as a yogi has won him the place assigned in the tradition to those who through rigorous discipline attain enlightenment.

The third figure, Mohandas K. Gāndhi (1869-1948), was very different from the others. This is partly because of his unique political role, but also because of his intense desire to express the values of the tradition in ethical terms that would be immediately understandable by the Indian masses. His achievements are so well-known that they neither need nor permit summarization, and the selections chosen for inclusion emphasize his attempt to find sanctions for a revolutionary social ethic within the Hindu tradition. Building on the work of previous reformers, but chiefly relying on his own genius for creative improvisation, he gave the Indian independence movement a quality unique in human history. Non-violence, ahimsa, was more than a technique to be used by the weak against the strong: it was primarily a way of life, of which political freedom was but one manifestation. Equally important was the creation of self-respect, which was impossible, he believed, under the conditions imposed by foreign rule.

hile he drew freely upon Western ideas and ideals—
om the New Testament, Ruskin, and Tolstoy—his ethi-
l positions can be seen as derived from the ancient
dian insistence on an order that undergirds both the
smos and the life of man. He called his autobiography
xperiments with Truth, and in this he was faithful to the
indu understanding of truth as an experience to be real-
ed and made manifest in one's own personal life.

Sarvepalli Rādhakrishnan (b. 1888) crowned a career of
eat academic distinction that included the posts of Vice
hancellorship of Banaras Hindu University and the
alding Professorship of Eastern Religions at Oxford
ith his election to the Vice Presidency of India in 1952
d to the Presidency in 1962. His many publications on
ligion and philosophy have made him the best-known
terpreter of Indian thought. To his commitment to the
indu religious and philosophical tradition he adds a deep
d sympathetic knowledge of the Western tradition. Out
this has come a persuasive statement of Hindu thought
pressed in a felicitous literary style. For him, Hinduism
above all a union of reason and mystical intuition that
fuses to define its creed, and that is continually being
riched by its hospitable attitude to new ideas and expe-
ences. His interpretation has been widely accepted by
ucated Hindus as the statement of their faith that
rmits an attachment to the past but which is not cir-
mscribed by it. From Rādhakrishnan, as from Tagore,
urobindo and Gandhi, comes the assurance that as India
ters a period of great social change her central values will
d eloquent spokesmen. In a world utterly remote in
me and spirit from the one that gave them birth, these
lues remain to provide form and color to the new age.

RABĪNDRANĀTH TAGORE:
A VISION OF INDIA

Tagore did not throw himself whole-heartedly into the n
tionalist movement because he questioned the direction
seemed to be taking. The leaders of the Indian moveme
had, he believed, accepted a Western conception of the mea
ing of the nation that was alien to India. His own visio
was of India as the center of a new and revitalized humanit
and it seemed to him that nationalism was the enemy of th
dream. In the first selection, which is taken from a spee
made to a Bengali nationalist meeting in 1910, he presente
his view that the English had performed a notable work
India. They had broken down the walls of separation betwe
East and West, and because of this the spirit of India w
free to spread throughout the world. Nothing should be do
to hinder this possibility. In the poem the same ideas a
expressed in a different form. When the West has spent itse
in the madness of nationalist wars, it will turn to "the patie
dark" of India for a message of healing peace.

In the evolving History of India, the principle at work
not the ultimate glorification of the Hindu, or any oth
race. In India, the history of humanity is seeking to elab
rate a specific ideal, to give to general perfection a speci
form which shall be for the gain of all humanity;—nothir
less than this is its end and aim. . . .

. . . So, for ourselves, we must bear in mind that In
dia is not engaged in recording solely our story, but that
is we who are called upon to take our place in the gre
Drama, which has India for its stage. If we do not fit ou
selves to play our part, it is we who shall have to go. If w
stand aloof from the rest, in the pride of past achievemen
content with heaping up obstacles around ourselves, Go
will punish us, either by afflicting us with sorrow unceasir
till He has brought us to a level with the rest, or by castir

us aside as mere impediments. If we insist on segregating ourselves in our pride of exclusiveness, fondly clinging to the belief that Providence is specially concerned in our own particular development; if we persist in regarding our *dharma* as ours alone, our institutions as specially fit only for ourselves, our places of worship as requiring to be carefully guarded against all incomers, our wisdom as dependent for its safety on being locked up in our strong rooms; then we shall simply await, in the prison of our own contriving, for the execution of the death sentence which in that case the world of humanity will surely pronounce against us.

Of late the British have come in and occupied an important place in India's history. This was not an uncalled for, accidental intrusion. If India had been deprived of touch with the West, she would have lacked an element essential for her attainment of perfection. Europe now has her lamp ablaze. We must light our torches at its wick and make a fresh start on the highway of time. That our forefathers, three thousand years ago, had finished extracting all that was of value from the universe, is not a worthy thought. We are not so unfortunate, nor the universe, so poor. Had it been true that all that is to be done has been done in the past, once for all, then our continued existence could only be a burden to the earth, and so would not be possible.

With what present duty, in what future hope, can they live who imagine that they have attained completeness in their great grandfathers,—whose sole idea is to shield themselves against the influence of the Modern behind the barriers of antiquated belief and custom?

The Englishman has come through the breach in our crumbling walls, as the messenger of the Lord of the world-festival, to tell us that the world has need of us; not where we are petty, but where we can help with the force of our Life, to rouse the World in wisdom, love and work, in the expansion of insight, knowledge and mutuality. . . .

The India to which the Englishman has come with his

message, is the India which is shooting up towards the future from within the bursting seed of the past. This new India belongs to humanity. What right have we to say who shall and who shall not find a place therein. Who is this "We"? Bengali, Marathi or Panjabi, Hindu or Mussalman? Only the larger "We" in whom all these,—Hindu Moslem and Englishman, and whosoever else there be— may eventually unite shall have the right to dictate who is to remain and who is to leave.

On us to-day is thrown the responsibility of building up this greater India, and for that purpose our immediate duty is to justify our meeting with the Englishman. It shall not be permitted to us to say that we would rather remain aloof, inactive, irresponsive, unwilling to give and to take, and thus to make poorer the India that is to be.

(R. Tagore, *Greater India*, pp. 82-87)

Nationalism

1

The last sun of the century sets amidst the blood-red clouds of the West and the whirlwind of hatred.
The naked passion of self-love of Nations, in its drunken delirium of greed, is dancing to the clash of steel and the howling verses of vengeance.

2

The hungry self of the Nation shall burst in a violence of fury from its own shameless feeding.
For it has made the world its food.
And licking it, crunching it, and swallowing it in big morsels,
It swells and swells,
Till in the midst of its unholy feast descends the sudden shaft of heaven piercing its heart of grossness.

3.

The crimson glow of light on the horizon is not the light
   of thy dawn of peace, my Motherland.
It is the glimmer of the funeral pyre burning to ashes the
   vast flesh—the self-love of the Nation—dead under its
   own excess.
Thy morning waits behind the patient dark of the East,
Meek and silent.

4

Keep watch, India.
Bring your offerings of worship for that sacred sunrise.
Let the first hymn of its welcome sound in your voice and
   sing
"Come, Peace, thou daughter of God's own great suffer-
   ing.
Come with thy treasure of contentment, the sword of for-
   titude,
And meekness crowning thy forehead."

5

Be not ashamed, my brothers, to stand before the proud
   and the powerful
With your white robe of simpleness.
Let your crown be of humility, your freedom the freedom
   of the soul.
Build God's throne daily upon the ample bareness of your
   poverty
And know that what is huge is not great and pride is not
   everlasting.

(R. Tagore, *Nationalism*, pp. 157-59)

SRI AUROBINDO:
A VISION OF SPIRITUAL EVOLUTION

In *The Life Divine*, which was first published as a series of
articles in the journal *Arya* from 1914 to 1916, Aurobindo
stated his theory of spiritual evolution. Man must progress
from the normal state of mental awareness to what he calls
Supermind, "the truth-consciousness, the Real-Idea which
knows itself and all that it becomes." The achievement of
this state of Divine Life would lead to an enriched order of
humanity. Aurobindo's concern with the social results of mystical intuition is in rather striking contrast with that of many
other mystics. As man developed, he argued, he would become
"acutely aware of the discord and ignorance that governs his
relations with the world, acutely intolerant of it, more and
more set upon finding a principle of harmony, peace, joy and
unity."

The earliest preoccupation of man in his awakened
thoughts and, as it seems, his inevitable and ultimate preoccupation,—for it survives the longest periods of scepticism and returns after every banishment,—is also the highest which his thought can envisage. It manifests itself in
the divination of Godhead, the impulse towards perfection, the search after pure Truth and unmixed Bliss, the
sense of a secret immortality. The ancient dawns of human knowledge have left us their witness to this constant
aspiration; to-day we see a humanity satiated but not satisfied by victorious analysis of the externalities of Nature
preparing to return to its primeval longings. The earliest
formula of Wisdom promises to be its last,—God, Light,
Freedom, Immortality.

These persistent ideals of the race are at once the con-
tradition of its normal experience and the affirmation of
higher and deeper experiences which are abnormal to hu-

manity and only to be attained, in their organised entirety, by a revolutionary individual effort or an evolutionary general progression. To know, possess and be the divine being in an animal and egoistic consciousness, to convert our twilit or obscure physical mentality into the plenary supramental illumination, to build peace and a self-existent bliss where there is only a stress of transitory satisfactions besieged by physical pain and emotional suffering, to establish an infinite freedom in a world which presents itself as a group of mechanical necessities, to discover and realise the immortal life in a body subjected to death and constant mutation,—this is offered to us as the manifestation of God in Matter and the goal of Nature in her terrestrial evolution. To the ordinary material intellect which takes its present organisation of consciousness for the limit of its possibilities, the direct contradiction of the unrealised ideals with the realised fact is a final argument against their validity. But if we take a more deliberate view of the world's workings, that direct opposition appears rather as part of Nature's profoundest method and the seal of her completest sanction.

For all problems of existence are essentially problems of harmony. They arise from the perception of an unsolved discord and the instinct of an undiscovered agreement or unity. To rest content with an unsolved discord is possible for the practical and more animal part of man, but impossible for his fully awakened mind, and usually even his practical parts only escape from the general necessity either by shutting out the problem or by accepting a rough, utilitarian and unillumined compromise. For essentially, all Nature seeks a harmony, life and matter in their own sphere as much as mind in the arrangement of its perceptions. The greater the apparent disorder of the materials offered or the apparent disparateness, even to irreconcilable opposition, of the elements that have to be utilised, the stronger is the spur, and it drives towards a more subtle and puissant order than can normally be the result of a less difficult endeavour. The accordance of active

Life with a material of form in which the condition of activity itself seems to be inertia, is one problem of opposites that Nature has solved and seeks always to solve better with greater complexities; for its perfect solution would be the material immorality of a fully organised mind-supporting animal body. The accordance of conscious mind and conscious will with a form and a life in themselves not overtly self-conscious and capable at best of a mechanical or subconscious will is another problem of opposites in which she has produced astonishing results and aims always at higher marvels; for there her ultimate miracle would be an animal consciousness no longer seeking but possessed of Truth and Light, with the practical omnipotence which would result from the possession of a direct and perfected knowledge. Not only, then, is the upward impulse of man towards the accordance of yet higher opposites rational in itself, but it is the only logical completion of a rule and an effort that seem to be a fundamental method of Nature and the very sense of her universal strivings.

We speak of the evolution of Life in Matter, the evolution of Mind in Matter; but evolution is a word which merely states the phenomenon without explaining it. For there seems to be no reason why Life should evolve out of material elements or Mind out of living form, unless we accept the Vedantic solution that Life is already involved in Matter and Mind in Life because in essence Matter is a form of veiled Life, Life a form of veiled Consciousness. And then there seems to be little objection to a farther step in the series and the admission that mental consciousness may itself be only a form and a veil of higher states which are beyond Mind. In that case, the unconquerable impulse of man towards God, Light, Bliss, Freedom, Immortality presents itself in its right place in the chain as simply the imperative impulse by which Nature is seeking to evolve beyond Mind, and appears to be as natural, true and just as the impulse towards Life which she has planted in certain forms of Matter or the impulse towards Mind which she has planted in certain forms of Life. As there, so here, the impulse exists more or less obscurely in her different vessels with an ever-ascending series in the power of its will-to-be; as there, so here it is gradually evolving and bound fully to evolve the necessary organs and faculties. As the impulse towards Mind ranges from the more sensitive reactions of Life in the metal and the plant up to its full organisation in man, so in man himself there is the same ascending series, the preparation, if nothing more, of a higher and divine life. The animal is a living laboratory in which Nature has, it is said, worked out man. Man himself may well be a thinking and living laboratory in whom and with whose conscious co-operation she wills to work out the superman, the god. Or shall we not say, rather, to manifest God? For if evolution is the progressive manifestation by Nature of that which slept or worked in her, involved, it is also the overt realisation of that which she secretly is. We cannot, then, bid her pause at a given stage of her evolution, nor have we the right to condemn with the religionist as perverse and presumptuous or with the Rationalist as a disease or hallucination any intention she may evince or effort she may make to go beyond. If it be true that Spirit is involved in Matter and apparent Nature is secret God, then the manifestation of the divine in himself and the realisation of God within and without are the highest and most legitimate aim possible to man upon earth.

Thus the eternal paradox and eternal truth of a divine life in an animal body, an immortal aspiration or reality inhabiting a mortal tenement, a single and universal consciousness representing itself in limited minds and divided egos, a transcendent, indefinable, timeless and spaceless Being who alone renders time and space and cosmos possible, and in all these the higher truth realisable by the lower term, justify themselves to the deliberate reason as well as to the persistent instinct or intuition of mankind. Attempts are sometimes made to have done finally with questionings which have so often been declared insoluble by logical thought and to persuade men to limit their mental activities to the practical and immediate problems of their material existence in the universe; but such evasions are never permanent in their effect. Mankind returns from them with a more vehement impulse of inquiry or a more violent hunger for an immediate solution. By that hunger mysticism profits and new religions arise to replace the old that have been destroyed or stripped of significance by a scepticism which itself could not satisfy because, although its business was inquiry, it was unwilling sufficiently to inquire. The attempt to deny or stifle a truth because it is yet obscure in its outward workings and too often represented by obscurantist superstition or a crude faith, is itself a kind of obscurantism. The will to escape from a cosmic necessity because it is arduous, difficult to justify by immediate tangible results, slow in regulating its operations, must turn out eventually to have been no acceptance of the truth of Nature but a revolt against the secret, mightier will of the great Mother. It is better and more rational to accept what she will not allow us as a race to reject and lift it from the sphere of blind instinct, obscure intuition and random aspiration into the light of reason and an instructed and consciously self-guiding will. And if there is any higher light of illumined intuition or self-revealing truth which is now in man either obstructed and inoperative or works with intermittent glancings as if from behind a veil or with occasional displays as of the northern lights in our material skies, then there also we need not fear to aspire. For it is likely that such is the next higher state of consciousness of which Mind is only a form and veil, and through the splendours of that light may lie the path of our progressive self-enlargement into whatever highest state is humanity's ultimate resting-place.

(Aurobindo Ghose, *The Life Divine,* pp. 1-7)

MAHĀTMA GĀNDHI:
A VISION OF THE GOOD LIFE

Gāndhi was aware that there were very great differences between his teachings and those of Hinduism in general. Other reformers, including such notable ones as Rāmmohan Roy and Dayānanda Saraswatī, had argued that the original religion had been corrupted, and that the true teachings of Hinduism could be recovered by a return to the great scriptures. But Gāndhi, with the frankness that was part of the secret of his power, admitted that his teachings were reinterpretations of the past. "I have endeavoured," he once wrote, "in the light of prayerful study of the other faiths of the world, and what is more, in the light of my own experiences in trying to live the teachings of Hinduism, . . . to give an extended but by no means strained meaning to Hinduism, not as buried in its simple scriptures, but as a living faith speaking like a mother to her aching children." In his interpretation of the *Bhagavad Gītā*, one of the two religious books of the Hindus that he claimed to know (the other was the Rāmāyana of Tulasīdās), he expounded his central idea of non-violence, although admitting that the *Gītā* apparently approves of war. His explanation was that the great stories of Hinduism are allegories, not historical accounts, and that each age must read them in the light of their spiritual knowledge. For him, therefore, the *Gītā* becomes above all a book of ethics, emphasizing selfless devotion in the cause of human brotherhood.

Krishna of the *Gita* is perfection and right knowledge personified; but the picture is imaginary. That does not mean that Krishna, the adored of his people, never lived. But perfection is imagined. The idea of a perfect incarnation is an aftergrowth.

In Hinduism, incarnation is ascribed to one who has performed some extraordinary service of mankind. All embodied life is in reality an incarnation of God, but it is not

usual to consider every living being an incarnation. Futur
generations pay this homage to one who, in his own gener
ation, has been extraordinarily religious in his conduct.
can see nothing wrong in this procedure; it takes nothin
from God's greatness, and there is no violence done t
Truth. There is an Urdu saying which means, "Adam i
not God but he is a spark of the Divine." And therefore h
who is the most religiously behaved has most of the divin
spark in him. It is in accordance with this train of though
that Krishna enjoys, in Hinduism, the status of the mo
perfect incarnation.

This belief in incarnation is a testimony of man's loft
spiritual ambition. Man is not at peace with himself till h
has become like unto God. The endeavour to reach thi
state is the supreme, the only ambition worth having. An
this is self-realization. This self-realization is the subject c
the *Gita*, as it is of all scriptures. But its author surely di
not write it to establish that doctrine. The object of th
Gita appears to me to be that of showing the most exce
lent way to attain self-realization. That which is to b
found, more or less clearly, spread out here and there i
Hindu religious books, has been brought out in the clea
est possible language in the *Gita* even at the risk of repe
tion.

*That matchless remedy is renunciation of fruits of a
tion.*

This is the centre round which the *Gita* is woven. Th
renunciation is the central sun, round which devotio
knowledge and the rest revolve like planets. The body h
been likened to a prison. There must be action whe
there is body. Not one embodied being is exempted fro
labour. And yet all religions proclaim that it is possible f
man, by treating the body as the temple of God, to atta
freedom. Every action is tainted, be it ever so trivial. Ho
can the body be made the temple of God? In other wor
how can one be free from action, i.e. from the taint of si
The *Gita* has answered the question in decisive languag
"By desireless action; by renouncing fruits of action;

edicating all activities to God, i.e., by surrendering one-
elf to Him body and soul."

But desirelessness or renunciation does not come for the
nere talking about it. It is not attained by an intellectual
eat. It is attainable only by a constant heart-churn. Right
nowledge is necessary for attaining renunciation. Learned
nen possess a knowledge of a kind. They may recite the
'edas from memory, yet they may be steeped in self-
adulgence. In order that knowledge may not run riot, the
uthor of the *Gita* has insisted on devotion accompanying
and has given it the first place. Knowledge without de-
otion will be like a misfire. Therefore, says the *Gita*,
Have devotion, and knowledge will follow." This devo-
on is not mere lip worship, it is a wrestling with death.
Tence the *Gita's* assessment of the devotee's qualities is
milar to that of the sage's.

Thus the devotion required by the *Gita* is no soft-
earted effusiveness. It certainly is not blind faith. The
evotion of the *Gita* has the least to do with externals. A
evotee may use, if he likes, rosaries, forehead marks, make
fferings, but these things are no test of his devotion. He is
ne devotee who is jealous of none, who is a fount of
ercy, who is without egotism, who is selfless, who treats
like cold and heat, happiness and misery, who is ever for-
iving, who is always contented, whose resolutions are
rm, who has dedicated mind and soul to God, who causes
o dread, who is not afraid of others, who is free from
xultation, sorrow and fear, who is pure, who is versed in
ction and yet remains unaffected by it, who renounces all
uit, good or bad, who treats friend and foe alike, who is
ntouched by respect or disrespect, who is not puffed up
y praise, who does not go under when people speak ill of
im, who loves silence and solitude, who has a disciplined
ason. Such devotion is inconsistent with the existence at
ne same time of strong attachments. . . .

While on the one hand it is beyond dispute that all ac-
on binds, on the other hand it is equally true that all
ving beings have to do some work, whether they will or

no. Here all activity, whether mental or physical, is to b
included in the term of action. Then how is one to be fre
from the bondage of action, even though he may be ac
ing? The manner in which the *Gita* has solved the prol
lem is to my knowledge unique. The *Gita* says: 'Do you
allotted work but renounce its fruit—be detached an
work—have no desire for reward and work.'

This is the unmistakable teaching of the *Gita*. He wh
gives up action falls. He who gives up only the rewar
rises. But renunciation of fruit in no way means indiffe
ence to the result. In regard to every action one mu
know the result that is expected to follow, the mea
thereto, and the capacity for it. He, who, being th
equipped is, without desire for the result and is yet whol
engrossed in the due fulfillment of the task before him
said to have renounced the fruits of his action.

Again let no one consider renunciation to mean want
fruit for the renouncer. The *Gita* reading does not warra
such a meaning. Renunciation means absence of hank
ing after fruit. As a matter of fact, he who renounc
reaps a thousandfold. The renunciation of the *Gita* is tl
acid test of faith. He who is ever brooding over result oft
loses nerve in the performance of his duty. He becom
impatient and then gives vent to anger and begins to
unworthy things; he jumps from action to action never
maining faithful to any. He who broods over results is li
a man given to objects of senses; he is ever distracted,
says goodbye to all scruples, everything is right in his es
mation and he therefore resorts to means fair and foul
attain his end.

From the bitter experiences of desire for fruit the auth
of the *Gita* discovered the path of renunciation of fr
and put it before the world in a most convincing mann
The common belief is that religion is always opposed
material good. "One cannot act religiously in mercant
and such other matters. There is no place for religion
such pursuits; religion is only for attainment of salvatio
we hear many worldly-wise people say. In my opinion t

author of the *Gita* has dispelled this delusion. He has drawn no line of demarcation between salvation and worldly pursuits. On the contrary he has shown that religion must rule even our worldly pursuits. I have felt that the *Gita* teaches us that what cannot be followed out in day-to-day practice cannot be called religion. Thus, according to the *Gita*, all acts that are incapable of being performed without attachment are taboo. This golden rule saves mankind from many a pitfall. According to this interpretation murder, lying, dissoluteness and the like must be regarded as sinful and therefore taboo. Man's life then becomes simple, and from that simpleness springs peace.

Thinking along these lines, I have felt that in trying to enforce in one's life the central teaching of the *Gita*, one is bound to follow Truth and *ahimsa*. When there is no desire for fruit, there is no temptation for untruth or *himsa*. Take any instance of untruth or violence, and it will be found that at its back was the desire to attain the cherished end.

(M. Gāndhi, in Desai, *The Gita According to Gāndhi*, pp. 128-32)

SARVEPALLI RĀDHAKRISHNAN:
A VISION OF HINDUISM

In a series of lectures delivered in England and the United States in 1926 Rādhakrishnan developed the interpretation of Hinduism that has since become associated with his name. Many of the ideas had been expressed by previous Indian thinkers, but the combination of systematic presentation, great erudition, and deep religious feeling, gave his views a wide audience. Especially significant has been his argument that Hinduism finds a place within itself for all the varieties of religious experience, thus creating a religion of tolerance, while Christianity and Islam, the inheritors of Judaism, display "the intolerance of narrow monotheism." The selection given here summarizes his understanding of the nature of Hinduism.

We are now at the end of our course. We see that the Hindu recognises one supreme spirit, though different names are given to it. In his social economy he has many castes, but one society. In the population there are many races and tribes, but all are bound together by one common spirit. Though many forms of marriage are permitted, there is only one ideal aimed at. There is a unity of purpose underlying the multitudinous ramifications. It may perhaps be useful to conclude this course with a brief résumé of the central spirit of Hinduism and its application to the problems of religion and society.

The world which is a perpetual flow is not all. Its subjection to law and tendency to perfection indicate that it is based on a spiritual reality which is not exhausted in any particular object or group of objects. God is *in* the world, though not *as* the world. His creative activity is not confined to the significant stages in the evolutionary process. He does not merely intervene to create life or consciousness, but is working continuously. There is no dualism of the natural and the supernatural. The spiritual is an emergent of the natural in which it is rooted. The Hindu spirit is that attitude towards life which regards the endless variety of the visible and the temporal world as sustained and supported by the invisible and eternal spirit.

Evil, error and ugliness are not ultimate. Evil has reference to the distance which good has to traverse. Ugliness is half-way to beauty. Error is a stage on the road to truth. They have all to be outgrown. No view is so utterly erroneous, no man is so absolutely evil as to deserve complete castigation. If one human soul fails to reach its divine destiny, to that extent the universe is a failure. As every soul is unlike all others in the world, the destruction of even the most wicked soul will create a void in God's scheme. There is no Hell, for that means there is a place where

God is not, and there are sins which exceed his love. If the infinite love of God is not a myth, universal salvation is a certainty. But until it is achieved, we shall have error and imperfection. In a continuously evolving universe evil and error are inevitable, though they are gradually diminishing.

In religion, Hinduism takes its stand on a life of spirit, and affirms that the theological expressions of religious experience are bound to be varied. One metaphor succeeds another in the history of theology until God is felt as the central reality in the life of man and the world. Hinduism repudiates the belief resulting from a dualistic attitude that the plants in my garden are of God, while those in my neighbour's are weeds planted by the Devil which we should destroy at any cost. On the principle that the best is not the enemy of the good, Hinduism accepts all forms of belief and lifts them to a higher level. The cure for error is not the stake or the cudgel, not force or persecution, but the quiet diffusion of light.

In practical religion, Hinduism recognises that there are those who wish to see God face to face, others who delight in the endeavour to know the truth of it all. Some find peace in action, others in non-action. A comprehensive religion guides each along his path to the common goal, as all woo the same goddess though with different gifts. We must not give supreme and sole importance to our specialty. Perfection can be attained as a celibate, or a householder, or an anchorite. A rigid uniform outlook is wrong. The saintliness of the holy man does not render the steadfastness of the devoted wife or the simple innocence of the child superfluous. The perfection of every type is divine. "Whatsoever is glorious, good, beautiful and mighty, understand that it goes forth from out of a fragment of my splendour." [1]

The law of Karma tells us that the individual life is not a term, but a series. Fresh opportunities will be open to us until we reach the end of the journey. The historical forms we assume will depend on our work in the past. Heaven

[1] *Bhagavadgītā*, x. 41.

and Hell are higher and lower stages in one continuous movement. They are not external to the experiencing individuals. Purification is by means of purgation. The wages of sin is suffering. We need not regard sin as original and virtue as vicarious. We should do our duty in that state of life to which we happen to be called. Most of us have not a free hand in selecting our vocation. Freedom consists in making the best of what we have, our perentage, our physical nature and mental gifts. Every kind of capacity, every form of vocation, if rightly used, will lead us to the centre.

While the ideal of monogamy is held up as the best means for a complete mental and spiritual as well as physical understanding between husband and wife, other forms were permitted in view of the conditions of people with different ideals and interests, habits and desires. A happy marriage requires to be made by slow steps and with much patient effort. If incompatibility of temper is enough to justify divorce, many of us will be divorced. While women's functions are distinguished from those of men, there is no suggestion of their inferiority.

While caste has resulted in much evil, there are some sound principles underlying it. Our attitude to those whom we are pleased to call primitive must be one of sympathy. The task of the civilised is to respect and foster the live impulses of backward communities and not destroy them. Society is an organism of different grades, and human activities differ in kind and significance. But each of them is of value so long as it serves the common end. Every type has its own nature which should be followed. No one can be at the same time a perfect saint, a perfect artist, and a perfect philosopher. Every definite type is limited by boundaries which deprive it of other possibilities. The worker should realise his potentialities through his work, and should perform it in a spirit of service to the common weal. Work is craftsmanship and service. Our class conflicts are due to the fact that a warm living sense of unity does not bind together the different groups.

These are some of the central principles of the Hindu

faith. If Hinduism lives to-day, it is due to them, but it lives so little. Listlessness reigns now where life was once like a bubbling spring. We are to-day drifting, not advancing, waiting for the future to turn up. There is a lack of vitality, a spiritual flagging. Owing to our political vicissitudes, we ignored the law of growth. In the great days of Hindu civilisation it was quick with life, crossing the seas, planting colonies, teaching the world as well as learning from it. In sciences and arts, in trade and commerce it was not behind the most advanced nations of the world till the middle of this millennium. To-day we seem to be afraid of ourselves, and are therefore clinging to the shell of our religion for self-preservation. The envelope by which we try to protect life checks its expansion. The bark which protects the interior of a tree must be as living as that which it contains. It must not stifle the tree's growth, but must expand in response to the inner compulsion. An institution appropriate and wholesome for one stage of human development becomes inadequate and even dangerous when another stage has been reached. The cry of conservatism "it has always been thus" ignores the fundamentals of the theory of relativity in philosophy and practice, in taste and morals, in politics and society, of which the ancient Hindus had a clear grasp. The notion that in India time has stood still for uncounted centuries, and nought has been changed since the primeval sea dried up, is altogether wrong. While there has been continuity with the past, there has also been progress. The Upanisads are products of a perfectly spiritual movement which implicitly superseded the cruder ceremonial religion of the Vedas. When the movement of the Upanisads became lost in dogmatic controversies, when the fever of disputes and dialectics lulled the free spirit of religion, Buddhism called upon the people to adhere to the simplicity of truth and the majesty of the moral law. About the same period, when canonical culture and useless learning made religion inhuman scholasticism, and filled those learned in this difficult trifling with ridiculous pride, the *Bhagavadgītā* opened the gates

of heaven to all those who are pure in heart. When th
ritualists succeeded in imprisoning the living faith in rigi
creeds, the true prophets of the spirit, the Śaiva and th
Vaisnava saints, and the theologians like Śamkara an
Rāmānuja, summoned the people to the worship of th
living God. The influence of Madhva and Caitanya, Basav
and Rāmānanda, Kabīr and Nānak is not inconsiderable
There has been no such thing as a uniform stationary un
alterable Hinduism whether in point of belief or practice
Hinduism is a movement, not a position; a process, not ;
result; a growing tradition, not a fixed revelation. Its pas
history encourages us to believe that it will be found equa
to any emergency that the future may throw up, whethe
on the field of thought or of history.

After a long winter of some centuries, we are to-day i
one of the creative periods of Hinduism. We are begin
ning to look upon our ancient faith with fresh eyes. W
feel that our society is in a condition of unstable equilib
rium. There is much wood that is dead and diseased tha
has to be cleared away. Leaders of Hindu thought an
practice are convinced that the times require, not a sur
render of the basic principles of Hinduism, but a restate
ment of them with special reference to the needs of ;
more complex and mobile social order. Such an attemp
will only be the repetition of a process which has occurre
a number of times in the history of Hinduism. The wor
of readjustment is in process. Growth is slow when root
are deep. But those who light a little candle in the dark
ness will help to make the whole sky aflame.

(S. Rādhakrishnan, *The Hindu View of Life*, pp. 124-30)

SOURCES OF ENGLISH
TRANSLATIONS
AND SELECTIONS

Apastamba Dharma Sūtra. Translated by George Buhler, in *Sacred Books of the East*, Vol. II, Part I, American Edition. New York: Christian Literature Company, 1898.

Atharva Veda. Translated by R. T. H. Griffith in *The Hymns of the Atharva Veda*. Benares: E. J. Lazarus and Co., 1896.

Bāna. *The Harsacarita of Bāna.* Translated by E. B. Cowell and F. W. Thomas. London: Royal Asiatic Society, 1897.

de Bary, W. T., Stephen Hay, Royal Weiler and Andrew Yarrow, *The Sources of Indian Tradition*. New York: Columbia University Press, 1958.

Besant, Annie. *Avatāras.* London: Theosophical Society, 1900.

Bhagavad Gītā. Translated by Sir Edwin Arnold in *The Song Celestial*. Boston: Roberts, 1885. Translated by K. T. Telang in *Sacred Books of the East*, Vol. VIII. Oxford: Clarendon Press, 1882.

Bhartrihari. *The Satakas or Wise Sayings.* Translated by J. M. Kennedy. London: Laurie, 1910.

Bhavabhūti. *Mālati and Mādhava.* Translated by H. H. Wilson in *The Theatre of the Hindus*. London: Trubner, 1871.

Dayānanda, Saraswatī. *Satyārtha Prākāsh.* Translated by C. Bharadwaja. Lahore, 1906.

Desai, M. K., *The Gita According to Gandhi*. Ahmedabad: Navjivan Trust, 1956.

Ghose, Aurobindo. *The Life Divine.* Calcutta: Arya Publishing House, 1939.

Gotama. *Nyāya Sūtras.* Translated by S. C. Vidyābhusana in *Sacred Books of the Hindus*, Vol. VIII. Allahabad: Panini Office, 1913.

Griffith, R. T. H. See *Rig Veda.*

Hitopadeśa. Translated by Sir Edwin Arnold. London: Smith, Elder, 1861.

Hume, R. E., *The Thirteen Principal Upanishads.* Bombay: Oxford University Press, 1954.

Jayadeva. *Gītā Govinda.* Translated by George Keyt. Bombay: Kutub 1947.

Kabīr. Translated by Rabīndranāth Tagore in *Songs of Kabīr.* New York: Macmillan, 1915; also translated by G. H. Westcott in *Kabīr and the Kabīr Panth.* Cawnpore: Christ Church Mission Press, 1907.

Kaegi, Adolf. *The Rig Veda: the Oldest Literature of the Indians.* Translated by R. Arrowsmith. Boston: Ginn and Co., 1886.

Kālidās. *Shakuntalā.* Translated by Monier Williams. New York Dodd, Mead, 1885.

Kanāda. *The Vaiśeṣika Sūtras of Kanāda* in *Sacred Books of the Hindus,* Vol. VI. Allahabad: Panini Office, 1911.

Kautilya. *Arthaśāstra.* Translated by R. Shamasastry. Mysore: Sri Raghuveer Press, 1956.

Kennedy, M. T. *The Chaitanya Movement.* Calcutta: Association Press, 1925.

Kingsbury, F., and G. E. Phillips. *Hymns of the Tamil Saivite Saints.* Calcutta: Association Press, 1921.

Kumārila. *Ślokavārtika.* Translated by G. N. Jha. Calcutta: The Asiatic Society, 1902-1908.

Macauliffe, M. A., *The Sikh Religion.* Vol. I. Oxford: Clarendon Press, 1909.

Macdonnell, A. A. See *Rig Veda* below.

Mahābhārata. Translated by P. C. Roy. 14 vols. Calcutta: Bharat Press, 1883-1890; selections from this translation edited by S. C Nott in *The Mahabharata.* New York: Philosophical Library, 1956.

Majumdar, R. C., editor. *The Classical Age.* Vol. III, *The History and Culture of the Indian People.* Bombay: Bharatiya Vidya Bhavan, 1954.

Mānikkavāchakar. *Tiruvācagam.* Translated by G. U. Pope. Oxford Clarendon Press, 1900.

Manu. *Manu Smriti.* Translated by George Buhler in *Sacred Books of the East,* Vol. XXV. Oxford: Clarendon Press, 1886.

Muir, John. *Original Sanskrit Texts.* 5 vols. London: Trubner, 1884-1890.

Orr, W. G., *A Sixteenth Century Indian Mystic.* London: Lutterworth Press, 1949.

Patanjali. *Yogasūtra.* Translated by Rama Prasad in *Sacred Book of the Hindus,* Vol. IV. Allahabad: Panini Office, 1924.

Rādhakrishnan, S., *The Hindu View of Life.* London: Allen & Unwin, 1927.

Rāmakrishna. *The Gospel of Rāmakrishna.* Translated by "M." New York: Vedanta Society, 1947.

Rāmānuja. *The Vedānta Sūtra with Commentary of Rāmānuja.* Translated by George Thibaut in *Sacred Books of the East,* Vol. XLVIII. Oxford: Clarendon Press, 1906.

Rammohan Roy. *Translation of the Isa Upanishad.* Calcutta, 1816; and *The English Works of Raja Rammohan Roy.* Allahabad: Panini Office, 1906.

Rānade, M. G., *Religious and Social Reform.* Bombay: Gopal Narayan, 1902.

Rig Veda. Translated by R. T. H. Griffith, in *The Hymns from the Rig Veda.* 2 vols. Benares: E. J. Lazarus, 1920; also, A. A. Macdonnell, *Hymns from the Rigveda.* Calcutta: Association Press, 1923.

Śatapatha Brāhmana. Translated by Julius Eggeling in *Sacred Books of the East,* Vol. XII. Oxford: Clarendon Press, 1882.

Sen, K. C. *Lectures in India.* Calcutta: Brahmo Tract Society, 1899.

Sources of Indian Tradition. See de Bary, W. T., *et al.,* above.

Tagore, Debendranāth. *The Autobiography of Maharishi Devendranath Tagore.* Translated by S. Tagore and I. Devi. London: Macmillan, 1914.

Tagore, Rabīndranāth. *Greater India.* Madras: Ganesan, 1921.

Tagore, Rabīndranāth. *Nationalism.* New York: Macmillan, 1917.

Tilak, B. G. *Writings and Speeches.* Madras: Ganesan, n.d.

Tukārām. *The Poems of Tukārām.* Translated by J. N. Fraser and K. B. Marathe. Madras: Christian Literature Society, 1909.

Tulasīdās. *Rāmacaritamānasa.* Translated by F. S. Growse in *The Rāmāyana of Tulsīdās.* Allahabad: NWP and Oudh Government Press, 1887.

Valmiki. *Rāmāyana.* Translated by H. P. Shastri. Vol. I. London: Shanti Sadan, 1952.

Vishnu Purāna. Translated by H. H. Wilson. London: John Murray, 1840.

Vivekānanda, Swami. *Complete Works,* Vol. I. Almora: Prabuddha Bharata, 1919.

INDEX

AINSLIE THOMAS EMBREE was born in Nova Scotia and educated at Dalhousie University in Halifax and Columbia University. He taught Indian history at Columbia University from 1958 to 1969, and is now Professor of History at Duke University. He is the President of the American Institute of Indian Studies.

Mr. Embree is the author of *Charles Grant and British Rule in India* and *India's Search for National Identity.* He has been co-editor of several books, including *Approaches to Asian Civilizations, Guide to Oriental Classics* and *The Development of Civilization.* With S. M. Ikram, Mr. Embree has written *Muslim Civilization in India.*